CF... renew/return this item by the last date shown.

... your telephone call is charged at local rate,
...se call the numbers as set out below:

	From Area codes 01923 or 0208:	From the rest of Herts:
Renewals:	01923 471373	01438 737373
Enquiries:	01923 471333	01438 737333
Minicom:	01923 471599	01438 737599

L32b

Hertfordshire
COUNTY COUNCIL

Library Service

Please return this book
on or before the last
date shown or ask for
It to be renewed.

L32

Hertfordshire
COUNTY COUNCIL
Community Information

2 1 FEB 2005

2 3 MAY 200

1 2 JUN 200

1 2 NOV 2008

0 3 AUG 2009

1 6 AUG 2009

- 8 NOV 2009

L32a

1 6 OCT 2006

1 3 NOV 2006

0 4 DEC 2006

JAN 2007

1 4 AUG 2   8 JAN 2007

- 5 SEP 2006

1 9 APR 2008

2 4 JUL 2

2 5 SEP 2006

D1610303

Britain's Living Folklore

Britain's Living Folklore

ROY PALMER

DAVID & CHARLES
Newton Abbot   London

HERTFORDSHIRE
LIBRARY SERVICE

No.		
Class	398.0941	
Supplier	Price	Date
JMLS	13.99	13/6

1 8 JUN 1991

British Library Cataloguing in Publication Data

Palmer, Roy
  Britain's living folklore.
  1. Great Britain. Folklore
  I. Title
  398.0941

  ISBN 0-7153-9384-7

Copyright © Roy Palmer 1991

The right of Roy Palmer to be identified as
author of this work has been asserted by him in accordance
with the Copyright, Designs and Patents Act 1988.

All rights reserved. No part of this publication may be
reproduced, stored in a retrieval system, or transmitted, in any
form or by any means, electronic, mechanical, photocopying,
recording or otherwise, without the prior permission
of David & Charles plc.

Typeset by Typesetters (Birmingham) Ltd,
Smethwick, Warley, West Midlands
and printed in Great Britain
by Billing & Sons Ltd, Worcester
for David & Charles plc
Brunel House Newton Abbot Devon

Contents

ACKNOWLEDGEMENTS

I should like to thank the following people and organisations for advice and help: Gordon Ashman, British Tourist Authority, Folklore Society Library, D. S. Goodbrand, Bill Hall, Inverness, Loch Ness and Nairn Tourist Board, Tony Marcovecchio, Museum of London, North Yorkshire County Library, Pat, Simon, Adam and Thomas Palmer, Peak District National Park, Paul Sibellas, Cyril Tawney, F. H. J. Thomas, Vaughan Williams Memorial Library, Welsh Tourist Board, Welsh Folk Museum, F. Wonbell and Working Class Movement Library.

Introduction

What is folklore? Funk and Wagnall's *Standard Dictionary of Folklore, Mythology and Legend (1972)* offers a staggering twenty-two definitions, running to half a dozen pages. In recent years definitions have tended to be all-embracing in their simplicity: folklore is made up of 'the traditional stories, customs and habits of a particular community or nation' says the *Collins Cobuild Dictionary* of 1987. More specific definitions also abound; perhaps folklore should be identified as the community's commitment to maintaining stories, customs and habits purely for their own sake. (A perfect example of this would be the famous horse race at Siena in Italy: the *palio* attracts many thousands of tourists, yet if not a single outsider attended the people of the community would still support the event year after year.)

But what about those events or beliefs which have been recently initiated or which are sustained for reasons of commercial gain or tourism? Many customs are not as ancient as their participants may claim but it would be foolish to dismiss them as irrelevant. Some apparently 'ancient' customs are, in fact, relatively modern but does this mean they cannot be termed as folklore? The spectacular fire festival at Allendale, for instance, feels utterly authentic despite the fact that there is no record of the event prior to 1853. There are

7

many other cases of new events or stories which have rapidly assumed organic growth and therefore deserve, in my view, the status of being recognised as folklore.

Any book on folklore has to be selective, but here we shall attempt to explore and celebrate the variety and vigour of Britain's folklore. A wide geographical area is covered: England, Scotland and Wales, with some reference to Ireland and North America; and we also look at the contributions immigrant communities – Caribbean, Indian and Chinese – have made to the folklore of Britain. These deserve more extensive treatment than they are granted in most books on the subject and in years to come will probably be regarded as as much a part of our folklore heritage as the Floral Dance and Whuppity Stourie; Notting Hill Carnival already makes the national headlines every year.

Entire books – indeed, whole libraries of books – have been written on every aspect of folklore covered here: on epitaphs and weather lore, folk medicine and calendar customs, traditional drama, sports and pastimes, superstitions, ghosts and witchcraft, fairs, sea monsters and many others. While trying to cram much into little we have avoided generalisations. Precise details such as names, dates and localities are given wherever possible and there are many references to features which can still be seen – a mountain, a bridge, a standing stone or a carving in a church.

Classic folklore belongs within the country to the basic unit of the parish. Most parishes could produce at least a booklet and in some cases a substantial volume on their own folklore, past and present. It would be a mistake, however, to think that rural customs, dance and tale were the whole picture, and this book attempts to give a fair showing to urban and industrial folklore as well – from the office girl's pre-wedding ceremonies to urban tales of phantom hitchhikers and stolen corpses.

In this age of fragmentation, speed and stress, people often seem to thirst for something in which they can take an active part. There is a need to rediscover something which is more permanent and part of a continuing tradition. By tapping into our heritage of song and story, ritual and celebration, our lives are given shape and meaning. In some cases all we need to do is to join in with an activity which is already happening; in others it will perhaps mean reviving a dance or a traditional play. But however we choose to participate, as long as we continue to use, adapt and develop the elements of our folklore heritage it will survive.

This book is an attempt to encourage us all to seek out the stories and the customs of country, county, town and village, to understand and enjoy them and to pass them on.

1
The Watery World

Not a single town or village in England is situated more than a hundred miles from the sea, except for a few places in the Midlands, and most of those in Wales and Scotland are nearer still. The coastline runs for thousands of miles, with a host of off-shore islands ranging from Scilly to Shetland and Wight to Lewis. It is hardly surprising then that our long and eventful maritime history is complemented by a rich heritage of nautical stories and superstitions, beliefs and customs, many of which continue to affect our daily lives – even oil rigs, very much a twentieth-century phenomenon, have tales of their own. Inland water, too, are the subjects of stories which echo the folklore of the coasts and seas.

BENEATH THE WAVES

Many tales are told of submerged lands, and of church bells ringing ominously from beneath the waves. Between Land's End and the Scilly Islands lies a group of rocks called the Seven Stones, known to fishermen as 'The City' and near to which the land of Lyonesse is believed to lie, lost under the sea. There is a rhyme which proclaims:

> Between Land's End and Scilly Rocks
> Sunk lies a town that ocean mocks.

Lyonesse was said to have had 140 churches. These and most of its people were reputed to have been engulfed during the great storm of 11 November 1099. One man called Trevilian foresaw the deluge, and moved his family and stock inland – he was making a last journey when the waters rose, but managed to outrun the advancing waves thanks to the fleetness of his horse. Since then the arms of the grateful Trevilians have carried the likeness of a horse issuing from the sea. A second man who avoided the catastrophe erected a chapel in thanksgiving which stood for centuries near Sennen Cove.

Another area lost under water is Cantre'r Gwaelod, which lies in Cardigan Bay somewhere between the River Teifi and Bardsey Island. Sixteen towns and most of their inhabitants were apparently overwhelmed by the sea when the sluice gates in the protective dyke were left open. There are two versions of the story as to who was responsible: in one it is a drunken watchman called Seithenin; in another, Seithenin was a king who preferred to spend his revenue in dissipation rather than in paying for the upkeep of the coastal defences.

A moral of one kind or another will often be the basis of tales about inland settlements lost beneath water. For example Bomere Lake in Shropshire – now visited as a beauty spot – was created one Easter Eve when the town which stood there was submerged as a punishment for reverting to paganism. One Roman soldier was spared because he had attempted to bring the people back to Christianity, but he then lost his life while trying to save the woman he loved. It is said that his ghost can sometimes be seen rowing across the lake at Easter, and that the town's bells can be heard ringing. There is another version of the same story in the same place but set in Saxon times: the people turn to Thor and Woden at a time when the priest is warning that the barrier which holds back the mere needs strengthening. He is ignored, but as the townsfolk are carousing at Yuletide the water bursts in and destroys them.

There is a cautionary tale told of Semerwater, another lake with a lost village in its depths. Semerwater lies in north Yorkshire not far from Askrigg, which is perhaps better known as the centre of 'Herriot country', from the veterinary stories of James Herriot. The story goes that a traveller – variously given as an angel, St Paul, Joseph of Arimathea, a witch, and Christ in the guise of a poor old man – visited house after house seeking food and drink but at each one was turned away, until he reached a Quaker's home, just beyond the village: this was the only building spared in the avenging flood which followed.

The Goodwin Sands

One lost land off the Kent coast can be partially seen at high tide: originally, the Goodwin Sands were in fact an island, the island of Lomea which according to one version disappeared under the waves in the eleventh century when funds for its sea defences were diverted to pay for the building of a church tower at Tenterden. The blame for this is laid at the door of an abbot of St Augustine's at Canterbury who was both owner of Lomea and rector of Tenterden. However, sceptics say that Tenterden had no tower before the sixteenth century, nor can archaeologists find any trace of habitation or cultivation on the Sands. Even so, the tales continue to be told; one of these blames Earl Godwin, father of King Harold, for the loss of the island. The earl promised to build a steeple at Tenterden in return for safe delivery from a battle, but having survived the battle, he forgot the vow and in retribution Lomea, which he owned, was flooded during a great storm. The Sands still bear his name.

Yet worse was to follow, for scores of ships and the lives of some 50,000 seafarers have been lost on the Goodwins, and ill-fortune seems to dog the area. For example, in 1748 the *Lady Lovibond* was deliberately steered to her destruction on the Sands by the mate of the vessel, John Rivers. Rivers was insanely jealous because his intended bride, Annetta, had forsaken him to marry his captain, Simon Reed. The entire wedding party perished with the ship in the midst of the celebrations, but the remarkable thing is that the scene made a phantom reappearance once every fifty years – until 1948, when the *Lady Lovibond* at last failed to re-enact the drama.

Another fifty-year reappearance concerns the *Northumberland*; she was lost on the Goodwind Sands in 1703 in a storm, along with twelve other men-of-war, but in 1753 seen again by the crew of an East Indiaman – sailors were leaping into the water from the stricken vessel though their shouts and screams could not be heard.

The *Northumberland* was under the command of Sir Cloudesley Shovel, to whom is attached a further tale. Three years afterwards, the admiral's flagship, the *Association*, was wrecked on the Gilstone Rock near the Scilly Isles. The fleet was homeward bound after a triumphant campaign against the French and some maintain that the crews were drunk. But the story which Scillonians believe to this day is that a sailor aboard the flagship warned that the fleet was dangerously near the islands, and that for this he was hanged at the yardarm for insubordination, on the admiral's orders. The man was granted a last request to read from the bible, and turned to the 109th psalm: 'Let his days be few and another take his place. Let his children be fatherless and his wife a widow'. As he read, the ships began to strike the rocks.

The admiral was a very stout man and his natural buoyancy was sufficient to carry him ashore alive, though very weak. However, official searchers found him dead, stripped of his clothing and valuables, including a fine emerald ring. The body was taken to Westminster Abbey for interment, and his widow appealed in vain for the return of the ring. Many years later a St Mary's islander confessed on her deathbed that she had found Sir Cloudesley and had 'squeezed the life out of him' before taking his belongings. The hue and cry had forced her to abandon the idea of selling the emerald, but she had felt unable to die in peace before revealing her crime.

A commemorative stone marks the place where the admiral's body was temporarily buried in the shingle of Porth Hellick, on St Mary's Island. No grass grows over the grave.

The Wreck of the Ramillies

Many hundreds of shipwrecks have their own songs and stories. Although the *Ramillies*, for example, was wrecked well over 200 years ago, tradition perpetuates the event as clearly as if it had happened only yesterday. In February 1760 the majestic, ninety-gun, triple-decked ship was outward bound from Plymouth to Quiberon Bay when hurricane-force winds blew up in the Channel and forced the captain to turn back and run for shelter. Sailing east, the master thought he had passed Looe Island, and had only to round Rame Head to reach the safety of Plymouth Sound. In fact the ship was a bay further on and the land sighted was Burgh Island, in Bigbury Bay. The promontory was Bolt Tail with its four hundred foot cliffs, and beyond lay no safe harbour at all but several miles of precipitous rocks. As soon as the sailing master realised his mistake the ship was hove to, but the wind was so violent that the masts immediately snapped and went overboard. The two anchors which were dropped held fast but their cables fouled each other, and after hours of fierce friction, they parted and the ship was driven to destruction on the rocks.

Of more than seven hundred men on board only about two dozen reached safety. Led by Midshipman John Harrold, they scrambled up the cliffs, by pure luck choosing the one place where this was possible. Next day a certain William Locker travelled to the scene to try to find the body of his friend, one of the officers. Locker himself would have been aboard the *Ramillies* but his lieutenant's commission had come from the admiralty too late, arriving just a few hours after she had sailed. He found the shores of Bigbury Bay strewn with hundreds of corpses, their clothing torn away by the sea's pounding, their features unrecognisable. The village nearest to the scene of the wreck was Inner Hope, and some there still maintain that a Bigbury man aboard the *Ramillies* pleaded with the captain to alter course; but he was clapped in irons, and went down with the ship. They say that only one officer survived because others were prevented from leaving the stricken vessel.

Most of the bodies were washed ashore at Thurlestone, a few miles to the west. There used to be a depression in the village green which marked the place where many of the seamen had been buried in a mass grave; this has now been asphalted to make a carpark. Then in the mid-1960s a child digging in a sand dune found a bone. He showed it to a man on the beach who happened to be a doctor and identified it as human. Further digging revealed the skeletons of ten men, small in stature and buried at five-foot intervals – perhaps these had been washed up after the mass burial. No scrap of clothing or equipment was found, and finally the bones were thrown into a lorry and consigned to the rubbish tip. Even though two centuries have elapsed since their deaths, one feels that the men of the *Ramillies* deserved better. The ship still lies six fathoms down in the cove which has borne her name since 1760, and Wise's Spring on the cliffs is called after one of the seamen who scrambled ashore with the tiny band of survivors.

Portents of Disaster

Great pains are taken when first launching a vessel so as to ensure good fortune, and one of the most important portents is the ritual bottle of champagne which must break first time (the liquid may be a substitute for the blood of a sacrifice). It is interesting that the various ships to bear the name *Ark Royal* have always been lucky; for example, when the World War II vessel was sunk there was minimal loss of life. The original ship dated from Elizabethan times and had a crucifix placed beneath the mainmast by the captain's mistress; this apparently secured good fortune for all her successors. On the other hand there are vessels which seem perpetually unlucky, some even jinxed and quite incapable of escaping misfortune.

Brunel's fine ship the *Great Eastern* was launched in 1858 after several ominously unsuccessful attempts. She ruined the man in whose yard she was built, and caused a breakdown in Brunel's health – he died even before her maiden voyage. And despite her immense

13

technical advantages, she was never successful as a passenger-carrying vessel.

In 1859 she was in port at Holyhead. When the *Royal Charter* sailed by, homeward bound from Australia, the passengers expressed a desire to see her and their captain was only too pleased to oblige. However, the ship strayed off course and a wild storm blew up. The ship was wrecked, with great loss of life. Some of the trouble was attributed to the story of a riveter and his boy who were said to have been accidentally sealed into the famous double hull. Unexplained knockings were heard at various times but although searches were made, nothing was found. When the vessel was broken up at New Ferry, Cheshire, in 1888 it was rumoured that two skeletons were discovered, their bony fingers still clenched round the worn-down hammers which had beaten in vain for rescue.

The *Victoria* was commissioned in 1887 on Good Friday, the thirteenth of the month – and if this were not ill-luck enough, the fact that her name ended in 'a' was considered another bad sign. In 1893 she sank with heavy losses after a collision during manoeuvres in the Mediterranean off Beirut, and interestingly, various things happened which indicated calamity: two hours earlier a fakir had actually predicted disaster, and at the time of the collision crowds had gathered at the dockyard gates in Malta, drawn by an instinctive apprehension of impending doom. At the same moment during lunch at a Weymouth torpedo works the stem of a wine glass had suddenly cracked with a loud retort; and in London's Eaton Square the ship's Admiral Tryon was seen coming down the stairs at his home. He was in fact aboard the *Victoria*, where he survived the impact but made no effort to save himself. As he sank beneath the waves he is said to have lamented: 'It was all my fault' – and so it was, for he had given the incorrect order which led to the collision.

Generations after her loss the *Titanic* is still a byword for *hubris*. In 1912 the 'unsinkable ship' struck an iceberg on her maiden voyage and went down with 1,500 passengers and crew. Again, a variety of omens anticipated the disaster: a steward's badge came to pieces as his wife stitched it to his cap, and a picture fell from the wall in a stoker's home; then aboard the ship a signal halliard parted as it was used to acknowledge the *bon voyage* signal from the Head of Old Kinsale lighthouse – and the day before the collision rats were seen scurrying aft, away from the point of impact. After the calamity Captain Smith, who went down with the ship, is rumoured to have been seen ashore.

One cause of the *Titanic* disaster is said to have been an unlucky

Egyptian mummy case. This is the lid of an inner coffin with the representation of the head and upper body of an unknown lady of about 1000 BC. Ill-fortune certainly seemed to travel with the lid – first of all the man who bought it from the finder had an arm shattered by an accidental gun shot. He sold the lid, but the purchaser was soon afterwards the recipient of bad news, learning that he was bankrupt and that he had a fatal disease. The new owner, an English lady, placed the coffin lid in her drawing room: next morning she found everything there smashed. She moved it upstairs and the same thing happened, so she also sold it. When this purchaser had the lid photographed, a leering, diabolical face was seen in the print. And when it was eventually presented to the British Museum, members of staff began to contract mysterious ailments – one even died. It was sold yet again to an American, who arranged to take it home with him on the *Titanic*. After the catastrophe he managed to bribe the sailors to allow him to take it into a lifeboat, and it did reach America. Later he sold it to a Canadian, who in 1941 decided to ship it back to England; the vessel taking it, *Empress of Ireland*, sank in the River St Lawrence. So runs the story, but in reality the coffin lid did not leave the British Museum after being presented in 1889. It is still there; its reference number is: 22,542.

In his book *Sailing* (1975), the former prime minister, Edward Heath, revealed that he too had experienced warnings of ill omen. At the launch of *Morning Cloud I* the bottle twice refused to break, and at the same ceremony for *Morning Cloud III* the wife of a crew member fell and suffered severe concussion. This yacht was later wrecked off the south coast with the loss of two lives, and in the very same gale *Morning Cloud I* was blown from her moorings on the island of Jersey, and also wrecked. Meanwhile, *Morning Cloud II* had been launched without incident and was leading a trouble-free life with the Australian to whom she had been sold.

As recently as December 1987 a strange case came to light as a result of a Department of Health and Social Security enquiry into why members of a Bridlington trawler crew were spending so much time unemployed. In explanation, Derek Gates, skipper of the *Pickering*, said that putting to sea had become impossible: on board lights would flicker on and off; cabins stayed freezing cold even when the heating was on maximum; a coastguard confirmed that the ship's steering repeatedly turned her in erratic circles and in addition, the radar kept failing and the engine broke down regularly. One of the crewmen reported seeing a spectral, cloth-capped figure roaming the deck, and a former skipper, Michael Laws, told how he repeatedly sensed someone in the bunk above his, though it was always empty. He added: 'My three months on the *Pickering* were the worst in seventeen years at sea. I didn't earn a penny because things were always going wrong'.

The DHSS decided that the men's fears were a genuine reason for claiming unemployment benefit, and the vicar of Bridlington, the Rev. Tom Willis, was called in to conduct a ceremony of exorcism. He checked the ship's history, and concluded that the disturbances might be connected with the ghost of a deckhand who had been washed overboard when the trawler, then registered as *Family Crest*, was fishing off Ireland. He sprinkled water from stem to stern, led prayers, and called on the spirit of the dead to depart. His intervention proved effective because the problems ceased, and furthermore the crew began to earn bonuses for good catches.

SAILORS' LUCK

Sailors used to be very superstitious – maybe they still are – and greatly concerned to avoid ill-luck, both ashore and afloat. Wives must remember that 'Wash upon sailing day, and you will wash your man away', and must also be careful to smash any eggshells before they dispose of them, to prevent their being used by evil spirits as craft in which to put to sea and cause storms. Luck was brought by:

tattoos
a gold ear-ring worn in the left ear
a piece of coal carried
a coin thrown over the ship's bow when leaving port
a feather from a wren killed on St Stephen's Day
a caul
a hot cross bun or a piece of bread baked on a Good Friday

The last three all preserved from drowning. David Copperfield's caul was advertised for sale in the newspapers 'for the low price of fifteen guineas', and a woman from the port of Lymington in Hampshire offered one in the *Daily Express* as recently as 23 August 1904. One Grimsby man born with a caul has kept it to this day. When he joined the Royal Navy during World War II his mother insisted that he take the caul with him. Various other sailors offered him up to £20 – a large sum for those days – if he would part with it, but he declined.

For over two hundred years now a bun has been added every Good Friday to a collection preserved at the Widow's Son Tavern,

Bromley-by-Bow, London. The name and the custom derive from an eighteenth-century widow who hoped that her missing sailor son would eventually come home safely if she continued to save a bun every Easter. Some seamen had their own version of this, and would touch their sweetheart's bun (*pudenda*) for luck before sailing.

Other things had to be avoided because they brought ill-luck. For example:

meeting a pig, a priest or a woman on the way to one's ship
having a priest or a woman aboard
saying the words pig, priest, rabbit, fox, weasel, hare
dropping a bucket overboard
leaving a hatch cover upside down
leaving a broom, a mop or a squeegee with the head upwards
spitting in the sea
whistling
handing anything down a companionway
sailing on a Friday
finding a drowned body in the trawl (in the case of Yorkshire fishermen)

Although many of these beliefs are obscure in origin, others can be explained. For example, the pig had the devil's mark on his feet – cloven hoofs – and was a bringer of storms; furthermore the drowning of the Gadarene swine was a dangerous precedent. Then the priest was associated with funerals, and so taking him aboard was perhaps too blatant a challenge to the malign powers – if he were to be designated in conversation he was always 'The gentleman in black'. The pig was 'curly tail', or in Scotland 'cauld iron beastie' since if it were inadvertently mentioned the speaker and hearers had to touch cold iron to avoid evil consequences; if no cold iron were available, the studs of one's boots would do. The other four animals were taboo because they were thought to be the shapes assumed by witches who were notorious for summoning storms.

Perhaps women were also shunned because they were considered potential witches, although a good way to make a storm abate was for a woman to expose her naked body to the elements. Bare-breasted figure-heads were designed to achieve the same result. Nevertheless, during HMS *Durban*'s South American tour in the 1930s the captain allowed his wife to take passage on the ship. Before the tour was halfway through there were two accidental deaths on board, besides a series of mishaps, and feeling amongst the crew began to run high. At one port of call a group of men returning to the ship on a liberty boat were freely discussing the run of bad luck, attributing it to 'having that bloody woman on board'. They did not realise that the captain was separated from them by only a thin bulkhead and had overheard the whole conversation. But instead of taking disciplinary action, he put his wife ashore the next day; she travelled by land to other ports, and the ship's luck immediately changed for the better.

Fridays were anathema – 'Friday sail, Friday fail' was the saying – since the temptation of Adam, the banishment from the Garden of Eden, and the crucifixion of Christ had all taken place on a Friday. One old story, probably apocryphal, tells of a royal navy ship called HMS *Friday* which was launched, first sailed and then lost on a Friday; moreover her captain was also called Friday. Oddly enough, a ship of this name does appear in the admiralty records in 1919, but the story was in circulation some fifty years earlier. This fear of Fridays dies hard. A certain Paul Sibellas, seaman, was aboard the *Port Invercargill* in the 1960s when on one occasion she was ready to sail for home from New Zealand at 10pm on a Friday the thirteenth. The skipper, however, delayed his departure until midnight had passed and Saturday the fourteenth had arrived.

Whistling is preferably avoided because it can conjure up a wind, which might be acceptable aboard a becalmed sailing ship, but not otherwise. Another way of getting a wind was to stick a knife in the mast with its handle pointing in the direction from which a blow was required – this was done on the *Dreadnought* in 1869, in jury rig after being dismasted off Cape Horn. In 1588 Francis Drake is said to have met the devil and various wizards to whistle up tempests to disrupt the Spanish Armada; the spot near Plymouth where they gathered is now called Devil's Point. He is also said to have whittled a stick, of which the pieces became fireships as they fell into the sea; and his house at Buckland Abbey was apparently built with unaccountable speed, thanks to the devil's help. Drake's drum is preserved in the house and is believed to beat of its own accord when the country faces danger.

DENIZENS OF THE DEEP

With her mirror and comb, her long hair, bare breasts and fish tail, the mermaid is instantly recognisable, but nowadays only as an amusing convention. However, she once inspired real fear as well as fascination and sailors firmly believed she gave warning of tempest or calamity. As recently as seventy years ago, Sandy Gunn, a Cape Wrath shepherd, claimed he saw a mermaid on a spur of rock at Sandwood Bay. Other coastal dwellers also recalled such encounters, even naming various landmarks. In Cornwall there are several tales involving mermaids: at Padstow the harbour entrance is all but blocked by the Doom Bar, a sandbank put there by a mermaid, we are told, in retaliation for being fired at by a man of the town. And on the southern Cornish coast between the villages of Down Derry and Looe, the former town of Seaton was overwhelmed by sand because it was cursed by a mermaid injured by a sailor from the port. Mermaid's Rock near Lamorna Cove was the haunt of a mermaid who would sing before a storm and then swim out to sea – her beauty was such that young men would follow, never to re-appear. At Zennor a mermaid was so entranced by the singing of Matthew Trewella, the squire's son, that she persuaded him to follow her; he, too, failed to return, but his voice could be heard from time to time, coming from beneath the waves. The little church in which he sang on land has a fifteenth-century bench-end carved with a mermaid and her looking-glass and comb.

On the other hand, mermaids could sometimes be helpful. Mermaid's Rock at Saundersfoot in Wales is so called because a mermaid was once stranded there by the ebbing of the tide. She was returned to the sea by a passing mussel-gatherer, and later came back to present him with a bag of gold and silver as a reward. In the Mull of Kintyre a Mackenzie lad helped another stranded mermaid who in return granted him his wish, that he could build unsinkable boats from which no man would ever be lost.

Sexual unions between humans and both sea people and seals are the subject of many stories, and various families claim strange sea-borne ancestry: for example the McVeagh clan of Sutherland traces its descent from the alliance between a fisherman and a mermaid; on the western island of North Uist the MacCodums have an ancestor who married a seal maiden; and the familiar Welsh name of Morgan is sometimes held to mean 'born of the sea', again pointing to a family tree which includes a mermaid or merman. Human wives dwelling at sea with mermen were allowed occasional visits to the land, but they had to take care not to overstay – and if they chanced to hear the benediction said in church they were never able to rejoin their husbands. Matthew Arnold's poem *The Forsaken Merman* relates how one human wife decides to desert her sea husband and children. There is also a Shetland tale, this time concerning a sea wife married to a land husband:

On the island of Unst a man walking by the shore sees mermaids and mermen dancing naked in the moonlight, the seal skins which they have discarded lying on the sand. When they see the man, the dancers snatch up the skins, become sea creatures again, and all plunge into the waves – except one, for the man has taken hold of the skin. Its owner is a mermaid of outstanding beauty, and she has to stay on the shore. The man asks her to become his wife, and she accepts. He keeps the skin, and carefully hides it.

The marriage is successful, and the couple have several children. Yet the woman is often drawn at night to the sea shore, where she is heard conversing with a large seal in an unknown tongue. Years pass. During the course of a game one of the children finds a sealskin hidden in a cornstack. He mentions it to his mother, and she takes it and returns to the sea. Her husband hears the news and runs after her, arriving by the shore to be told by his wife: 'Farewell, and may all good attend you. I loved you very well when I lived on earth, but I always loved my first husband more'.

As we know from David Thomson's fine book *The People of the Sea* (1984), such stories are still widely told in parts of Ireland and Scotland and may explain why sailors were reluctant to kill seals. There was also a belief that seals embodied the souls of drowned mariners.

The friendly dolphin invariably brings good luck to seafarers, and has even been known to guide them in the right direction. As recently as January 1989 the newspapers reported that an Australian swimmer who had been attacked and wounded by a shark was saved from death only by the intervention of a group of dolphins which drove off the predator. Also worthy of mention here is another benevolent helper of seamen lost in open boats: a kindly ghost known as the pilot of the *Pinta*. When all seems lost he will appear in the bows of the boat and insistently point the way to safety.

Other denizens of the deep inspired fear and terror. The water horse of Wales and the Isle of Man – the kelpie of Scotland – grazes by the side of the sea or loch. If anyone is rash enough to get on him he rushes into the water and drowns the rider; furthermore his back can conveniently lengthen to accommodate any number of people. There are several tales believed of the water horse, for example, if he is harnessed to a plough he drags it into the sea; if he falls in love with a woman he may take the form of a man to court her – only if she recognises his true nature from the tell-tale sand in his hair will she have a chance of escaping, and then she must steal away while he sleeps. Legend says that the water horse also takes the shape of an old woman; in this guise he is put to bed with a bevy of beautiful maidens but kills them all by sucking their blood, save for one who manages to run away. He pursues her but she jumps a running brook which, water horse though he is, he dare not cross.

Still more terrible are the many sea monsters of which stories are told. One played havoc with the fish of the Solway Firth until the people planted a row of sharpened stakes on which it impaled itself. Another serpent-like creature, the Stoor Worm, was so huge that its body curled about the earth. It took up residence off northern Scotland and made it known that a weekly delivery of seven virgins was required, otherwise the towns and villages would be devastated. Soon it was the turn of the king's daughter to be sacrificed, but her father announced that he would give her in marriage to anyone who would rid him of the worm. Assipattle, the dreamy seventh son of a farmer, took up the challenge and put to sea in a small boat with an iron pot containing a glowing peat; he sailed into the monster's mouth, then down into its inside – after searching for some time he found the liver, cut a hole in it, and inserted the peat. The liver soon began to burn fiercely, and the worm retched out Assipattle and his boat. Its death throes shook the world: one of its teeth became the Orkney Islands, the other Shetland; the falling tongue scooped out the Baltic Sea, and the burning liver turned into the volcanos of Iceland. The king kept his promise, and the triumphant Assipattle married his daughter.

Perhaps the most famous of all water monsters is that of Loch Ness, first mentioned in a life of St Columba written in 700 AD. Some 150 years earlier one of the saint's followers was apparently swimming in the loch when the monster 'suddenly swam up to the surface, and with gaping mouth and with great roaring rushed towards the man'. Fortunately, Columba was watching and ordered the monster to turn back: it obeyed. The creature (or its successor) then lay dormant for some 1,300 years, for the next recorded sighting was in 1871. However, during the last fifty years there have been frequent reports and controversies. In 1987 a painstaking and expensive sonar scan of the loch revealed a moving object of some 400lb in weight which scientists were unable to identify. Sir Peter Scott dubbed the monster 'Nessiterras Rhombopteryx', after the diamond-shaped fin shown on a photograph taken by some American visitors; the Monster Exhibition Centre at Drumnadrochit on Loch Ness describes it as 'The World's Greatest Mystery'. Tourists from all over the world flock to visit Loch Ness, monster and centre.

NAUTICAL CUSTOMS

The seas will always be potentially dangerous for those who choose to sail them and most seafarers tried hard to avoid incurring the wrath of Davy Jones – they once were sometimes reluctant even to save drowning comrades lest they deprive the deep of a victim which would serve as a propitiatory sacrifice though the dilemma could be resolved by throwing the drowning man a rope or spar. This was a much less personal intervention than actually lending a hand or diving in to help and therefore less risky.

Various shipboard ceremonies were observed and maintained religiously: at Christmas a tree would be lashed to the top of the mast (the custom is still followed, and on ships lacking a mast the tree is tied to the railings on the highest deck); at midnight as New Year's Eve becomes New Year's Day the ship's bell is rung eight times for the old year and eight times for the new – midnight on a ship is normally eight bells – the oldest member of the crew giving the first eight rings, the youngest the second.

'Burying the Dead Horse' was a ceremony which was continued in merchant ships until late in the nineteenth century, and kept up most recently in vessels on the Australian run. The 'horse' was a symbol for the month's pay advanced on shore (and usually spent before sailing); after twenty-eight days at sea the advance was worked out. The horse's body was made from a barrel, its legs from hay, straw or shavings covered with canvas, and the mane and tail of hemp. The animal was hoisted to the main yardarm and set on fire; it was allowed to blaze for a short time and was then cut loose and dropped into the sea. Musical accompaniment was provided by the shanty 'Poor Old Horse':

> Now he is dead and will die no more,
> And we say so, for we know so.
> It makes his ribs feel very sore,
> Oh, poor old man.
> He is gone and will go no more,
> And we say so, for we know so.
> So goodbye, old horse,
> We say goodbye.

On sailing ships collective work at the capstan, windlass, pumps and halliards was often accompanied by particular songs known as shanties. In the late nineteenth and early twentieth centuries big, full-rigged vessels were bringing cargoes of nitrate, guano and saltpetre to Britain from South American ports. When a ship was loaded and ready to sail round Cape Horn and home, the carpenter would make a large wooden cross to which red and white lights were fixed in the shape of the constellation known as the Southern Cross. As this was hoisted to the head of the mainmast, the crew would sing the shanty 'Hurrah, my boys, we're homeward bound', and then the crew of every ship in harbour took turns to cheer the departing vessel.

Seafarers crossing the equator for the first time – and sometimes the tropics or the polar circles – are often put through a sort of baptism or initiation ceremony. The earliest recorded reference to such a ritual dates from 1529 on a French ship, but by the end of the following century English vessels were involved in the same custom, which continues to this day in both royal navy and merchant service. One of the crew appears as Neptune, complete with crown, trident and luxuriant beard; others represent Queen Amphitrite, a barber, a surgeon and various nymphs and bears. Neptune holds court by the side of a large canvas bath full of sea-water, and any on board who have not previously crossed 'the Line' are ceremonially shaved with huge wooden razors, then thoroughly ducked. Finally, the victim is given a certificate which protects him from the same ordeal on any future occasion. Even passengers are put through a modified form of the proceedings, though women are given a still softer version of the treatment.

When a naval captain leaves his ship he can expect a ritual farewell. Even Prince Charles was unable to escape when in 1976 he relinquished command of the minesweeper, HMS *Bronington*; he was seized by white-coated doctors (his officers), placed in a wheelchair and 'invalided out' to the cheers of his crew-members who held up a banner inscribed: 'Command has aged me'.

Other mariners departed in a less jovial manner. When a man died at sea his body would be sewn into canvas, weighted, and committed to the deep. The sailmaker was responsible for making the shroud, and would always put the last stitch through the corpse's nose, ensuring that there was no sign of life and that the body remained attached to the weighted canvas. This practice was followed at least until the 1960s, the sailmaker receiving a bottle of rum for his work. Nowadays bodies are seldom buried at sea but are refrigerated and brought back to land. However, those consigning a body in this way still receive the traditional bottle of rum for their trouble.

2
Down to Earth

In many instances folklore can be said literally to spring from the soil, since natural features such as hills, outcropping rocks and even forests often gave rise to beliefs which attempted to explain them or commented on their presence. Man-made additions to the landscape such as burial mounds and the great standing stones also attracted their share of both lore and awe, as did the huge figures cut into the chalk of downlands. Crossroads and bridges, too, were regarded as highly sensitive places, transitional points where the line dividing the normal world from that of the supernatural was believed to be easily breached. Caves and passages, both natural and artificial, also provided a focus for tales ranging from buried treasure to disappearing musicians.

FEATURES OF THE LANDSCAPE

Hills and High Places
Unusual features in the landscape such as a sudden hill or a giant boulder are frequently explained as the result of supernatural activity. There are numerous tales of the devil's hurling huge rocks which fell to earth and became hills, and mighty giants' scattering enormous stones during battle. Wiltshire's Silbury Hill has always

24

provoked diverse speculation: firstly, it is thought to be the burial place of King Sil, who can be seen galloping over the downs on certain moonlit nights. But there is also the local story that one day when the devil was flying towards Marlborough, with a sack of earth and chalk (planning to smother the townspeople who had for some reason annoyed him), the vigilant priests of Avebury saw him coming, and sent up such a barrage of prayers that he had to drop his burden and turn tail. Yet another explanation for the hill's origin is that the people of Marlborough were feuding with their neighbours at Devizes and asked the devil to drop a load of earth on them. The Devizes people appealed for help to St John, who advised them to adopt the following stratagem: an old man carrying a large sack of worn-out shoes was sent out to meet the devil, who was unsure of the exact location of Devizes; when he asked the old man how far it was, he was told 'I left there three years ago, and I've worn out all these shoes on the way'. The devil threw down his burden in disgust.

The Devil's Nightcap near Studland on the Dorset coast is a mass of rock which the devil is said to have thrown at Corfe Castle from the Isle of Wight. (In fact the projectile therefore missed its mark by several miles, and the devil in these stories appears to be as incompetent as he is gullible.) Another Devil's Nightcap can be found in Warwickshire, just off the A422 on the Stratford side of Alcester. The devil was apparently gathering nuts in the vicinity – a suitable enough activity since 21 September is known as the Devil's Nutting Day – but on this occasion he happened to come face to face with the Virgin Mary. His shock was so great that he ran off, abandoning his bag of nuts which became the hill.

Such tales and motifs tend to recur in different places all over the country. The story of hills being formed from the discarded burden of the devil after an encounter with a quick-thinking cobbler is one which pops up again and again: the hill known as Devil's Spittleful near Bewdley in Worcestershire, for example (where the Devil planned to punish the townspeople for their piety); and the Wrekin in Shropshire, where a giant bearing a grudge against the people of Shrewsbury was put off his intent to dam up the river Severn by yet another shrewd shoemaker and persuaded to dump his load of earth and rubble. Nearby Ercall Hill (alternatively Wenlock Edge) is made from the earth that the giant scraped off his boots.

Sometimes elevated features were regarded as holy – for example Glastonbury Tor in Somerset was once an island in time of flood or high water and the Celts believed it to be the shrine of the god of the underworld; some identify it as Avalon, the burial place of King Arthur. Other hills and barrows were used as sites for more secular purposes such as sports and fairs.

Fairy Hills
Fairy Hill, Fairy Knowe, Bryn-yr-Ellylon – all mean Hill of the Fairies and placenames such as these can be found in many different parts of Britain. Fairy Hill is at Bishopton in County Durham, Fairy Knowe at Aberfoyle in Perthshire (now Central Scotland) and Bryn-yr-Ellylon near Mold in Flintshire (now Clwyd), and all three have their stories.

It is well known that the fairies were passionately fond of music, and legend often tells of their luring a passing piper or fiddler underground to play for them – if they succeeded he would have to remain for a year and a day. There is even a story that the Queen of Fairyland paid two fiddlers to play for a night, and kept them for two hundred years. When they finally returned above ground, still thinking they had been away for only one night, they crumbled into dust. The same queen had dealings with Thomas the Rhymer, a historical figure who lived in the thirteenth century and made some fifty prophecies, including the one which foretold that England, Wales and Scotland would be ruled by a single monarch. He is said to have been buried in the Inverness town cemetery on Tom-na-Hurich (Hill of the Yews) together with his men and horses, and is ready to rise again if Scotland should have need of him. The tales of his consorting with the Queen of Fairyland usually begin on the slopes of the Eildon Hills in Roxburghshire (now the Border Region in Scotland):

Thomas is asleep on Huntley Bank by the Eildon Tree when he wakes to see the green-clad Queen of the Fairies. They make love under the tree, but the queen is turned temporarily into a hag and Thomas is put into her power for seven years. The queen leads him into the hill, and after a journey in darkness of three days and nights they come into a garden of forbidden fruit where she shows him roads leading to heaven, paradise, purgatory, hell and fairyland.

Before taking the road to fairyland the queen, who has now recovered her beauty, warns Thomas that he must speak to no one but her, otherwise he will never be able to leave. He stays in the land of music, dancing and revelry for what he thinks is seven days but is in fact seven years.

Before leaving he receives an apple from the queen, and with it the gift of a tongue that can never lie. Then he finds himself back on Huntley Bank, beneath the Eildon Tree.

Caves and Passages

The many caves and passages, both real and imagined, which exist below ground support a number of traditional tales. Many hidden mysteries lie beneath the landscape and one of the most enduring stories concerns Moel Arthur, a mountain overlooking the Welsh Vale of Clwyd. Moel Arthur is thought to be the burial place of Queen Boudicca. A vast treasure hoard is said to be at its heart, its location indicated at times by a supernatural ray of light – but anyone attempting to dig will be driven away by thunder, lightning and storm. Another hill in Wales with a history of folklore is Dinas Emrys, two miles from the village of Beddgelert (itself the centre of a controversial legend, see p196): one story associated with the hill is in the ancient collection of Welsh tales known as the *Mabinogion* and concerns King Llud of Britain (who incidentally gave his name to London – via Caer Llud, and Llundein).

Llud went to consult his brother, Llevelys, King of France, about the troubles affecting his kingdom, one of which was a plague caused by the fighting of two dragons.

'Find the centre of your kingdom', advised Llevelys, 'dig a pit there, and put in it a vat of the best mead, with a silk sheet over it. The dragons will appear in the air, fighting, but when they tire they will fall on to the sheet and turn into two little pigs – their weight will pull the sheet to the bottom of the vat. They will drink up the mead, then fall asleep. You must then wrap them in the sheet, put them in a stone chest, and bury it in the most secure place you can find.'

Llud returned home, and after careful measurements had been made decided that the centre of the country lay at Oxford. A pit was dug, and everything followed as predicted by Llevelys. The place chosen for burying the chest was Dinas Emrys.

All went well for many centuries but then a later king, Vortigern, ran into difficulties when he tried to build a fortress on top of Dinas Emrys. He consulted the wizard, Merlin, who told him that the two dragons were still fighting in an underground lake inside the hill. Merlin managed to deal with the dragons – one white, the other the famous red dragon of Wales – and later buried his own treasure under the hill in a golden vessel, predicting that the discoverer would be 'blue of eye and gold of hair' – when he or she approaches a bell will ring, and the cave will open of its own accord. The treasure still awaits the lucky finder.

Many of those venturing underground might well find that their quest ends in disaster. At least three underground passages boast the same story: from Old Grange to Flaxley Abbey near Cinderford in the Forest of Dean; from Malling Abbey (or Leybourne Grange) to Smuggler's Cave near Ryash, close to the M20 in Kent; and from Binham Priory to Walsingham Abbey, about three miles apart on the B1388 in Norfolk. In each case a wood called Fiddler's Copse stands about halfway along the route. The explanation is that two brothers wished to trace the subterranean passage; one was a fiddler and set off along the passage playing his instrument all the while so the other could follow the sound on the surface. But as he reached the copse the music ceased, and the brother was never seen again.

There is another tale concerning the Scilly Isles, where at the foot of a headland called Peninnis on St Mary's is a freshwater pool known as Piper's Hole; a cavern on the island of Tresco bears the same name and local lore maintains the two are linked by a passage running beneath the sea – but no-one who has ventured along it has returned to tell the tale. Perhaps one of those lost was the piper who provided the name.

Similarly the village of Morda and the castle at Chirk, both near Oswestry and about six miles apart, are supposed to be connected by an underground passage; another parallel is that people who went exploring did not come out again. Then a wandering fiddler called 'Iolo ap Hugh' (Ned Pugh) decided to try to solve the mystery: one Hallowe'en he took a basket of provisions, a candle and his fiddle, and set off down the dark passage. He played bravely as he walked, the lighted candle stuck to his fiddle and the basket strapped to his back. The music soon receded, and no more was heard of Iolo. Several years passed until again at Hallowe'en a shepherd was amazed to hear music coming from a cave. He looked in and there was Iolo dancing to his own fiddle, still looking young in body but with an agonised expression on his face. Two years later the shepherd heard the same tune coming from beneath the church floor, though this time it was early on Christmas morning; later on he whistled the tune to the vicar who took it down, and although Iolo never came back, the music exists to this day – it is called 'Farewell, Ned Pugh'.

Another version of the story relates that Ned took up a bugle instead not a fiddle, and became chief huntsman to Gwyn ap Nudd, God of the Underworld. At Hallowe'en he wanders below Mount Plynlimon, through the Black Mountains, and in the wild places around Aberdare. Travellers fear for their lives when they hear his bugle or his wild cries to the Dogs of Hell, for the sinister pack brings warning of death to all whom it encounters.

STONES

Unusual stones have made a profound mark on the popular mind, inspiring both awe and affection. They include outcropping rocks or glacial erratics, man-made monoliths or stone circles, and these may represent petrified giants and their missiles or possess magical and curative powers – there is, without doubt, a tremendous number of stories and beliefs still associated with them. A single stone is often enough to generate tales and anecdotes. For example at the village of Staunton, near Monmouth, the Buckstone is reputed to have been used for sacrificial purposes by the Druids. And nearby is another sacrificial stone where once an intended victim was apparently miraculously saved: a young bard called Tudor was waiting for the archdruid's dagger to fall and end his life, when a stag ambled out of the forest. All those present were struck by the coincidence and so the stag was taken for sacrifice, and Tudor was freed.

The Rufus Stone

Some contend that William Rufus was another sacrifice – the stone to his memory was erected in 1745 and stands in Canterton Glen on the northern edge of the New Forest, near the Hampshire village of Minstead. King William II of England, nicknamed Rufus because of his red hair, was killed on 2 August 1100 while out hunting when an arrow loosed by his chief huntsman, Walter Tyrell, glanced off a deer and accidentally hit him. Yet the death remains mysterious in many ways.

Rufus was unpopular because he had extended the forest and tightened the penalties for those who infringed its code, and it may be significant that although after his death Tyrell fled the country, he was not pursued, nor were his estates confiscated. Henry, William's younger brother, was not next in line to the throne, but within three days he had been crowned at Westminster. Furthermore Rufus had been instrumental in preventing Henry from marrying a young nun, Matilda, yet three months after Henry's accession the

Archbishop of Canterbury declared Matilda to be 'no nun', and so Henry was able to marry her.

One theory is that Henry engineered William's death so he could take both the kingdom and the wife he wanted. Another quite unassociated suggestion is that Rufus voluntarily allowed himself to be sacrificed in a fertility cult, though this seems highly doubtful, particularly if it is true that he was apparently reluctant to hunt on the fatal day, having dreamed of blood spouting from his chest and hiding the sun. This was not the only evil omen which presaged his death – another concerned the Earl of Cornwall, who met a wounded, naked man being carried through the forest on the back of a black goat. The man warned that he was a malevolent spirit who wished to procure Rufus' death because of the harm he had done the church – though why such a spirit should wish to help the church is not clear.

It is also claimed that William Rufus did not die near the place marked by his stone, but in the south-eastern corner of the New Forest. The traditional spot was known as Thorougham, and this was the original name of a farm now called Parks Farm on the Beaulieu Estate.

Moll Walbee

The village of Llowes is on the A438 near Hay-on-Wye and there is a stone in the church called Moll Walbee's Stone. Originally it stood outside; it commemorates one Matilda St Valéry who in the reign of King John married a baron, William de Braose. Many stories are told of Matilda, or Moll. She was hated by the Welsh because of her often high-handed actions – for example on one occasion she forced a chieftain called Madog to shoot an apple from his son's head (à la William Tell). Moll and her children were eventually captured by King John's men, and imprisoned at Windsor (her husband having escaped or been exiled to France). Hundreds of masons were employed to build a tower over the captives and when it was complete, they were left to die there. Another story is that Moll and her son were shut in a dungeon with a sheaf of wheat and a piece of raw bacon. Eleven days later when the door was opened they were found dead, but Moll, horribly, had half-eaten her son's cheeks.

She is said to have built the castle at Hay-on-Wye in a single night, aided by occult powers. She was of giant stature, and while she was working on the castle she carried the stones in her apron. One of them, nine feet long, fell into her shoe – in irritation she plucked it out and threw it away; it landed three miles away, in Llowes churchyard. An effigy in St Mary's Church at Hay is reputed to be that of Moll, but probably depicts a monk. It is probably not the unfortunate monk who interrupted Moll's midnight incantations as he was thrown into the middle of the Wye – hence the wailing and gurgling that can still sometimes be heard coming from the river at that spot.

Idris' Chair

Cadair Idris is a 3,000 foot mountain a few miles from Dolgellau in North Wales. The giant Idris, like Moll Walbee, was also troubled by his shoes and so took them off, together with what were to him three grains of sand. To ordinary people, however, they are three huge boulders – Tri Graienyn – and they can be seen to this day. Idris' Chair was a hollow near the top of the mountain, now partly filled by the waters of Llyn Cau, and local tradition maintains that anyone who spends the night on the summit will be found next morning dead, mad or a genius. There is no record of whether anyone has put it to the test.

Hangman's Stones

The following tale is told of at least twenty-five places in England and Wales, from Dorset as far as Northumberland and from Pembroke to Lincolnshire:

A sheepstealer carries a stolen animal home on his back, under cover of darkness, its tied legs round the front of his neck. Weary of the burden, he rests it on some convenient milestone or monolith but the creature struggles and the man is strangled by its weight. His dead body is found the next day, a warning to others.

At Rottingdean on the Sussex coast a hangman's stone was once sold to a collector for one guinea – however, it was a fake and the real one still stands above the bathing pool near the cliff edge.

Healing Stones

Cornwall, with its rocky terrain and archaeological richness, has more than its share of impressive stones including some which have (or had) healing powers. For example, not far from the village of Madron – near Penzance – is the famous Men-an-Tol (Holed Stone): if an infant suffering from rickets or scrofula was stripped naked and passed nine times through the two-foot aperture, it was expected to recover. Then at Morvah, three miles from Madron, is a forked rock called the Crick Stone. It was believed that those who could squeeze through the hole without touching the rock would be cured of a cricked back – though it must be said that anyone suffering such a problem would probably find the feat particularly difficult. The 'Cornish Pebble' at Perranarworthal, near Truro, is a large stone balanced on two others. Those willing to crawl round it and also through the aperture could leave their sciatica or rheumatism behind, provided they followed the procedure during the month of May.

Many other stones, large and small, portable and otherwise, are thought to have therapeutic powers. According to Merlin, at Stonehenge people poured water over the stones, then collected it and bathed in it, or mixed it with herbs and applied it to wounds. This was reported by Geoffrey of Monmouth in his *History of the Kings of Britain*, written early in the twelfth century.

Fruitful Stones

Some stones are associated with fertility. A cleft in one of the faces of the Wrekin known as the Needle's Eye is supposed to have been from when the rocks were 'rent asunder' at the moment of the crucifixion. On visiting the hill for the first time, every young woman would squeeze through, to be greeted by her sweetheart on the other side with a kiss – but if she turned round or looked back she would never marry.

The Odin Stone stood at Stenness on the Orkney mainland until it was broken up in 1814. It was visited regularly by young lovers who would clasp hands through a hole in it, take the Odin oath (of which the words are now lost), and thus become promised to each other. The pact was so binding that in one instance a woman travelled to London, took the hand of her dead pirate sweetheart who had been hanged in chains at Greenwich, and made sure the oath was retracted before committing herself elsewhere. A song still sung in Orkney tells this story:

A couple meet at the stone one Christmas Eve to pledge themselves. They kiss, then turn towards their respective homes but on his way the young man is stabbed and killed by a rival suitor. As the woman reaches her home she is startled by a cry, turns round, and for a moment sees her love standing there: 'His hand was pointing to the stars, and his eyes gave such a light; and with a smiling countenance he vanished from her sight'.

The phallic associations of standing stones may have helped the belief that they could ensure fertility. At least until the 1920s the pillars of St Paul's Cathedral in London were regularly embraced by women, with this end in mind. Further afield, a granite block on a hilltop in Glenavon, near Braemar in Aberdeenshire (now Grampian), was visited by women who believed that its influence would help them to conceive. Some went again when they were pregnant because they considered a second dose of the stone's powers would bring them an easy childbirth.

People Petrified

Some stones are thought to have human characteristics such as growing or bleeding, and those groups called 'Nine Stones' may originally have been known as 'Noon Stones', from the belief that they drank from nearby streams at noon. This idea of stones' drinking was not an altogether rare occurrence, apparently – the Whet Stone near the market town of Kington in Herefordshire, close to the Welsh border, is said to roll down to the brook for a drink at cockcrow, then to resume its place. The Four Stones at Old Radnor, near Kington, are said to drink at Hindwell Pool. The Nine Stones on Dartmoor's Belstone Common do not drink at noon – but they dance. Similarly the three monoliths standing a mile apart from each other near Stackpole, a village south of Pembroke, are called the Dancing Stones because on unspecified occasions they meet, go down to Sais's (Saxon's) Ford and dance there before making their way home.

Such notions are less surprising in view of the belief that many stones – sometimes whole groups of them – were thought to be petrified people. Carreg Lleidr (the Robber's Stone) for example, near the Anglesey village of Llandyfrydog, takes its name from the man who was turned into this very same stone when he was running away with the church bible which he had stolen. On Christmas Eve when the clock strikes midnight the stone apparently runs three times round the field; it is then stopped in its tracks for another year. There is also folklore attached to a limestone column near Clydach (off the A465 between Brynmawr and Abergavenny in Gwent): it is called the Lonely Shepherd and the story goes that a shepherd was so cruel to his wife that she drowned herself in the River Usk – as a punishment he was turned into stone, to keep eternal vigil. On Midsummer Night he goes down to the river to look in vain for his wife, then returns before daybreak.

On the island of Skye and situated five miles north of the main town of Portree, there is a prominent spike of stone known as the

33

Old Man of Storr; close by it lies another column, 'the wife', which once stood upright as well. The explanation offered is that an old couple were hunting a lost cow hereabouts when they came across a band of giants. They were deeply afraid and ran away, but made the mistake of looking back and so were turned to stone.

Such stories continue elsewhere; as a young Aberdeenshire woman, turned to stone in answer to her prayers to escape being raped by a warlock. The Maiden Stone also bears certain marks which are traditionally explained as the burns made on her apron by a hot bread-oven shovel which she took in self-defence as she fled from her home. Antiquarians, however, say that the marks are vestiges of the badges of two noble Pictish families. The woman's name was Janet of Drumdurno, and the story has inspired a sculptor, Shaun Crampton, to make his own statue of her – a powerful, bare-breasted figure which looks capable of putting any warlock to flight. Both stone and statue are to be found near Chapel of Garioch, off the B9002, five miles from Inverurie in Aberdeenshire (now Grampian).

Various stone circles in Cornwall are said to be young men and women punished for breaking the sabbath. To the east, near Liskeard, there are three circles on the moor in the parish of St Cleer known as the Hurlers – young men who were indulging in the sport of hurling on a Sunday. And in the far west, at St Buryan, are the nine Dawns Men (Dancing Stones). otherwise called the Merry Maidens, with two granite pillars nearby. Apparently one Sunday evening some of the young women of the village chose to wander into the fields instead of going to evening service. Two evil spirits took the guise of pipers and began to play dance tunes, forgetting that it was a holy day, the women started to dance. The music became wilder and wilder, the steps more and more abandoned, then out of a clear sky came a flash of lightning: pipers and dancers were transfixed and there they remain still.

A broadly similar story is told of two impressive stone circles at Stanton Drew, a few miles south of Bristol, off the A37:

Many hundreds of years ago a newly-married couple gathered with their relatives and friends on a Saturday evening to celebrate. They feasted and danced until they heard the clock strike midnight when the piper, a pious man, would play no longer. The guests, however, wanted to carry on dancing, and so did the bride. 'I'll not be baulked by a beggarly piper', she said. 'I'll go to hell and back to get one, if need be.' She had barely spoken when a grey-

34

haired old man appeared and offered his services. 'You're very welcome', said the bride. He sat down and played a slow air. 'Faster, faster,' called the guests, so the piper struck up a jig.

The dancers bounded joyfully along. The pace grew quicker and quicker, but they found themselves unable to stop. 'Let's have a rest, piper!' they shouted. He took no notice, and his shape gradually changed into that of the devil. On and on went the dance, remorselessly until daybreak, by which time the wedding party had been reduced to skeletons – and when the rest of the villagers came on the scene they found only large stones strewn about the meadow.

The only survivor was the pious piper. He was lying under the hedge half-dead with fright, having witnessed the whole drama.

Stonehenge

The most famous of all stone circles in Britain and perhaps even in the world is Stonehenge. Prehistoric temple, early astronomical observatory, ring of petrified giants: there are many theories and legends as to its origin and purpose, and one of the first must be that related by Geoffrey of Monmouth, writing in the twelfth century. He tells us that Aurelius Ambrosius, King of the Britons, wished to build a monument on the site of the place where some 450 people had been massacred by the Saxon invader, Hengist, and was advised by Merlin to send to Ireland for the Giants' Dance from Mount Killaurus (which some have identified with Kildare). Aurelius sent his brother, Uther Pendragon, with an army of 15,000 men which proceeded to defeat an Irish army, then brought back the stones and re-erected them.

In fact, the sixty so-called blue stones came from the Preseli Hills in Pembrokeshire; they were brought up the River Severn, which may explain the misconception that they came from Ireland. Stonehenge still inspires strong feelings, and there is now an annual confrontation at mid-summer between the 'hippies' who wish to celebrate the solstice there and the police who are required to keep them away in the interests of conservation (see Chapter 7).

CHALK FIGURES

As well as leaving their enduring mark in the shape of megaliths and stone circles, the peoples of the past cut huge figures into the turf of chalk hills. Near Uffington, a few miles west of Wantage in Berkshire, is the famous White Horse cut out some 2,000 years ago by a Celtic tribe, or possibly even earlier. It stands close to an earthworks known as Uffington Castle which some believe can be identified as Mount Badon, where King Arthur defeated the Saxons. The 374 foot long horse gives its name to the Vale of the White Horse and may have been the symbol of a god or a tribe. Local people used to think that it represented a dragon which St George killed nearby; each year they would go out to scour the weeds from the figure, and then hold a celebration. The event as it took place in 1857 was described by Thomas Hughes (the author of *Tom Brown's Schooldays*) in his classic book *The Scouring of the White Horse*. More recently erosion became a serious problem because of the enormous increase in the number of visitors, so now the horse is concreted, and the occasional coat of paint keeps it white. Even so it is still an impressive sight from afar, and it continues to draw many tourists.

There was also a scouring at Cerne Abbas, a Dorset village a few miles north of the county town, where the figure of a giant is cut in outline on a hillside. He is 180 feet tall and carries a huge club, but is particularly renowned for displaying massive and unabashed sexual power. In order that the masculine parts might be hidden by grass and weed, the clergy at one time forbade scourings of the chalk – Victorian mothers told their children that the giant was really a tailor with his shears in his lap. 'A Romano-British version of Hercules', said scholars; other suggestions included a cudgel player or a wrestler, and local people thought he was a Danish giant killed by peasants after feasting on stolen sheep, then falling asleep. Some say he goes down to the stream to drink when he hears the clock strike midnight – but does he ever 'hear'?

Most saw the giant as a fertility symbol, and sought to harness his latent energy. Barren women tried to find a cure by sitting at the appropriate place on the figure; others believed they needed to consummate their marriage there, though it must have been rather a draughty and public place for such an activity. Nevertheless childless couples continue to visit the giant. In 1982 the *Dorset Evening Echo* reported that the Marquis of Bath, his wife Virginia and his daughter Silvy make an annual pilgrimage: some twenty-two years earlier the marquis had called on its power after five years of childless marriage, and nine months later his daughter had arrived. Since then the three have visited the giant every year, and communed with it about their problems.

Another outline figure bigger even than the Cerne Abbas giant is the Long Man of Wilmington, cut out on Windover Hill between

Lewes and Polegate in East Sussex – this one is 230 feet long, though he lacks the sexual apparatus of his comrade at Cerne. His possible identities are many: he was Waendal (the Anglo-Saxon god of war), he was the badge of Harold II (the last of the Anglo-Saxon kings), a Saxon haymaker, a Roman soldier, Mohammed, St Paul, a pre-historic surveyor – or sometimes just a giant killed by a neighbour with whom he had quarrelled. In fact we are unlikely ever to know the true identification.

BRIDGES AND CROSSROADS

At Kirkby Lonsdale, a market town less than six miles east of the M6 in Cumbria, there is a dramatic fifteenth-century bridge spanning the River Lune and known as the Devil's Bridge. One of the stories associated with it goes as follows:

> An old woman's cow strayed across the river away from home but by the time she was missed the water was in spate. The devil appeared and offered to build a bridge overnight though on one condition – he was to have the first living thing to cross it. However, the old woman was not so simple as he thought because when the bridge was ready she threw a bun across it for her little dog to run after. The dog, having no soul, was of course no use to the devil who rushed off in a fury, leaving behind his collar (which he had taken off while working), his fingermarks (im-printed on the coping stones of the bridge), and some spare stones. All these can still be seen.

Similar stories are told of other bridges, including at least three in Wales: the Devil's Bridge near Aberystwyth over the River Mynach, another over the Monnow at Grosmont (see p182), and a third at Clydach, near the Lonely Shepherd (see p33). The Clydach bridge is reached by a subway under the A465 road from the Drum and Monkey Inn, and below the bridge is a pool believed to be the home of a spirit called Pwca, the Welsh version of Puck. It is claimed that part of the Clydach Valley – Cwm Pwca – was the original setting for *A Midsummer Night's Dream*, and that Shakespeare owed his knowledge of Cambrian fairies to his friend, Richard Price of Brecon. Pwca is best known, however, as a kind of will o' the wisp who leads the benighted traveller up a narrow path to the very edge of the ravine; as soon as the man is on the brink, Pwca laughs and blows out the candle, and leaves him to grope his way back as best he can.

The trick must have its dangers if it is played in the Clydach Gorge.

Robert Burns' famous poem 'Tam o' Shanter' tells how the man Tam comes across witches dancing in the churchyard at Alloway (Burns' birthplace, now part of the Ayr conurbation). He cannot withhold his admiration for the capers of one witch, dressed in a particularly short garment, and calls out 'Weel done, Cutty Sark!' ('cutty' meaning 'cut very short', and 'sark' a shirt or chemise). The witches are alarmed, and rush for Tam who has to fly for his life on his horse, Meg. However, he knows that witches cannot cross running water so he makes for the bridge over the River Doon – he and his horse manage to pass just in time, but run it so close that Cutty Sark at the head of the pursuing pack is left with Meg's tail in her hand.

Other bridges are associated with fairies. Near Dunvegan in the north of the Isle of Skye is Fairy Bridge – no-one has to cross it nowadays because a more modern structure has replaced it, but its reputation is not good; some say that it was the scene of a murder, and that the victim's ghost haunts it. In addition, two men have been found dead there on different occasions; some people wonder whether they might have died of fright. Fairies are supposed to dance there, invisible to people but presumably seen by horses because when riders passed their horses would always shy. An attempt was made to explain this away, in the suggestion that the first time a rider passed he or she would communicate his own fear to the horse, thus provoking a nervous reaction – the horse would remember afterwards, too, and shy every time. One man determined on an experiment, and sent a stranger who was unaware of these stories to try out a horse which was also new to the area. Obviously, the route chosen crossed the Fairy Bridge. 'Well, how did you get on?' he asked when the stranger returned. 'A good beast,' he said, 'but she shied twice at a bridge, on the way out and on the way home.' It was, of course, the Fairy Bridge.

The Fairy Bridge is close to a crossroads, and these frequently have an evil reputation, too. A gibbet was often set up at such a spot and suicides, witches and other undesirables were buried there, sometimes with a stake through the heart to stop them walking. There are two particular places in Gloucestershire which have given rise to interesting stories: on older maps, 'Ellis's Cross' is marked, close to the hamlet of Fours Oaks and a few miles from Newent (close to the present M50). This is thought to be the burial place of Sarah Ellis, who in the seventeenth century was the recipient of a curse and as a result went mad and committed suicide. The curse was inscribed on a lead sheet roughly three inches square; it was found in 1892 at Wilton Place, a mansion in the parish of Dymock some three miles from Ellis's Cross, and is now preserved in Gloucester Folk Museum.

The second instance is found in the village of Poulton where a minor road is crossed by the A417 from Cirencester to Lechlade: the so-called Betty's Grave was located here. Local lore identifies Betty as a woman who wagered that she would reap an acre of corn with a sickle in a certain time. She won the bet, but then dropped dead from her exertions, and was buried at the spot. Another story is that she was a Poulton woman who poisoned herself and her possibly illegitimate baby, and was buried at the crossroads.

There are many tales of ill-omened and melancholy crossroads in different parts of the country. Perhaps the greatest danger they pose in recent times, though, is that of traffic accidents.

ANCIENT WOODS AND TREES

The Forest of Arden still appears on the map, though it is scarcely a forest now; the story goes that once upon a time a squirrel could traverse the whole expanse without touching the ground. However, the deep forests of the past still loom dark in tales such as those of the brothers Grimm, and some British stories have a similar background. Moreover it is interesting to consider that a third of the place names of the British Isles feature trees, from Appletreewick (North Yorkshire) to Sevenoaks (Kent), and from Aspatria ('Patrick's ash', in Cumbria) and Birkenhead ('headland with birches' in Cheshire) to Poplar (London) and Salisbury ('sal' meaning willow, in Wiltshire); and various Mile Oaks and Gospel Oaks still exist, for trees were widely used as boundary markers and meeting places.

Different species have their own associations: the oak – at least in some areas – comes into its own on Oak Apple Day (29 May); Christmas for most people would be inconceivable without the holly, mistletoe and spruce; and the yew is invariably linked with melancholy because of its poisonous berries and its frequent siting in churchyards – on the other hand, it also symbolises immortality because of its extraordinary longevity. The apple, admired for its blossom and its fruit, stands for life and beauty, King Arthur's grievous wound was treated at Avalon, the Apple Vale of Celtic myth. In the same place the Glastonbury thorn – the hawthorn was once widely revered – blooms twice a year, in November or December and May. It is supposed to have sprung from the staff of

Joseph of Arimathea, and has scions in various parts of England.

The humble elder, on the one hand accursed as the tree on which Judas Iscariot hanged himself, is nonetheless believed to have widespread curative powers, in various forms able to heal quinsies, sore throats, erysipelas, rheumatism, snake bite, rabies, warts and fits. It can also give protection against witches, as can the mountain ash and the oak. In the nineteenth century ash and sycamore were planted together to mark dangerous places on the roads, such as intersections. Such trees were known as 'John and Mary' and many a pair still stand at crossroads.

Trees of Sorrow

Convenient trees were frequently used both for lynchings and for quasi-judicial executions; in Scotland they were called 'dool' (sorrow) trees and barons often used them to hang enemies, and even friends if they became recalcitrant. One still stands at the old castle of Cassilis on the banks of the River Doon in Ayrshire; amongst its victims are seven gipsies, including their leader Johnny Faa, who are said to have been hanged on it by Lord Cassilis for abducting his lady. The story is told in a ballad entitled 'Seven Gypsies', or 'The Gypsy Laddie':

> Lord Cassilis rode home last night,
> Enquiring for his lady-o.
> The servant girl made this reply:
> 'She's gone with a dark-eyed gypsy -o'.

Johnny Faa certainly existed, but scholars deny that this story has any historical basis. The ballad continues to be sung, however, on both sides of the Atlantic.

Still in Scotland, there is a famous tree in a suburb of Edinburgh known as the Corstorphine Sycamore, or the White Lady. One story says that Lord Forrester was murdered at its foot by his sister, after a quarrel – another that Forrester murdered his daughter's lover (because he considered him an unacceptable suitor) under the tree where the pair secretly met. After the murder the leaves turned white; and when the daughter died, her ghost haunted the spot – another kind of white lady.

In England the stories associated with individual trees continue: for example, on the Bournemouth side of Poole in Dorset stands an old pine which marked the meeting place in the eighteenth century used by Gulliver, the smuggler (see p198), and his gang. The area is still known as Lilliput and of course Jonathan Swift used both names in his book *Gulliver's Travels*. Another tree and another story have their roots just outside the town of Bidford-on-Avon, fourteen miles from Stratford; a crab apple tree once stood here, and Shakespeare is supposed to have spent the night underneath its branches, sleeping off the effects of a drinking contest in which he had taken part in Bidford. On waking up, he wrote the famous rhyme:

> Piping Pebworth, dancing Marston,
> Haunted Hillborough and hungry Grafton;
> With dodging Exhall, Papist Wixford,
> Beggarly Broom and drunken Bidford.

The tree is marked on the first edition of the Ordnance Survey map as 'Shakespeare's Crab'; however, it suffered greatly from the attentions of souvenir hunters, and its remains were grubbed up in 1824. Crab Tree Farm still exists, though, not far away from the spot, and the rhyme based on what have become known as 'the Shakespeare villages' continues to flourish.

Hard as Oak

The native oak has been revered by successive peoples – the Celts, Romans, Anglo-Saxons and the Normans – for centuries, and the very name is still synonymous with sturdiness and reliability; individual specimens have been landmarks for very many years. They often play a significant role in traditional folklore, too, and a well known story with an oak at its centre is 'Babes . . .' or 'Children in the Wood'. For four hundred years, as song, play, narrative and pantomime, the story has captivated audiences, old and young; Joseph Addison called the ballad 'one of the darling songs of the common people' and 'the delight of most Englishmen in some part of their age'. It was first printed in 1595, as 'The Norfolk gent his will and Testament and howe he Commytted the keepinge of his Children to his owne brother who delte most wickedly with them and howe God plagued him for it'. There is a theory that the murder of the children is a coded reference to Richard III's treatment of his nephews, but if this were so the allegory would surely have been revealed by Richard's opponents who were anxious to discredit him after his defeat and death in 1485. Furthermore the Norfolk connection is emphasised in the ballad, since the place of the murder is traditionally held to be Wayland Wood, near the village of Griston (some ten miles south of East Dereham, off the A1075). The wood

41

was called Wanelund in ancient times, the second syllable coming from the Old Norse *lundr* meaning 'a grove'; it was probably a grove of assembly, and perhaps of worship, before the Norman Conquest. In the wood was an oak under which the children were supposed to have died. When it was cut down (in 1879) after being struck by lightning people flocked to take home pieces as souvenirs. In a typically twentieth-century ending to the saga, Wayland Wood is now owned by the Norfolk Naturalists' Trust.

At Monkleigh near Bideford in Devon the oak known as Hankford's Oak still stands. It takes its name from Sir William Hankford, who was Lord Chief Justice of England in the early fifteenth century. The judge had told his keeper to shoot at anyone who was in his park at night who could not satisfactorily respond to a challenge; unfortunately this precaution went sadly wrong, for Hankford himself absentmindedly failed to give the correct answer and was therefore shot beneath the oak by his own keeper. More or less the same thing happened in Hampshire two hundred years later, though the roles were reversed, when the Archbishop of Canterbury, Dr George Abbot, shot his gamekeeper at Branshill under a tree still called the Keeper's Oak.

Other oaks have been less fortunate as regards survival. Carmarthen in central Wales is reputed to be Merlin's birthplace, and among the wizard's many predictions was one about the town:

> When Merlin's oak shall tumble down,
> Then shall fall Carmarthen town.

The tree in question was very carefully preserved until it was no more than a dead stump propped up by iron bars and concrete. In 1978 the local council decided that it was a hazard to traffic, and should be removed. When cars confront heritage they usually win, though admittedly in this case there was a tremendous amount of soul-searching, and the decision made headline news in Wales – Merlin's words still had force, seven hundred years after they were uttered. Even so, the oak went. The town remained, and there was a general sigh of relief when the prophecy proved unfounded (so far.)

The largest surviving tree in Sherwood Forest (at Edwinstowe, near Mansfield in Nottinghamshire) is called the Major Oak – it was already ancient when Robin Hood was roaming the forest and has survived wind and weather, vandalism and fire. It is now in the area administered by the Robin Hood Visitor Centre and Country Park, which is far removed from the wild greenwood of years gone by.

3
God's Acre

Most small towns and villages are still dominated by their parish church and the sacred plot within which it stands: God 's acre. In our cities the cathedrals are counted amongst our most highly-prized national treasures. These places of worship preserve a host of interesting objects, and also serve as a focus for a wealth of associations, stories and beliefs. At times it was a deliberate policy to build churches in places sacred in pre-Christian times – St Paul's Cathedral in London, for example, occupies the site of a Roman temple dedicated to Diana, goddess of the moon; and in Wales a considerable number of churches have oval or round churchyards, a shape indicating the previous existence of a grove of trees sacred to the Celts – these include Llanfechain (Powys), Cilcenin (Dyfed) and Derwen (Clwyd).

Yew trees are frequently found in churchyards, and they were planted for several reasons: their heavy foliage is emblematic of death, and was particularly hated by witches; their longevity symbolised immortality – a thousand year life-span is not exceptional, and the yew at Fortingall, near Loch Tay in Scotland is three thousand years old; in addition, the trees gave physical shelter to the church buildings. Especially famous are the ninety-nine yew trees at Painswick churchyard in the Cotswolds; and at Nevern in west

Wales, twelve miles or so from Fishguard, there is one yew in an avenue called 'the bleeding tree'. A branch was once removed from it, and a prophecy was made that it would bleed from that time until the castle (now just an overgrown mound on a hill north of the church) was again occupied by a Welshman.

CHURCH SITES AND CONSTRUCTION

Wells and Holy Waters

Churches are often sited close to a spring or well whose cool, clear water was worshipped by members of early religions. The Romans had their own celebration of wells and springs, called *fontinalia*, and the Derbyshire well dressings of today (see Chapter 6) are descended from these; the Druids attempted to predict the future by studying the water of streams and holy wells. Hundreds of wells are still reputed to be holy – there are seventy in Yorkshire alone. In the little north Somerset port of Watchet the church of St Decuman claims to have been standing by its holy well since the year 400. Another church with an interesting history is the one at Altarnun in Cornwall (just off the A30 between Launceston and Bodmin); both church and holy well nearby are dedicated to St Non, the mother of St David. The water of the well was once thought to cure madness, so lunatics were immersed in it.

The Worcestershire village of Clent, only a few miles from Birmingham, still boasts a healing well associated with St Kenelm. The historical Kenelm was the son of Kenulf, King of Mercia; he died before his father, in 812 or 821, possibly in battle with the Welsh, and was buried at Winchcombe Abbey in Gloucestershire. His sister, Kendrida, was the abbess of Minster in Kent. A legend grew up about Kenelm, and was written down by William of Malmesbury in the eleventh century:

On the death of his father Kenelm becomes king of Mercia, but as an infant of only seven he is placed under the tutelage of his older sister, Kendrida. Wishing to take the crown for herself, she persuades her lover, Askobert, to kill the child. So Kenelm is taken from the royal palace at Winchcombe on a hunting expedition which leads him many miles away to the slopes of the Clent hills. Knowing that he is about to die, Kenelm plants his staff in the ground, where it roots and becomes a thorn tree. As he kneels to say the *Te Deum* Askobert strikes off his head with a long-bladed knife.

A white dove flies out of Kenelm's head and makes its way to Rome, where it drops a scroll on the high altar at St Peter's. The scroll bears a message, which in modern English reads:

> In Clent cow-pasture under a thorn
> Of head bereft lies Kenelm, king born.

The pope orders enquiries to be made in England, and a procession of churchmen led by the Bishop of Mercia is guided to Kenelm's grave by a ray of light. [In an alternative version the spot is located because a cow remains there without eating but still grows fat.] As the body is disinterred, church bells ring of their own accord, and a spring of water gushes from the ground.

When the remains of Kenelm are taken to Winchcombe the false Queen Kendrida looks down from her window and attempts to read the 53rd psalm backwards, probably for magical purposes. The crowd shouts: 'Kenelm is truly God's martyr'. Kendrida replies: 'As truly as my eyes are lying on this book' and her eyes fall out on to the page.

A blood-stained psalter is preserved at Winchcombe Abbey, near Cheltenham, and in 1815 two stone coffins were discovered there, one containing a man, the other a few bones, a child's skull and a long-bladed knife. Unfortunately all these crumbled to dust on being exposed to the air. Kenelm's spring at Clent was found to have healing powers, and became a place of pilgrimage; a chapel was built, and then (in the eleventh century) a small church. The village of Kenelmstowe grew up round about, with some thirty houses and an inn called the Red Cow, named after the miraculous beast of the legend. The place was important enough for Henry III to grant it an annual fair, which used to start on the eve of St Kenelm's Day (17 July). However, pilgrimages were largely brought to an end by the Reformation, and Kenelmstowe – which by then was called Clent – went into a decline. Now, only the church and a single house remain.

One custom, that of 'crabbing the parson', survived until the mid-nineteenth century: people would assemble at St Kenelm's Wake, as they termed it, to pelt each other and also their clergyman with crab apples. The spring is still there too, but is diverted from its original position inside the east end of the church to a few yards away, outside. Certainly the Clent hills remain a powerful attraction to the people of Birmingham and the Black Country, but more for walking, picnicking and horse-riding than for making pilgrimage.

Persistent traditions hold that the siting of certain churches was determined by supernatural means. Durham Cathedral was built in honour of St Cuthbert, who died in 687 on the island of Lindisfarne just off the Northumbrian coast, and the story of how it came to be built on its present site shows just such a tradition:

> The danger of pirates caused the monks of Lindisfarne to abandon their island. They exhumed the remains of St Cuthbert, and carried them for several years, wandering from place to place in search of a home. Then at a place called Ward Law the bier stuck fast, and could not be moved. For three days the monks prayed for enlightenment, and became convinced that the saint's remains must go to Dunholme. They had no idea where this was, but happened to overhear a woman speaking of a cow which had strayed to Dunholme, and so decided to follow her. The bier moved without difficulty. They reached the now-famous spot on the banks of the River Wear and built the cathedral; the woman and her cow were carved on one of the pinnacles, and can be seen to this day.

It is ironic that the saint's followers should have been aided by a woman because Cuthbert was notoriously misogynic, his bias apparently having arisen when a Pictish princess accused him (falsely or otherwise) of fathering her child. In its monastic days Durham Cathedral was strictly out of bounds to women. When a Lady Chapel was added in the twelfth century it was first sited near St Cuthbert's tomb, but the story goes that the ground shook and the pillars swayed, so building was restarted further away at the west end of the cathedral.

Another legend concerns the village of Breedon-on-the-Hill near Ashby-de-la-Zouch in Leicestershire: it is situated – despite its name – at the bottom of a hill, yet the church stands all on its own at the top. Apparently building was begun at the bottom, but each night all the stones laid during the day were carried to the top by a number of doves, until the masons took the point and carried on building the church at the new site.

There are similar stories scattered all over Britain, with the supernatural agent changing to fairies, witches, various animals, and even devils. For example, a spirit voice crying 'Bryn-y-Grog' (literally, 'hill at the crossroads') caused builders at Wrexham in Clwyd to change their plans and adopt the location indicated; at both Hanchurch and Walsall in Staffordshire fairies persistently moved materials until new sites were adopted; and a cat – perhaps a spirit in this form – somehow managed the same feat at Leyland, near Preston in Lancashire.

The village of Winwick, now in Cheshire, owes its site to the actions of a pig: the animal spent a whole night carrying stones in its mouth to the place where St Oswald, the martyr king of Northumberland, was believed to have been killed in 642. (It should be mentioned here that other places lay claim to this honour, including a spot between Oswestry and Maesbury in Shropshire, where one of the saint's arms was hung in the Mile Oak. In fact, Oswald's body was sacrificially dismembered as a sacrifice to Woden, and his arms, legs, head and body were dispersed. Many churches claimed the relics, and over seventy are still dedicated to St Oswald.) The story continues that in between carrying stones, the inspired pig was continually screaming 'We-ee-wick, we-ee-wick', and this gave the village its name. Its likeness was carved in stone just above the west door of the church and can still be seen. The same building is distinguished by a rather less reverent belief concerning the local young women's purity, or lack of it; it is encapsulated in the following rhyme:

> The church at little Winwick,
> It stand upon a sod,
> And when a maid is married there
> The steeple gives a nod.

The church at Wendover in Buckinghamshire stands half a mile from the town, and witchés – or alternatively fairies – are said to have carried materials there from the original site, which is still called Witches' Meadow. A similar transfer was accomplished at Bisley in Gloucestershire by unseen hands, where the first site has also retained its original name, Church Piece. When the church was restored in 1862 a Roman altar bearing the figure of a horseman was found built into a wall; it may well have been brought from Church Piece where there are many Roman remains, thus providing the kernel of the story.

Other explanations for changes of site may lie in simple changes of mind, in difficulties with geology or in dispute with landowners. Primitive fears may well have counted, too.

Devils and Churches
People believed the devil was powerful enough even to bring about a change in the location of a church. For example at Altarnun in

Cornwall he moved materials with the help of a deer and a hare; and at Worfield, near Bridgnorth in Shropshire, he caused the place chosen for the church to be moved from a hilltop to a lower position. Three fine churches near Banbury in Oxfordshire – at Adderbury, Bloxham and King's Sutton – are said to have been built with the devil's help: three brothers working as masons were delighted with the assistance of a labourer who possessed superlative but uncanny skill. Eventually, however, they decided his powers must be of infernal origin and challenged him. He fled, but not before flinging away a hodful of mortar which became Crouch Hill.

On the other hand, some churches are celebrated because the devil tried to destroy them. At Rudston, a few miles inland from Bridlington in East Yorkshire, a monolith only yards from the church wall is said to be the devil's shot at the building which fell just wide of the mark. The round church at Bowmore on the Inner Hebridean island of Islay is apparently shaped thus so as to deny the devil any corner behind which to hide. And several hundred miles south there is a stone in the graveyard at Llanarth near Cardigan which has curious marks: legend has it that the devil once tried to steal a bell from the church. Awakened by the noise, the vicar climbed to the belfry and when he saw what was going on, started intoning the name of Jesus Christ. The devil backed away till he reached the edge of the tower, then jumped to the ground below, leaving marks on a stone.

The devil also prevented the completion of the church tower at Towednack, near St Ives in Cornwall. Each night he pulled down everything the masons had erected by day until finally they lost heart and gave up the struggle. Another tower, at West Walton near Wisbech in Norfolk, purports to show his influence in even more spectacular manner. It is significant that it stands a short way from the body of the church: local lore has it that there was a great deal of wickedness in the surrounding fenland, and the devil was able to recharge his batteries from it, so to speak, to such an extent that sufficient power was produced for him to move the tower away from the church. There were many such beliefs; one of the functions of gargoyles was to frighten off the devil and other evil spirits, and the same was true of the weathercock (as well as its purpose of showing how the wind blows). The land to the north side of the church (and also the door in it) was traditionally regarded as the devil's, and for this reason the north door was kept locked; moreover it usually still is, though there are exceptions where for all practical purposes it provides the best entrance.

For the same reason people avoided burying their dear ones on the north side of the churchyard, which was used instead for paupers, itinerants and strangers. And in a new graveyard it was considered unlucky to be the first buried, since the devil was reputed to take the first corpse. The sunny south would tend to be filled first, then the east – which faced the direction from which the resurrection would come – and next the west; only when all other space was exhausted would the north side be used. A belief also grew up that the dead buried in the tiny village of Orleton, four miles north of Leominster in Herefordshire, would be the first to be raised on the day of judgement. At one time, therefore, Orleton became an extremely sought-after place in which to be buried.

EPITAPHS

Inscriptions to the dead, both inside our churches and in their graveyards, make a fascinating study. Among the commonest of epitaphs was:

> As you are now, so once was I.
> As I am now, so shall you be.
> Therefore prepare to follow me.

Similar moralising is frequently found. For example at Hinckley in Leicestershire, John Stevens (died 1721, aged thirty-eight) warns:

> You readers all both old and young,
> Your time on earth will not be long;
> For Death shall come, and die thou must,
> And like to me return to dust.

At the tiny village of Ripple, close to the River Severn between Worcester and Tewkesbury, a tombstone marks what is locally known as the Giant's Grave – in fact that of Robert Reeve, who died in 1626 from the exertion of mowing a huge meadow for a wager. The inscription warns:

> As you passe by, behold my length,
> But never glory in your Strength.

Another moralising epitaph, which is found throughout the country, runs:

> This world's a city of crooked streets,
> Death is the Market-place where all men meet;
> If life was merchandise that men could buy,
> The rich would live, the poor might die.

At Kingsbridge in south Devon Robert Phillip (died 1793, aged sixty-three) makes a pointed comment from beyond the grave. The inscription states that 'the following lines' were inscribed at his request:

> Here lie I at the Chancel door
> Here lie I because I'm poor
> The further in the more you'll pay
> Here lie I as warm as they.

The manner of death – by illness, accident, or even murder – is often the subject of comment. 'I in a moment fell And had not time to bid my friends farewell' says one, which might indicate a heart attack. And that dread disease of the past, tuberculosis, is often mentioned in words such as these:

> A pale consumption gave the final blow.
> The stroke was fatal, though th'effect came slow.

Drowning, lightning, fire, brawls, accidents – all these make their contributions. A monument in the south porch of Ely Cathedral commemorates the deaths of two men killed in 1845 while they were working on the construction of the railway line from Ely to Norwich. Entitled 'The Spiritual Railway', the epitaph concludes:

> Come then poor Sinners, now's the time
> At any Station on the Line,
> If you'll repent and turn from sin
> The Train will stop and take you in.

Many epitaphs are full of imagery appropriate to particular trades and professions; from here it is an easy step to jokes and puns, and there is a strain of graveyard humour which produces such lines as 'Death is the broom which sweeps us all away'. The name of one man from Bromsgrove in Worcestershire was too good to be missed:

> Here lies a man that was Knott born.
> His father was Knott before him.
> He lived Knott, and did Knott die,
> Yet underneath this stone doth lie.
> Knott christened, Knott begot,
> And here he lies, and yet was Knott.

Another famous inscription, is reported from several places, including Upton-on-Severn in Worcestershire:

> Beneath this stone in hopes of Zion
> Doth lie the landlord of the Lion.
> His son keeps on the business still,
> Resigned upon the heavenly will.

Other epitaphs retain the power to move the reader over many centuries. William Fox and Helen, his wife, were both buried at Castle Donington in Leicestershire on the same July day in 1585, and their life and death are recorded on a brass tablet fixed to the favoured south wall of the church:

> The fatal scyth which cuts in two
> Most nuptiall knots this closer drew;
> Life made them one, death left them so,
> And love more constant who can show?

And at Lydney in Gloucestershire a child is remembered with this simple verse:

> Here a pretty baby lies,
> Sung asleep with lullabies.
> Pray be silent and not stir
> The easy earth that covers her.

An old man at Welton, near Hull, has this memorial:

> Jeremiah Found has eight times married been;
> But now old age has caught him in his cage,
> And he lies under the grass so green.

BELLS AND BELL RINGING

Every church has its bell, however humble, and some have magnificent peals. The curfew bell once did indeed toll 'the knell of parting day' – the custom continued in many places until 1914, and some still keep it up even now. At Durham Cathedral curfew is rung at 9pm every day except Saturdays, and at Shipston-on-Stour, near Stratford-on-Avon in Warwickshire, at 8pm in summer and 7pm in winter from Tuesday to Saturday; here the expense is borne by Horniblow's Charity, which dates from 1826.

Until well within living memory the passing bell gave news of a death. Originally this was rung while the person was dying to drive away evil spirits – surely an added ordeal for the sufferer. Later it was sounded to announce that a death had taken place: for a man it was rung three times three – hence the saying 'Nine tellers mark a man', later corrupted to 'Nine tailors make a man'; for a woman, three times two; and for a child, three times only. Two rhymes comment on the practice, and the first goes:

> When the bell begins to toll
> Lord have mercy upon thy soul.

And the second one as follows:

> When thou dost hear a toll or knell,
> Then think upon thy passing bell.

One of the most famous lines in English prose is John Donne's 'Never send to know for whom the bell tolls. It tolls for thee'.

On the other hand, a joyous peal always rings for seasonal celebrations such as the arrival of the New Year, and for family occasions such as weddings. National rejoicings are also marked: in 1945 the bells rang again after six years' silence during the war; and in 1988 they pealed to celebrate the defeat of the Spanish Armada, three centuries earlier.

Many towns are remarked in legend as being places where the bells tolled of their own accord. For example, the little market town of Ledbury in Herefordshire just west of the Malvern Hills, has an association with St Katherine which, thanks to its peal of bells, dates back to the fourteenth century. Two poets, William Wordsworth and John Masefield, were both inspired by the story:

Katherine Audley, the cousin of King Edward II, was both noble and holy. She had a revelation that she should settle and found a hermitage in a town where the bells rang of themselves. So she and her faithful maid, Mabel, travelled far, but their long search was fruitless until they approached Ledbury. There, the bells 'broke forth in concert' (as Wordsworth put it) of their own accord. Katherine duly stayed and built a hermitage, its inmates living on herbs and milk paid for by an annual grant of £30 from King Edward. Before her death, Katherine prophesied that a door in the chapel dedicated to her in Ledbury Church should stay closed until it opened of itself: if this happened the town would become one of the richest in England – but if human hands opened the door, Ledbury would remain poor. So naturally the towns-people were very careful to keep the door closed, until one night some men in a drunken frolic threw it open.

The prophecy was fulfilled, but only for a time. The town is now prosperous, if not rich. Katherine's Acre (where the saint heard the bells) and Mabel's Furlong are now covered with houses, though St Katherine's Almshouses remain a prominent feature of the town, and an ancient female effigy resting on a tomb behind the organ in the church is said to represent Katherine herself.

The fourteenth-century White Cross is situated a mile from Hereford on the road to Hay-on-Wye and is said to mark the spot where the cathedral bells rang without human agency to greet Bishop Cantelupe as he was returning to the city. The notion of bells tolling of their own accord was once widely held – even sceptical Londoners once believed that the great bell of St Paul's could be rung by unseen hands, and that when this happened some calamity would befall a member of the royal family. In Pembrokeshire the people thought that when their bells rang in this way they warned of storm at sea or disaster on land.

Bells deliberately rung had the power of calming storms, and also of frightening witches or devils. At Heighington in County Durham, near Darlington, one of the church bells bears the inscription: 'Thou Peter When beaten calm the angry waves'. This is something of a mystery since the village – just off the A1(M) – is many miles from the sea.

Dorchester-on-Thames, eight miles south of Oxford, was once a Romano–British town with its own bishop, St Berin or Birinnus. In 650 Berin was bitten by a snake; the poison proved to be fatal, but before dying the saint announced that henceforth local people would be protected from snakebite as long as they were within the range of sound of a bell in the church. Snakes are still said to be unable to stand the sound of the present tenor bell. (This was hung in the fourteenth century, but may have replaced an earlier bell.)

Another tenor bell, at Lanivet near Bodmin in Cornwall, has an inscription reminding us that 'I to the Church the living call, And to the Grave do summon all'. Also in Cornwall, the eight bells of St Austell bear a more cheerful message:

1 By music minds an equal temper know
2 Nor swell too high nor sink too low
3 Music the fiercest grief can charm
4 And fate's severest rage disarm
5 Music can soften pain to ease
6 And make despair and madness please
7 Our joys below it can improve
8 And antedate the bliss above.

Ringers' Rhymes

If bells have their rhymes, so do ringers. Many belfries have boards with carefully painted instructions, often cast into verses which are remarkably similar in different parts of the country. Although it dates from 1694, this one is still to be seen at Tong, the little Shropshire village (now just off the M54) where Dickens set the imaginary death and burial of Little Nell:

> If that to Ring you doe come here,
> you must Ring well with hand and eare.
> Keep stroak of time and goe not out;
> or else you forfeit out of doubt.
> Our law is so concluded here;
> for every fault a jugg of beer,
> if that you Ring with Spurr or Hat;
> a jugg of beer must pay for that.
> If that you take a Rope in hand;
> these forfeits you must not withstand,
> or if that you a Bell ov'rthrow;
> it must cost Six pence e'ere youe goe.
> If in this place you sweare or curse;
> Six pence to pay pull out your purse;
> come pay the Clerk it is his fee;
> for one that swears shall not goe free.
> These Laws are old, and are not new;
> therefore the Clerk must have his due.

The keen rivalry between ringers of different villages was also expressed in verse and song. Some of the men of Egloshayle, near Wadebridge in Cornwall, are still remembered in a local song, and their epitaphs can be seen in the churchyard:

> There's Craddock the cordwainer first who rings the treble bell,
> The second is John Ellery who none could e'er excel.
> The third is Pollard, carpenter, the fourth is Thomas Cleave,
> And Goodfellow the tenor-man who rings 'em round so brave.

Another song describes a ringing match between several Devon and Cornish villages and towns. After contesting on various peals of bells, the men of North Lew on Broadbury Down, west of Dartmoor, were the winners:

'Twas at Ashwater town, then at Callington town,
They rang for a belt and a hat laced with gold.
The men of North Lew rang so steady and true
That there never was better in Devon I'm told.

STORIES IN STAINED GLASS

Scenes from the bible and the lives of the saints were frequently depicted in the stained glass of church windows for the education and edification of the people. The secluded fifteenth-century church of St Neot, not far from Liskeard in Cornwall, has windows showing the Creation, and also the legends of St George and St Neot himself. Neot (who also gave his name to St Neots in Cambridgeshire) was said to be so small that he had to stand on a stone to insert the key in the church lock, and on a stool to celebrate mass. He is renowned for working miracles with animals, and one of these is pictured in the glass in the church; the story is:

An angel appeared to Neot and said: 'I bring you three fish for your well. So long as you eat only one each day their number will never decrease'. Neot was careful to obey, but when he fell ill one day his servant, thinking to be helpful, cooked two fishes for him. Neot was deeply concerned, and prayed for a long time. Then he said to the servant: 'Please put the fishes back in the well'. She could not see what good this would do, but did as she was asked – and as soon as the cooked fishes touched the water they came back to life again.

St Nicholas is another figure who frequently appears in stained glass, and he brought back to life more than fishes: he resuscitated three young boys who had been slaughtered by a rascally butcher and put into pickle. The story is retold in Benjamin Britten's cantata 'Saint Nicholas'. Nicholas, bishop of Myra in the fourth century, is the patron of children, sailors, unmarried mothers, merchants, pawnbrokers, apothecaries and perfumiers. On one occasion he gave a bag of gold to each of three young women as a marriage dowry so as to save them from prostitution; this is thought to be one possible origin of the three gold balls of the pawnbrokers' sign. In a window of the church of the small south Devon port of Brixham, St Nicholas is shown bringing gifts to three little sleeping girls: he is, of course, also known as Santa Claus. At one time he was so popular that in England alone four hundred churches were dedicated to him.

Other saints, often more obscure, also have their memorials. At Hentland, close to the River Wye in Herefordshire, a window shows St Dubricius or Dyrif who, as a bishop, crowned King Arthur. The window includes a hedgehog (locally called an 'erchin') which is part of the county emblem. This is the legend of St Dubricius' birth:

Pebiau of the Anglo-Saxon domain of Archenfield returned from an expedition and ordered his daughter, Eurddil, to wash his hair. When she approached he noticed from her shape that she was expecting a baby. He flew into a rage because she was not married, and ordered that she should be put in a sack and thrown into the Wye. Three times she was thrown in. Three times she was gently washed back to the bank.

The king then gave instructions that she should be burnt alive. Accordingly, she was thrown into a blazing funeral pyre. Next morning, people were sent to collect her bones but they found her unharmed, and holding an infant son. On hearing this news the king had a change of heart, and welcomed his daughter and grandson. The child reached up and touched his face, whereupon he was cured of the affliction of constant foaming at the mouth from which he had always suffered.

The place of Eurddil's funeral pyre at Madley was originally marked by a stone, and although this is no longer there, the cross which stands in the centre of the village may have replaced it.

The death of another saint, Wistan, is shown in glass at the church of Wistanstow near Craven Arms in Shropshire. Wistan was of royal blood and could have become king of Mercia, but preferred to devote his life to prayer. He was murdered by a cousin jealous of his piety, and for a month afterwards a beam of light is said to have lit up the fatal spot. Wistanstow is not, however, the only place to claim it is the site of Wistan's death; another candidate is Wistow, a hamlet a few miles from Leicester – the story here, too, is that Wistan was murdered by his cousin, but for a different reason. Wistan was asked to consent to a marriage between his widowed mother Elfleda and his cousin Behrtric, but he refused, maintaining that such a match would be incestuous. The murder was revealed both by a column of light which hovered over the place where Wistan's body had been buried, and by hair sprouting from the ground where his blood had run. Behrtric went mad. Wistan's remains were taken first to Repton and then to Evesham Abbey, where they were visited by pilgrims until the Reformation. There is a belief that hair still sprouts from the ground at Wistow every year on the first of June, the anniversary of the murder; however, no-one seems to know the exact spot in which to look.

SCULPTURE AND CARVING

Various effigies, monuments and even natural objects in churches and graveyards have served as a starting point for traditions and beliefs. Always of particular interest were people whose enormous proportions gave rise to stories and legend. At Penrith, stone shafts standing fifteen feet apart are said to mark the grave of Ewan Caesarius, a fifth century ruler of Cumbria renowned as a boarslayer – there is a story that when the grave was opened in the sixteenth century the bones of a huge man were found. And at Weston, near Baldock in Hertfordshire, there is another giant, this time fourteen feet in height if the stones which stand at his head and feet are to be believed. Jack o' Legs (for this was his name) lived during the Middle Ages in a cave outside the village, and could easily converse with his friends through their upstairs windows. He was capable of shooting an arrow over a distance of three miles, and could bring down a bird in flight half a mile away.

He made a living as a highwayman, chiefly near a spot still known as Jack's Hill, and like others after him, he took from the rich and gave to the poor. Many of his victims were bakers from Baldock, who eventually ambushed him as he was walking through the town; he was struck down from behind with a heavy pole, tied up, and blinded with a red-hot poker. Before they killed him the bakers told him to shoot a last arrow, and said they would bury him where it fell. His arrow landed in Weston churchyard, over three miles away.

There are giants to be found in Aldworth, too, about nine miles from Reading in Berkshire. In the church are nine life-sized effigies, funeral monuments to men of the Norman family, de la Beche – some of them are seven feet tall. Three of the statues have become known as Long John, John Strong and John Never-afraid; originally there was a tenth effigy, that of John Ever-afraid, which once stood half inside and half outside the church, but this one is now missing. Apparently Ever-afraid made a pact with the devil, to exchange his soul after death for riches in life. The devil made a condition that the pact should stand wherever the body was buried, inside or outside the church; however, Ever-afraid obviously cheated him by making sure that he was placed neither in nor out.

Most sculpture, however, concerns figures of more conventional size. At Broad Hinton church, just off the A4136 to the south of Swindon in Wiltshire, there is a monument depicting Sir Thomas Wroughton, his wife Anne and their four children – the hands of Anne are clasped in prayer, but those of Thomas and his children have all been broken off. The reason for this is given in the following story: Thomas apparently returned from hunting one day to find his wife reading the bible, with no supper ready. Flying into a rage he seized the book and threw it into the fire. However, Anne pulled it out again, but at the cost of badly burned fingers. In divine retribution for this deed the hands not only of Thomas, but for some reason those of the children also, withered away; the monument also shows a bible with a corner missing. A more prosaic explanation might be that the sculpture had been damaged over the years.

This is indeed the case concerning the medieval effigies of a knight and his wife at Wickhampton, a mile or so inland from Great Yarmouth, where each statue once held a small stone heart. The local belief is that the figures were in fact those of two brothers named Hampton who in a fight occasioned by disputes over boundaries tore out each other's heart. God turned them into stone as a punishment, and they were placed in the church as a warning to others.

The mis-identification of statues often occurs. At Orlingbury in Northamptonshire, near Wellingborough, the recumbent effigy of a knight is that of a church benefactor, John de Withmayle – though not according to local lore, which believes it to be Jack of Batsaddle, the man who in 1375 killed the last wolf in England; after this momentous achievement, however, he drank from a spring and the shock of the cold water put paid to him.

Not far away, at the village of Ayston near Uppingham in what was Rutland (now Leicestershire), is a monument described by the guide books as 'a double effigy, weathered beyond description'; it perhaps represents two priests, but once again, local people have the last word. They say it shows one-armed twin sisters who despite their handicap worked so hard as spinners that they were able to save enough money to buy a field. After their deaths they left it to the parish so that its revenue could benefit the poor. There is another effigy at Berrington, near Shrewsbury, which seems to have lost half its face; it portrays a former lord of the manor, and the fact that he has a lion at his feet is significant because he is popularly identified as 'Owd Scriven', a local character supposed to have killed a lion in a nearby field.

In similar vein, at the village of Nunnington near the Hambleton Hills in north Yorkshire, the church holds the stone figure of Sir

Walter de Teyes, who died in 1325. The story is nevertheless told that it shows one Peter Loschy, who killed a magic dragon in the area. The fight went on for hours, because every time Peter struck home the dragon simply rolled on the ground, and its wounds immediately healed. It succumbed only when he had the idea of hacking pieces off – his dog carried each one away until there was nothing left.

Sir Roger Smith of Edmondthorpe near Melton Mowbray in Leicestershire died in about 1655, and his tomb at St Michael's Church has life-sized alabaster figures of himself and his two wives. It is significant that the statue of Lady Anne has a red stain on the wrist: the traditional story is that she was a witch, and could turn herself into a cat. In this guise she was wounded, the butler at her home (Edmondthorpe Hall) having struck at her with a cleaver – blood from the injured paw fell on a kitchen flagstone although the cat itself escaped. Anne regained her normal form but thenceforth bore a mark on her wrist, and after her death this appeared on her statue. The stain on the flagstone proved to be equally indelible, and as late as the 1920s maids were complaining that however much they scrubbed the kitchen floor at the Hall, the stone would not come clean.

There is another house worthy of note called Hergest Court, situated near Kington, a small Herefordshire market town close to the Welsh border. Firstly, the Red Book of Hergest, dating from about 1400, was found there in the nineteenth century by Lady Charlotte Guest, who translated it into English. It contains the earliest complete copy of the *Mabinogion*, a cycle of Welsh hero tales. Hergest was also the home of another knight, Sir Thomas Vaughan, who was killed in 1469 at the battle of Banbury while fighting in the Yorkist cause; the Welsh bard, Lewis Glyn Cothi, composed a lament for him. His body was brought back to Kington and lies, together with that of his wife, Ellen, in a tomb in the church, surmounted by their effigies in alabaster. Thomas was known locally as 'Black Vaughan' and his wife as 'Ellen Gethin' (Ellen the Terrible), because of their alleged cruelty. The story of Black Vaughan's troublesome ghost was told by parents to their children until well within living memory:

Vaughan's wickedness meant that his spirit could not rest after death. In broad daylight it would upset farmers' waggons, frighten their wives by jumping up behind them as they rode to Kington market, and torment the horses in the shape of a fly – it even charged into the church in the guise of a roaring bull. People were so afraid that they avoided the town, and its prosperity started to suffer.

One day, twelve parsons assembled to lay the ghost by reading from scripture, the plan being that as they read the ghost would become smaller and smaller until it would go into a silver snuffbox. Each parson held a lighted candle, but as they read the candles one by one went out, and one by one eleven of the clerics fell silent. The twelfth, however, stood fast – it was perhaps helpful that he was almost blind, and not particularly sober. At one stage he called out: 'Vaughan, why art thou so fierce?' The answer came back: 'I was fierce as a man. Now I am fiercer, for I am a devil.'

Undeterred, the parson read on. His candle flickered, but it continued to burn and Vaughan became smaller and smaller until at last the lid of the snuffbox began to close on him. Then the parson asked: 'Vaughan, where wilt thou be laid?' 'Anywhere, except in the Red Sea.' When the lid was closed they buried the box at the bottom of Hergest Pool, and put a large stone on top. There it will remain for a thousand years.

Footmarks used to be visible on the grass beneath a certain oak tree at Hergest Court because Black Vaughan loved to stand there, watching the deer in the park; however, his wickedness was such that grass would not grow there afterwards. The spot was pointed out until the late nineteenth century, but sadly even the oak has now disappeared. They say that the man who felled it went mad, and died in an asylum. The wife of the present owner of Hergest reports that there was a proposal to fill in Black Vaughan's pool. When JCBs arrived to do the work the water started to bubble ominously, and the plan was abandoned.

Grotesques

Alongside what might be called the 'official' sculptures of churches are many which seem to have been left to the fantasy of the masons involved. Roof bosses often show different kinds of 'green men': one, which is perhaps more common on inn signs, is similar to the Jack-in-the-Green of spring rituals, and shows a man almost hidden in greenery; another type has the tortured face and protruding tongue of a victim sacrificed by strangling in an ancient fertility rite; a third is that of the wood spirit, with no human connection.

A green man of the first kind can be seen as a roof boss in

Worcester Cathedral. Then there is the imp of Lincoln Cathedral, which is much more famous; it appears in the cleft of a pillar near the great east window, and this is its story:

One day the devil let his imps out to play: one rode on a rainbow without falling; another jumped into a furnace without getting burnt; a third dived into the sea without getting wet – and a fourth rode the east wind to Lincoln. There he threatened to knock over the bishop, blow up the dean, singers and organist, smash the windows, and put out the candles. The wind refused to take the imp inside, so he went on alone. He ripped tapestries from the walls, scratched the wood of the choir stalls and lectern, broke the candlesticks, and threatened to pluck feathers from the stone angels' wings. His antics were stopped by the smallest angel, which said: 'O impious imp, be thou turned into stone'. And he was. He still sits there, and the wind waits outside for his return.

In contrast to these great cathedrals is Kilpeck, one of the smallest churches in England situated off the A465 to the south-west of Hereford. In spite of its small size, it has a wealth of stone carvings, many of them dating from Norman times and including some eighty figures on corbels. Among their subjects are real and imaginary birds and beasts, a strange creature playing an unrecognisable instrument, a whirling kilted dancer, and two lovers embracing. Some figures are missing, deliberately smashed in Victorian times because they portrayed naked men in a state of arousal. However, the people responsible obviously overlooked one on the south side of the apse, the caricatural representation of a female figure holding open its genitals. This is a fertility symbol known as a sheila-na-gig, of which there are eighteen examples scattered in churches throughout the country, always outside. In January 1990 a five hundred year old sheila-na-gig was stolen in Fethard, County Tipperary, by thieves who scaled the walls of the ruined church to reach it.

A whole bestiary of fabulous animals can be found in churches. At Adderbury, near Banbury, there is a two-tailed mermaid, as well as a gryphon and a dragon. Dragons are almost commonplace, partly because of their association with both St George and St Michael. The church at Deerhurst near Tewkesbury in Gloucestershire has six stone carvings of a dragon's head which purport to show the beast which once ravaged the locality. It was said to feed on cattle, and many people were killed by its poisonous breath. The king issued a proclamation promising land to anyone who could kill it, and a certain John Smith (perhaps the village blacksmith) set out to try. He put out a huge quantity of milk for the animal, which drank it and fell asleep. Smith then crept up with his axe, smote between the scales, and struck off the dragon's head. He was rewarded by a grant of land on Walton Hill, and this passed to his descendants for many generations. The axe used was preserved until the eighteenth century.

Some spectacular dragons are reported from Somerset, a county which seems to have had a good share of them. For example in the village of Norton Fitzwarren, now almost a suburb of Taunton, the church has a fine roodscreen carving which shows a long, scaly dragon eating a naked woman whose hands are joined in prayer. (The carver is known to be Ralph Harris, who died in 1509 and is buried in the church.) Legend has it that the dragon was generated from the heaps of decaying corpses which lay on the hill above Taunton after a battle; it terrorised the surrounding area for some time until it was killed by Fulk Fitzwarin, who lived in the thirteenth century.

Only about ten miles from Norton is the village of Crowcombe, near the Quantock Hills. Its famous 'worm' or dragon is shown on a sixteenth century bench end in the church; it has wings and two heads, and is under attack from two strong, naked men with stout spears. Local tradition, however, tells a different story, and relates that the dragon's ultimate demise was due to an old woman who persuaded a woodcutter to go gathering bilberries with her in the worm's favourite haunt, Shervage Wood. The woodcutter sat down to rest on what he thought was a log but was in fact the dragon. As soon as he realised his mistake he cut it in two with his axe. Normally this would have done no good because a dragon can join up again, but this one lost its bearings and one half went towards Taunton and the other towards Minehead. The two parts failed to reunite, and so the ceature died.

Misericords

Even more favoured than bench-ends for unofficial carvings were misericords. These were wooden brackets fixed to the underside of choirstall seats so that when the seats were raised singers standing up could rest against them and take some of the weight off their feet (hence the name, misericord, or mercy seat). Carvings placed in such an ignoble position were left to the whim of the artisans, some of whom were well known and highly skilled. For instance a family from Ripon called, appropriately, Carver was responsible for the fine set of sixty-eight misericords – the most extensive in the country –

at Beverley Minster in east Yorkshire. Other work, relatively crude in execution, was probably done by village carpenters.

Misericords are found in cathedrals, such as those at Carlisle, Chester, Durham, Ely, Gloucester, Hereford, Lincoln, Ripon and Wells; in great churches, such as Malvern (Worcestershire) and Lavenham (Suffolk); and even in humble parish churches. Some misericords are purely decorative, with motifs of flowers and foliage. Biblical scenes, strangely enough, are not common, although one does find such subjects as the adoration of the Magi, the cutting of Samson's hair, the death of John the Baptist, the Annunciation, the Resurrection, Noah's Ark, and Adam and Eve. There are also lesser known scenes such as Jael driving a nail into Sisera's head, and the Israelites' return after spying in Canaan.

Mythical beasts and creatures abound – the dragon (sometimes symbolising the devil), wyvern and griffin occur over and over again. The merman is less common, but there are plenty of mermaids – there is one at Hereford suckling a large dog. Foliate heads or green men also occur repeatedly, for example at Holy Trinity in Coventry. Scenes of daily life are often illustrated. At Ripple (see p49), a series of twelve carvings depicts occupations which would be typical for each month of the year:

> January: collecting dead boughs
> February: hedging and ditching
> March: sowing corn
> April: scaring birds from the crops
> May: blessing the crops at Rogationtide
> June: hawking
> July: Lammas eve
> August: harvesting
> September: taking grain for malting
> October: knocking down acorns for the pigs
> November: pig killing
> December: sitting by the fire and spinning

Besides these, traditional sports such as hare-hunting, bear-baiting, deer-stalking, fox-hunting and football are favourite subjects. For example at St Mary's Church, Nantwich (near Crewe in Cheshire) a fighting cock is being taken to a game-pit, a man is about to skin a deer, and two wrestlers are engaged in a contest. Music is also a frequent topic, with all sorts of fiddlers and bagpipers, some grotesque, some angelic.

Rough humour is often present, especially in portrayals of domestic life – the sufferings of the hen-pecked husband in particular come up again and again. For example, in King Henry VII's chapel at Westminster Abbey a woman is thrashing a man; and in a carving at Beverley a shrew beats her husband – though in another she is going to be ducked as a punishment. Themes such as these appeared both in the carvings and the songs and stories of the day. At Nantwich, one misericord tells a story which was printed in 1481 in Caxton's *Reynard the Fox*: by shamming death a fox entices a pair of crows close enough to be able to catch and eat one – the female, Sharpebek – leaving only the feathers. And in Gloucester Cathedral, a Norse folk tale is illustrated, the story of the woman Disa who is clothed in a net; she rides a goat (while keeping one foot on the ground) and carries a rabbit. The explanation is that because of her outspoken criticism of the king's council she was commanded to appear neither riding nor walking, naked nor clothed, and bearing a gift that was not a gift. The king was so impressed by her ingenuity that he made her queen.

Graffiti

Mindless doodlings are no doubt still a problem for many public buildings, but at one time cutting one's initials on the fabric of a church or on statues inside it was thought to bring good luck. Especially favoured places were the effigies of founders or of various medieval kings and heroes. Some people carefully inscribed pictures which reflected their traditional – as opposed to religious – beliefs. In Gloucestershire alone, Churchdown has a mermaid cut into the outer jamb of the north porch; in Tewkesbury Abbey there are two guardian cats in one place and an owl and another cat elsewhere; and in Gloucester Cathedral at the east end of the choir a king is fighting both a monstrous worm and a winged serpent. At North Cerney near Cirencester, two large manticoras are carefully cut into the outside walls of the church. The manticora is a mythical beast noted for its ferocity, and these two may have been incised as a kind of protection for the building.

Not all graffiti are inscribed for serious purposes: in the fine fifteenth-century church at Leighton Buzzard, Bedfordshire, a tiny scratching on the south-west pier of the tower shows a quarrelling couple. According to local tradition the two people, Simon and Nell, were falling out over a cake for Mothering Sunday. The only ingredients they had were a little dough and the remains of a Christmas pudding. Simon insisted that the mixture should be boiled as a pudding, and Nell that it should be baked as a cake. As a compromise they did both, and the result was the first simnel cake.

BELIEFS AND CEREMONIES

Strange and varied beliefs associated with churches in many different places have grown up over the years. In Shropshire people thought that a death would ensue during the following week if the clock struck on a Sunday morning while the text of the sermon was being given out. In part of Yorkshire it was considered unlucky for the hour to strike while a wedding party was in church; times were therefore carefully arranged to avoid this. Churchyards are often thought to be haunted, which is hardly surprising, but Staffordshire people believed that a ghost could be prevented from walking if a turf were cut from the person's grave and laid under the altar for four days. One Cornish parson, the Rev. Thomas Flavel, took to wandering round churchyards with his horsewhip to frighten ghosts off. On the other hand one spirit – known as the Church Grim – was deliberately set up: a pig or boar would be buried alive beneath one of the cornerstones of the church when it was being built, this barbarous practice ensuring (or so it was thought) that the animal's perturbed spirit would frighten off ill-intentioned visitors such as witches.

Some churches without doubt do have a strange presence, and Hanbury, perched on its Worcestershire hill a few miles south of Birmingham, is a case in point. Workmen regularly refuse to work in the church alone by day and will not go in at all after dark. One young man in recent years was playing the church piano – alone, but in broad daylight – when he was seized by an overwhelming feeling of sudden terror, and his hair stood on end.

There was widespread belief in the curative properties of various items illicitly taken from churches and graveyards; these are described in Chapter 8. Divination, the means whereby one might foresee the future, was also widely practised. For example many believed that on St Mark's Eve (24 April) the spirits of all those due to die in the following year passed in procession into the church. They were invisible unless one took the trouble to keep watch in the churchyard for three successive years from 11pm on St Mark's Eve until 1am on St Mark's Day: on the third occasion the procession would be visible. However, if the watcher were amongst those who were going to die, he or she would fall asleep during the third vigil.

It was also thought that a woman could see her future husband in the churchyard if she followed a certain ritual of behaviour: she had to be there as midnight struck on Midsummer Eve (23 June) and run round the church three times, scattering hempseed and saying:

> Hempseed I sow, let hempseed grow.
> He that will my sweetheart be, come after me and mow.

If she dared to look back at the end of her run she would see her future husband mowing after her. One old lady reported that when her grandmother followed the ritual she had felt her lover's scythe so close at her heels she was afraid her feet would be cut off.

The church was once a centre for all kinds of sports, as well as its own services. However in Wales, Victorian restoration removed the stairways which connected chancels to local taverns, filled in niches where the parson kept the prize ale awarded to the winners of the Sunday sports, and occupied with graves those areas of the churchyards which had traditionally been kept for dances and sport. Cock-fighting, fives, quoits, even football, were once staged there. Other church customs included those known as clipping, bound-beating, rush-strewing, well-dressing and the distribution of food and drink; these are discussed more fully in Chapter 6. Nevertheless, the pattern of church services goes on all the year round, with climactic events or rites of passage – baptism, marriage and funeral – celebrated as the occasion demands.

Baptism

Originally baptism required complete or partial immersion, and both infants and adults were baptised in the open, in streams or pools. In cathedrals the ceremony was then moved into a special building, a baptistery, and finally, from about the eighth century, fonts were set up in ordinary churches and baptism came to be by sprinkling only – though some sects to this day still insist on complete immersion. Fonts are normally octagonal, a shape which symbolises renewal, and are placed by the door of the church since baptism celebrates entry to the Christian community.

It was considered unlucky for a child not to cry during baptism; crying showed that the devil was going out of it, or alternatively not crying indicated that it was 'too good to live'. The upper tier of the wedding cake was traditionally saved to be eaten at the christening. In former times, names given were from the bible only; then there was a vogue for virtuous names like Faith, Grace or Prudence. This has still not entirely died out, though not many children are called

'Praise-God' nowadays – the current vogue is to adopt the names of soccer, pop music or television stars; for example the popularity of today's Australian soap-opera *Neighbours* will guarantee that a great many children of the 1990s will be called Jason or Kylie.

Marriage

A host of beliefs and customs surround the marriage ceremony. Many people still consider it unlucky for a man and a woman to marry if their surnames begin with the same letter: 'Change the name and not the letter, Change for worse and not for better'. Some times of the year were considered inauspicious for weddings. May, for example, has been considered unlucky since Roman times – April is consecrated to Venus, and June to Juno, so to marry in May would slight both goddesses. Lent was also to be avoided: 'Marry in Lent, live to repent'. So was Christmas. The choice of day needed careful consideration, too: Friday was bad for any undertaking, whereas for reasons which remain mysterious, Wednesday was 'the best day of all'. Even the weather has significance, though it cannot be selected. 'Happy the bride the sun shines on', says one adage.

The colour of the bride's outfit was particularly important. Green – the fairies' colour – is still considered by some to be unlucky, even for everyday wear. In the Middle Ages, yellow was used for the dress of slaves and bankrupts, and as such was despised. (A relic of this belief occurs in the yellow stockings worn by the boys of Christ's Hospital School which originally was a charitable foundation. And during the Nazi years in Germany, Jews were forced to wear a yellow Star of David). Blue is the colour of heaven and shows constancy: 'Blue is love true', which no doubt is why it appears in the traditional formula for the bride's clothes 'Something old, something new, Something borrowed, something blue'. White indicates purity, and is still very popular; in some cases it is worn even when the bride's party includes her children born from another marriage or out of wedlock.

If the ring is dropped during the ceremony it is a sign of very bad luck. The wedding ring is worn on the fourth finger of the left hand because it has a vein which was thought to lead straight to the heart. When a couple could not afford rings the circle of the great church key was passed over their fingers instead – for generations the expression 'married by church key' was a proverbial way of saying a couple was poor. Regarding riches, there was once an amazing belief that if a wealthy woman should marry a man with debts, the creditors would be unable to touch her money as long as she was married naked. Just such a wedding took place in 1797 in St Philip's Church, Birmingham, and was reported in the local newspaper:

> In consequence of this prejudice, a woman of some property came with her intended husband into the vestry, and the moment she understood the priest was ready at the altar, she threw off a large cloak, and in the exact state of Eve in Paradise, walked deliberately to the spot, and remained in that state till the ceremony was ended.

A similar incident at Gedney in Lincolnshire – though this time with the woman covered by a sheet – was reported in *The Times* of 15 December 1842.

To return to more conventional weddings: as the couple leaves the church confetti is thrown by the guests – formerly this was wheat, and it symbolised fertility. When rice became more readily available it was used instead, and later confetti was substituted; a recent development is to have bio-degradable confetti, so the problem of litter solves itself. In the case of brides who were unpopular – mainly on the grounds of alleged immorality – chaff would be scattered on the doorstep to await their return. The same mark of public censure was also used for wife- and husband-beaters.

The old shoes customarily tied to honeymoon cars are a relic of the practice of throwing shoes after a married couple to bring them good luck. This in turn goes back to shoe-throwing which symbolised the transfer of authority from the bride's father to the groom. The chief bridesmaid threw the shoe and the other bridesmaids would scramble to retrieve it, since the one to claim it would be the next to marry. There was also a belief that throwing shoes brought luck and prosperity to any undertaking.

Death and burial

Numerous portents of death are listed in Chapter 9, p158. In Wales a *canwyll corff* (corpse candle) was a powerful sign: the traditional belief is that St David prayed for people to be given a warning of their impending death, so as to prepare themselves. He was told in a vision that corpse candles would hover round the place where a person was to die or an accident happen, would flutter on the shore where a shipwreck was to take place, and pass along the route to be taken by a funeral cortège. A red flame signified a man, blue was for a woman, and yellow for a child, and if there were more than one light, more than one person would die. Many a Welshman has testified to watching a flame flickering over a house where a person later died, and seeing it slither away down the road to the cemetery.

The Welsh also had a custom of 'sin-eating', and this was shared with some of the neighbouring English counties. A pinch of salt was placed on the breast of the corpse, and over it a piece of bread; a man or woman was paid a fee – of not less than half-a-crown (12½p) – to recite the Lord's Prayer or the Apostles' Creed over the bread and salt, which they would then eat. This was said to transfer the sins of the dead to the living. Sin-eaters, though, were loathed and despised for such actions and the custom lasted only until the end of the eighteenth century. Later, the chief mourners attending the corpse drank port wine and ate biscuits, believing that this took away its sins but without transferring them to the living.

The whole ceremony of burial was surrounded by traditional beliefs. For example, a virgin's grave was often marked by a white rose, and garlands made of white paper or linen would be carried before the coffin, then carefully placed in the church. At Abbots Ann, a village just outside Andover in Hampshire, some forty 'maidens' garlands' (for both sexes) are preserved, the last dating from 1953. At one time it was considered unlucky to use numbers when measuring a coffin; instead, knots were tied in a piece of string, one showing the height, one the width at the shoulders, and the third for the width at the hips. Another tradition is to carry a coffin out of a church after the funeral service with the feet of the deceased coming first, this being a seemly way to the 'long home'.

When earth is scattered on the coffin before a grave is filled, someone hearing it a long way off can expect a death in his own family. (In any case deaths come in threes.) And if while at the graveside a mourner is picked out by a ray of bright sunshine, he or she will be the next to die. In general, wet weather is preferred, in the belief that 'Blessed is the corpse the rain rains on'. At Bidborough, near Tunbridge Wells in Kent, the pendulum of St Lawrence's Church clock bears this inscription:

> When as a child I laughed and wept, time crept.
> When as a youth I dreamed and talked, time walked.
> When I became a full grown man, time ran.
> And later as I older grew, time flew.
> Soon I shall find when travelling on, time gone.
> Will Christ have saved my soul by then? Amen.

4
It Takes All Sorts

As they say in Yorkshire 'There's nowt so queer as folk', and without a doubt it is people, with all their foibles and passions, that constitute the very stuff of folklore. Many stories and rhymes derive from the intense rivalry which existed between villages, towns and even counties, and of course family relationships have always been significant (see p75). The nucleus of any community is the household, and the interaction between married (or unmarried) partners is as old as Adam and Eve, and as frequently the subject for comment. For example, customs such as that of 'rough music' (see p76) were used to indicate community disapproval should one or other marriage partner offend accepted norms of behaviour; and when tensions within a marriage became intolerable a form of popular divorce known as 'wife selling' was practised.

People were also inspired by a huge gallery of folk heroes and heroines, historical characters like Lady Godiva, Oliver Cromwell and Charles II (see p81) – even some who might objectively be considered as villains, from Dick Turpin to a large number of poachers and smugglers, were regarded with admiration. And King Arthur is at least one mythical hero who has retained a powerful hold over the imagination of ordinary people (see p78); sites associated with him in England, Scotland and Wales continue to attract large numbers of visitors to this day.

NICKNAMES

The stories associated with nicknames are legion, and for centuries anonymous dwellers in parish or county, village and town, have found nicknames for themselves or their neighbours, both complimentary and insulting – and sometimes intended to be insulting but taken as complimentary. Various counties have generic nicknames for their inhabitants: the Tykes of Yorkshire bear their name with pride, and so do the Yellowbellies of Lincolnshire; whether the Pigs of Pembrokeshire feel the same is questionable, but now that their county has ceased to exist (having become part of Dyfed) the term may drop out of use. The Wiltshire name, Moonrakers, is said to derive from a particular incident two or three hundred years ago involving the villagers of Bishops Cannings and All Cannings, near Devizes:

> Local people were engaged in smuggling kegs of spirits, which were hidden by day in any suitable place such as a pond. One moonlit night the smugglers met to drag the weighted barrels from the bottom of a pond with hayrakes. They had barely begun their work when a patrol of excisemen rode up. The officers were very suspicious, and asked what was going on. Feigning stupidity, the villagers replied that they had seen the moon [another version says a cheese] in the pool, and were trying to rake it out. Much amused by such rustic backwardness, the excisemen rode on.

The same story is told of at least forty different places, but the name of Moonrakers has stuck to the people of Wiltshire. Many towns and villages have nicknames for their inhabitants, it seems particularly in Wales: for example, those of Conwy will always be 'poor' because they were cursed by a stranded mermaid as she died of exhaustion when they refused her pleas to be put back in the sea. The people of Llantrisant, near Cwmbran, are the 'Black Army' because they fought on the side of the English Black Prince against the Welsh. Others are whelps (Carmarthen), mules (Flint), snakes (Aberdare), one-a-wantings and vipers (Llantwit Major), thieves (Merioneth), call-again-tomorrows (Cowbridge), cuckoos (Risca); and in each case there is a story to provide an explanation.

Incidents of unusual characteristics relating to particular towns are often still remembered today. To most people the two questions 'Who hung the monkey?' and 'Who killed the bears?' mean very little, but at one time if they were addressed to the right (or wrong) people, they would have incurred a violent response. In fact the first continues to irritate, at the very least, the people of Hartlepool whose ancestors were responsible for hanging a monkey. At the beginning of the nineteenth century, during the war with France, a monkey dressed in a kind of naval uniform fell overboard from the ship on which it was a mascot. It was washed ashore alive at Hartlepool but its outlandish appearance, coupled with its inability to express itself in English, caused local people to think it was a French spy and it was summarily hanged on the Town Moor. To the present day, the people of Hartlepool have been unable to live down the reputation which this action gave them.

The second question relates to a village in the Forest of Dean, Ruardean, where in 1889 two performing bears and their French mentors were attacked by a crowd. Both of the animals were killed because of a rumour that they were responsible for the death of a child and the mauling of a woman, and the Frenchmen, who were unable to make themselves understood, were beaten up. The rumour, however, was unfounded, but Ruardean has come to terms with its past and the centenary of the incident was celebrated with great good humour in 1989. A Gloucestershire poet, F. W. Harvey, put the original story into verse, combining it with wry jokes on village names and an allusion to a village (Dymock) where a farm sack was used as the shroud for a dead itinerant harvester.

FOOLS AND SIMPLETONS

A favourite theme has always been that of fools and simpletons. Throughout the country – including the whole of the Isle of Wight as far as Sutherland in Scotland, and from Risca (near Cwmbran) in Wales to the Lincolnshire Fens – some fifty places have the reputation of being peopled by fools. The sorts of things they have done to earn the reputation are putting a pig on the wall to watch the band go by, trying to rake the moon out of a well, and mucking the church tower to make it grow higher. Stories of the foolish wise men of Gotham, for example (a village six miles south of Nottingham) have been told since at least the sixteenth century – amongst their deeds was that of hedging in the cuckoo so that she would sing all the year round. When she flew away they concluded: 'We didn't make the hedge high enough'. (Gotham City, incidentally, was the name given to New York in a 1930s strip-cartoon series which satirised the ineptitude of its politicians, and the principal hero was Batman, an imaginative human do-gooder with enormous bat-like wings who flew about helping combat crime.)

Coggeshall (on the A120, east of Braintree in Essex) has won renown because its name has been coined for 'Coggleshall Jobs', a phrase used to describe any ludicrous or pointless undertakings; these might include fixing hurdles in a meadow to stop a flood (or in the bed of a stream to divert it); chaining up a wheelbarrow after it had been bitten by a mad dog to stop it doing any harm; and lighting fires beneath plum trees to help the fruit ripen. Even more obscure activities have been recorded, such as demolishing a windmill to leave more wind for another; hanging up blankets to stop the wind blowing any infection into the village; and collecting light in hampers and carrying them into the church to provide additional illumination.

Some villages even take a pride in their reputation for foolishness. At fêtes in Countesthorpe, just outside Leicester, the people are indeed happy to be photographed with a pig on the wall in a re-enactment of their having put it there to see the band go by; in fact this foible is shared with many other places, including Yorkley Slad in Gloucestershire. At the tiny settlement of Wing, near Oakham in Rutland (now Leicestershire), there is a public house called The Cuckoo Inn; the name is a pun on the local people's attempt to hedge the cuckoo in.

Three villages in Leicestershire – Debdale, Foxton and Glooston – boast of having treacle mines. Mocking outsiders claim that such mines show laziness, since work in treacle mines must be easy; poverty, indicated by living on bread and treacle; luxury, with treacle the symbol of a sweet and easy life; or just plain daftness. Insiders can refer to treacle mines to mystify others, or to suggest exclusive-ness. Both outsiders and insiders use them as a source for knowing jokes and verbal jousting. The concept must be popular, because it is shared with a wide variety of other villages in Gloucestershire, Lancashire, Surrey, Sussex, Wiltshire, and no doubt elsewhere.

The label of fool is sometimes deliberately assumed as a defence mechanism, as in this case, when the fool turns out to be wise after all. Deep in the country a yokel is berated by a lost motorist for being unable to give him directions to where he wants to go; the yokel has the last laugh with the retort: 'At least I know where *I* be', or 'Well, I wouldn't start from 'ere'.

RHYMES AND RIVALRIES

Many stories derive from local pride and the intense rivalry between villages, towns and counties, which found expression in a wide range of traditional rhymes, a sort of poor man's Baedeker. Small villages near large towns like to claim primacy – the saying, 'Bosbury was a town before Hereford was a city', compares a village of a few hundreds with a city of some 50,000 people. 'Plympton was a borough town When Plymouth was a vuzzy [furzy] down' has similar implications, and many other major towns and their small neighbours feature in such sayings. A great many rhymes describe or sum up places and their inhabitants: some are perhaps simply mnemonics for the landmarks encountered on journeys; others list the products or activities typical of different towns. Sometimes the characteristics of the inhabitants are summed up, charitably or otherwise – sometimes ancient enmities or antipathies are reflected, while others remain objective. Here are some examples:

> Pakefield for poverty,
> Lowestoft for poor.
> Gorleston for pretty girls,
> Yarmouth for whores.
> Caister for water dogs,
> California for pluck.
> Damn and bugger old Winterton,
> How black she do look.
> (Norfolk)

> Beccles for a puritan,
> Bungay for the poor.
> Halesworth for a drunkard,
> And Blythburgh for a whore.
> (Suffolk)

The Quayside for sailors,
The Castle-garth for tailors,
The Gateshead Hills for millers,
The north shore for keelers.
(Newcastle-upon-Tyne and neighbourhood)

> I was temptit at Pittempton,
> Draiglit [drenched] at Baldragon,
> Stricken at Strike-Martin,
> And killed at Martin's Stane.
> (Near Dundee, Tayside)

The last of these is very mysterious and requires a full explanation; the places mentioned are in Strathmartin, about three miles from

Dundee. The story goes that a man and his wife and their nine beautiful daughters lived at Pittempton. At sunset one day, one of the daughters was sent to fetch a pitcher of water from the well a short distance from the house. After a time she failed to return, so one of her sisters was sent to look for her – another followed, then another, until all nine had gone. By this time the father – who must have been either drunk or very slow on the uptake – had become alarmed. He seized his fish spear and ran to the well; of the daughters there was no trace, but a monstrous serpent or dragon, all besmeared with blood, was coiled by the well.

The man was afraid to tackle the dragon alone, so he ran back to summon help. He returned with a crowd of neighbours which included Martin, a young man who was in love with one of the daughters. The dragon made off towards the north. One assault on it was made at what came to be called Baldragon (then a marsh, and hence 'draiglit'). Two miles further on Martin managed to give the dragon a great blow with his club. The beast was stung into turning on him, and the people shouted a warning: 'Strike, Martin'. He landed a second blow, after which the dragon could barely crawl away – this place from then onwards was known as Strike-Martin. The dragon managed only a further half-mile before it was again surrounded by the villagers and Martin was able to deliver the *coup de grâce*, at a spot marked by a stone – Martin's Stone. The well where the girls perished (some say for attempting to carry water on the Sabbath) still exists, and is known as the Nine Maidens' Well.

FAMILY RELATIONSHIPS

Rivalries between neighbours are at least equalled by disputes between marriage partners, and relationships between the sexes are an important part of folklore, as of literature in general. A great wealth of folk song, for example, deals both with such matters as incompatibility and infidelity, and also – it should be said – constancy and marital harmony. Occasionally the community would intervene either to praise or blame a married couple for their conduct. The small town of Great Dunmow near Braintree in Essex, for example, maintains a traditional ceremony known as 'the Dunmow flitch', a custom mentioned by both Chaucer and Langland, which has existed for perhaps nine hundred years. The ceremony is held each Leap Year on a Saturday in mid-June, when a side of bacon is awarded to a married couple who have lived together for a year and a day without a single argument or wrong word. Contenders – four couples are usually short-listed – appear before a jury of six men and six maidens from Great Dunmow; a judge presides and there are both supporting and opposing counsel, though none of these is a real lawyer – various celebrities take on the role. If the jury finds 'for the flitch' the claimants go away empty-handed. However, if it is convinced that a year of concord has truly been achieved, the famous prize is awarded.

Far more frequent were customs under which the community punished a marriage partner who exceeded the limits of accepted social behaviour. For example, in the Priory Church at Leominster in Herefordshire a ducking stool is still preserved. The seat is fixed to a sort of wooden crane mounted on a trolley, and the last person for whom it was used was Jenny Pipes in 1809, who by order of the magistrates was paraded round the town and then ducked into water. 'Scolds' – women with too ready a tongue – were punished in this way, and also tradesmen who gave short measure or offered adulterated food. Scolds might also be gagged, literally, with a piece of iron held in place by a sort of cage round the head, called a 'scold's bridle', a 'gossip's bridle' or a 'branks'. Examples of such objects can still be found in some museums, such as the one at Ludlow in Shropshire, for instance.

Rough Music

Signs of community (as opposed to magistral) disapproval were applied to both sexes. The strewing of chaff on a doorstep, for example, could point to ill-treatment of either party by the other, or to infidelity, and extreme displeasure was indicated if a person were the subject of 'rough music', given on such instruments as 'pokers and tongs, marrow-bones and cleavers, warming pans and kettles, cherry clacks and whistles, constable's rattles, bladders with peas in them, cow's horns and tea trays'. An effigy of the offender would be carried round on a pole or astride a cart, and the whole process repeated for three successive nights; it was otherwise known as skimmington, tin-panning, randan, riding the stang, horn fair and lewbelling.

The procedure was applied to those who blatantly overstepped accepted limits. The most famous instance is probably that in Thomas Hardy's novel *The Mayor of Casterbridge*, when two characters, Henchard and Lucetta, are paraded in effigy on the back of a donkey. This is fiction, but undoubtedly based on real life, and as late as 1917 another skimmington was broken up in a Dorset village by police. There are many other cases on record: at the market town of Northallerton in North Yorkshire a man was unfaithful to his wife for just a few weeks before the community intervened – his effigy was carried round for three nights, then burned. In *The Changed Village* (1945) Ursula Bloom gives details of a suspected case of incest at Whitchurch, south of Stratford-on-Avon in Warwickshire; effigies were again burned, to the accompaniment of rough music.

Similar action was taken against an individual at Woodley, just outside Reading; whether it had the desired effect is not known, but rough music in fact often caused people to move elsewhere. Part of the ceremony at Woodley included the singing of hymns, but this was unusual and normally the songs were rather more specific. For example at South Stoke, near Wallingford in Oxfordshire, a wife-beater was greeted with:

> There is a man in our town who often beats his wife;
> And any man who beats his wife deserves to lose his life.
> So if he does it any more we'll pull his nose right out before.
> Holler, boys, holler, boys, make the bells ring.
> Holler, boys, holler, boys, God save the king.

In parts of Lincolnshire and Yorkshire there was a whole repertoire of songs and chants for riding the stang, remembered until at least the 1930s. One of them runs:

> Ran tan tan, the sound of the old tin can.
> Mr Timothy Wobblechops has been beating his good woman;
> Nather for wop not for why
> He up wi' his fist and he blacked her eye,
> But if he does it again,
> Which I suppose he will,
> We'll take him to the beck
> And give him a good swill.
> If that won't do we'll skin him
> And send him to the tanner,
> And if they won't tan him well
> We'll hang 'im on the nail o' 'ell.
> If the nail o' 'ell should happen to crack
> We'll put him on the devil's back.
> If the devil should happen to run
> We'll shoot him with a gun.
> If the gun should happen to miss
> We'll scald him to death with a barrel o' redhot piss.

This was applied to two men at the village of Clayworth, west of Gainsborough in Lincolnshire. One of them eventually hanged himself and the other ended his days in a madhouse, though these results should not necessarily be attributed to the stanging.

In domestic matters rough music now seems to have died out. As we see in Chapter 10, though, it is still occasionally found in an industrial context.

Wife Selling

A further climactic scene in Hardy's *Mayor of Casterbridge* is provided when Michael Henchard sells his wife. Critics said this went beyond the bounds of credibility, but it was based on a custom which obtained throughout the British Isles. The earliest recorded case was in Scotland or Ireland – it is not clear which – in 1073; we know of it because of a complaint made by Pope Gregory VII. One writer, S. P. Menefee, has investigated a total of almost four hundred instances, of which the latest occurred in Northumberland in 1972. The usual procedure (though this was not necessarily followed in full in all cases) was for the husband to lead his wife to market with a halter round her neck, and to sell her by auction. Disgusting, barbarous, outrageous and deplorable were some of the epithets applied to the practice, yet it was a form of divorce or separation agreed by both parties, and felt to be binding – even legal. The purchaser or new husband normally consented in advance to take on the woman in question. The serious underlying purpose did not prevent court cases, scandals, and also light-hearted commentaries and songs.

HISTORICAL HEROES AND HEROINES

Some figures of the past have faded quickly from the collective memory of ordinary people, and are remembered only in learned works; others have caught the popular imagination, and live on in song and story. In Scotland such people as Bruce, Wallace, Bonnie Prince Charlie and Flora Macdonald are still household names. Owain Glyndŵr is invoked by the Welsh, though his cult seems to date only from the 1770s, several centuries after his death. Tales of ancient and mythical heroes are widely told, and none more so than those of King Arthur and his Knights of the Round Table.

The Arthurian Legend

King Arthur was probably a Romano–British prince or chieftain of the sixth century, but he continues to fascinate after 1,400 years. Many places associated with him have been identified, and various others claim association, with England, Scotland and Wales all involved. Uther Pendragon, King of Britain, did certainly build many castles, including Pendragon itself, four miles south of Kirkby Stephen in Cumbria, though Uther's would have been a forerunner of the present twelfth-century structure. He tried to divert the river there to make a moat, but its waters kept to their course:

> Let Uther Pendragon do as he can,
> The River Eden shall run as it ran.

The story goes that Uther fell in love with Ygraine, wife to Gorlois, Duke of Cornwall, and reputedly the most beautiful woman in the kingdom. For safety, the duke sent her to Tintagel Castle on the north Cornish coast, and raised an army to resist the king. Gorlois was killed while defending a nearby camp, but in the meantime Uther (disguised with the help of Merlin as the duke) had slipped into the castle and spent the night with Ygraine; Arthur was born to her nine months later.

After Uther's death the Saxons invaded again. Arthur was crowned at Silchester (nine miles south-west of Reading), and led his army into battle at Badon Hill; he was victorious, and so set up his court at Camelot – quarrels over precedence among his knights were overcome by the introduction of the great round table, presented by Queen Quenevere. From Camelot the knights set out in quest of the Holy Grail, the chalice from which Christ had drunk at the Last Supper (Chalice Well at the foot of Glastonbury Tor is said to be where it was found). Eventually Arthur had to face a revolt led by Mordred, the bastard son of Quenevere and Lancelot; the armies of the king met the rebels at Camlann where Arthur was mortally wounded. He handed his sword, Excalibur, to Bedevere, with instructions that it be returned to the so-called Lady of the Lake: as the knight threw the sword into the pool an arm rose above the surface and caught it, brandishing it three times before withdrawing from sight.

Legend maintains that Arthur did not die, but sailed to the isle of Avalon where he lies sleeping with his knights until the day comes when he will rise again to save the kingdom in its hour of peril. Merlin, too, sleeps: the wily magician fell in love with an enchantress who put him under a spell. Merlin's cave has been identified as the cave in Merlin's Hill – Bryn Myrddin, above the village of Abergwili, just east of Carmarthen on the A40. Only when Arthur himself rises from his slumbers will Merlin be free.

Queen Quenevere played a significant part in history and legend, but few women are remembered in this way, which probably reflects the depressed status most of them had down the centuries; however, the epic deeds of Boudicca are well known, and the famous ride of Lady Godiva continues to attract interest.

Lady Godiva

The story goes that Lady Godiva rode naked through the streets of Coventry because her husband, Leofric, had promised that he would reduce taxes if she did so. All the townspeople were so touched by Godiva's generous action that they stayed indoors and refrained from looking: all, that is, except Peeping Tom – he was struck blind as a punishment.

Godiva and Leofric certainly existed, and Leofric, as Earl of Mercia, was a powerful man, owning vast areas of Midland England. He died in 1057, but there is no record of when he married Godiva, although their names were coupled in a document dated 1035. Godiva herself is shown in the Domesday Book as a major landowner in Warwickshire; she died in 1067, a year after William the Conqueror's invasion. There is actually no evidence that she and Leofric ever lived in Coventry. The ride is supposed to have taken place in 1057, but the first account dates from almost two hundred years later and makes no mention of Peeping Tom – for the first definite reference to him we have to wait until 1659. Even so, the story continues to be told. The wooden statue of a man with sightless eyes and agonised expression which stands in the Leofric Hotel at Coventry purports to be Peeping Tom, and a bronze Lady Godiva sits naked on her horse a few yards away in the city's main square or did so until 1990, when it was removed to make way for development. If the story is true, Godiva was a brave and generous woman who helped the people of Coventry, and her boldness anticipated that of the feminists of today. Each age seems to have its own re-interpretation of her story, which is why it continues to be told.

Oliver Cromwell

Oliver Cromwell is another historical character recalled in numerous tales. Some of them are no more than fancy – for example part of Barcheston (a Warwickshire village near Stratford), said to have been destroyed on his orders, was in fact abandoned and had fallen into ruin before he was even born. However, another story in the same county has perhaps greater substance: in 1642 Cromwell, then a captain of horse, apparently climbed the church tower at Burton Dassett to see how the battle of Edgehill was going. He must have been anxious about the outcome, for in his haste to rejoin the fighting he slid down a bell rope to reach the ground as quickly as possible.

Cromwell's name is naturally bound up with those of his opponents, Charles I and Charles II. Before the battle of Naseby in 1645 Charles I spent the night at Thorpe Lubenham Hall (just outside Market Harborough in Leicestershire, and four miles from the battlefield) – the chair in which he sat for his evening meal is preserved in the church. A local story tells how after being defeated at Naseby, Charles and a few followers galloped back to the hall, closely pursued by Cromwell's troopers. Charles and his party dashed in and barricaded the doors, but almost immediately their pursuers arrived, surrounded the hall, and started to smash their way in. Charles, though, was making his way down a secret tunnel which led to the church, 150 yards away, where fresh horses were waiting, and was able to make good his escape. However, as history relates, he was later captured, tried and sentenced to death. There is a tale that on the eve of the execution a messenger went to Cromwell, who was a Huntingdon man:

'Sir, his majesty is too proud to ask for mercy, but he asks for the help due to anyone who shows this', and then threw a split goose feather on to the table. This was a sign among the people of the Fens that help was needed, and any Fenman worth his salt was bound to give it to the best of his ability. Cromwell brooded all night, but did nothing to stop the execution. Some of his men heard of his failure to honour the appeal. They sent back to him their split feathers, bent or broken, and returned to the Fens.

Cromwell defeated Charles II at the battle of Worcester in 1651. After many adventures (including his miraculous escape at Boscobel, see p113) Charles made his way to France, and eventually returned to become king. Cromwell is said to have conferred with the devil on the morning of the battle in Perry Wood, near Worcester. He offered his soul in exchange for victory, but wanted twenty-one more years of life. The devil haggled, and in the end a bargain was made, but only seven years were granted. Cromwell died on 3 September 1658, seven years to the day after the battle of Worcester.

A Tragic Dynasty

In 1716 James Ratcliffe, 3rd Earl of Derwentwater, was executed on Tower Hill in London, found guilty of treason for joining the Jacobite rebels who wished to put James (known as the Old Pretender) on the throne instead of George I. There was a great deal of sympathy for Derwentwater, who was only twenty-six years of age and had vast estates in Cumberland and Northumberland where he was held in considerable affection. For well over a century afterwards people related that on the day of his death the stream by his seat at Dilston Hall (near Corbridge, west of Newcastle-upon-Tyne) ran red, and that the sun was the colour of blood (though both phenomena could in fact have been caused by the *aurora borealis*, and the Northern Lights were thereafter called Lord Derwentwater Lights).

At one time the family lived on a Derwentwater island in the Lake District. The mansion there was abandoned in the seventeenth century, but local tradition still holds that this was where the earl's wife received the news of his death, and that in her grief she cast her jewels into the lake. Lord's Island and Lady's Lake are still shown on the map. Derwentwater's estates were confiscated by the Crown, and later bestowed on Greenwich Hospital in London. Thirty years after Derwentwater's execution his son also died at the block, for fighting for the Young Pretender, Bonnie Prince Charles. A tune entitled 'Derwentwater's Farewell' is still played in the north of England, and a ballad is sung in both Britain and North America:

> O then stood up an old grey-headed man,
> With a poleaxe in his hand:
> "Tis your head, 'tis your head, Lord Derwentwater,
> 'Tis your head that I demand'.

> He laid his head upon the block,
> His eyes with weeping sore,
> He laid his head upon the block,
> And words spake never more.

Rogues and Smugglers

Popular sympathies have often gone to criminals such as outlaws, highwaymen, poachers, bank robbers – there was Robin Hood, for instance, who after a long career of robbing the rich to give to the poor, died in 1247, or so one tradition would have us believe; though another holds that he was alive in 1265, when he helped to defeat

Simon de Montfort at the battle of Evesham. One scholar, Professor F. J. Child, maintained that Robin Hood was 'absolutely a creation of the ballad-muse' and had no historical existence at all; though more recently J. C. Holt has identified him as Robert Hode, a tenant of the archbishopric of York who fled the jurisdiction of the king's justices at York in 1225. Whatever the historical justification, once the legend got under way, all sorts of incidents and situations were drawn into it. Most English-speaking countries still know of Robin Hood, partly through ballads, but mainly because of a flood of novels, poems, plays, films and television programmes – his phenomenal popularity is remarkable.

Another household name is that of Dick Turpin, who certainly did exist and who moreover was cruel, disloyal, unscrupulous and arrogant. The feat of riding from London to York was in fact accomplished some sixty years earlier by another highwayman, 'Swift' John Nevison, and Black Bess, the wonder horse, was invented by a novelist, W. H. Ainsworth, a century after Turpin's death. Yet the memory of the dashing, chivalrous outlaw continues to thrive, helped again by the modern media, and also by the innumerable inns in which he apparently slept.

There are stories of smugglers and their doings all round the British coasts, and in addition, smugglers often made up their own tales of ghosts so as to frighten people away from their hiding places. The customs men were often outwitted, but sometimes there was a tragic ending, as the following tale shows:

A young man from Ramsay in the Isle of Man decided to run some bags of salt to the Solway Firth in Scotland (there was a heavy duty on salt at the time). The expedition, on the eve of his wedding, was intended to defray some of the expense. Family and friends advised against the venture, but the bridegroom set off, accompanied by his future brother-in-law.

In the Solway Firth their vessel was intercepted by a revenue cutter, and ordered to heave to. Pretending not to understand English – the Manx people had their own language at the time – they held their course. A single musket ball was fired from the cutter, and the bridegroom fell dead. The other man ran the boat ashore near the village of Colvend (on the present A710, near Dalbeattie), and escaped, making his way back to Ramsay with the terrible news. The dead man was buried on the shore, but later re-interred in the churchyard at Colvend; the ship was impounded, and towed to Kircudbright.

The dead man's father decided to bring back his son's remains to the Isle of Man, and the bride and her brother insisted on joining the party. They obtained permission to remove the body from Colvend, and set off with it on the return journey. However, before they had sailed even three miles down the coast to Hestan Island a hurricane sprang up and a huge wave overwhelmed their boat: all aboard were lost. The bridegroom's body found its final resting place together with those of father, bride and brother-in-law in the treacherous seas of the Solway, though for many years local people pointed out the spot on the shore near Colvend where the unfortunate man was first buried.

5

The People's Games

The capacity for play is one of mankind's essential characteristics; it has given rise to a huge variety of games and pastimes, both individual and collective, and is responsible for the immense leisure and entertainment industry of the present day. Many of today's sports have traditional origins. For instance, knur and spell, one of the forerunners of golf, was played over the streets and fields of northern England up to the 1930s; and Association Football, the national sport, has ancient – and far rougher – forms which co-exist with the modern game. Blood sports (see p89) still seem to be widely supported despite the illegality of many of them, and the RSPCA is seriously concerned about cock-fighting, badger-baiting and dog-fighting – fox-hunting remains legal, but opponents campaign strongly against it, even though supporters argue that it is part of traditional country life.

Other traditional sports continue without controversy, and appeal to large numbers of people. Hound trailing (p91) has a passionate following in the north of England and parts of Scotland, and so have gatherings such as the Grasmere Sports and the many Highland Games meetings. Of more minority interest are such pastimes as marbles championships and the ancient form of handball. Performances of traditional music, drama and dance continue to draw large crowds, and some uniquely twentieth-century pastimes – motor cycling, for example – have developed their own colourful rituals.

SOCCER AND RUGBY

Association Football dates from 1863 and claims pride of place as the national game in England and Scotland, if not in Wales. It constantly commands media attention, often more for events off the pitch than on it – hooliganism on the part of spectators and disasters such as that at Hillsborough in 1989 have received extensive coverage. The government's scheme for identity cards for supporters at major clubs, also controversial, has now been dropped. Despite such things, the sport remains almost a religion for many. Teams are followed with fervent loyalty, sometimes by people living at the other end of the country, and clubs have affectionate nicknames derived from various sources. Local legend, for instance, supplies 'The Rams' for Derby County, and a town's dominant trade may provide a name: 'The Saddlers' for Walsall, and 'The Cobblers' for Northampton Town. 'The Magpies' reflects Newcastle United's black and white stripes, and West Bromwich's thrush emblem gives 'The Throstles', though the team is also known as 'The Baggies'. Badges and colours, songs and chants – all these help to foster a passionate sense of identity.

Players are idolised, and their doings are chronicled with the same kind of devotion offered to the saints of the early church. They are often highly superstitious: one individual will always put his left boot on first – another always insists on being last out on the pitch – a third wears a lucky charm, and so on. The epic struggles at matches inspire deep emotion with good and bad luck often playing an important part, and very often spectators feel that they are participating in vivid experiences on a heroic scale. At clubs such as Liverpool and Everton they often leave instructions that after death their ashes should be sprinkled on the hallowed turf of the pitch.

At one time no difference was made between soccer and rugby, and football was a mass free-for-all played in the streets and lanes of towns and villages. Games took place only on special occasions – on Shrove Tuesday, for example, over forty places in England, Scotland and Wales staged a match. The game in this form is undoubtedly ancient. Sedgefield in County Durham claims that its playing record goes back to 1027, but the earliest written record in fact belongs to Chester – 1533. Old as it is, the sport did not lack opponents and as early as 1583 the puritan, Philip Stubbes, wrote in his famous diatribe *The Anatomie of Abuses*:

> For as concerning football playing, I protest unto you it may rather be called a friendly kind of fight than a play or recreation, a bloody and murdering practice than a fellowly sport or pastime . . . And hereof groweth envy, malice, rancour, choler, hatred, displeasure, enmity, and what not else; and sometimes fighting, brawling, contention, quarrel picking, murder, homicide and great effusion of blood, as experience daily teacheth.

It is hardly surprising that modern ideas of law and order, trade and traffic, together with new notions of social decorum caused most of the old football games to die out; what is remarkable is that several have managed to survive. Stories of how football first came into being are still heard, and in Kirkwall, for instance, the origins of the game are explained in a suitably morbid tale: apparently there was a hated tyrant called Tusker (after his protruding teeth), whom at last a local man managed to kill, riding home afterwards with his head in a bag. Unfortunately one of the teeth wore through the cloth and pierced the skin of the victor's thigh; poisoning rapidly set in. No sooner had the man arrived before St Magnus' Cathedral and flung down the head in triumph than he fell from the saddle, dead. In grief and rage the crowd kicked Tusker's head round the streets, thus initiating the 'Ba' Game'.

Jedburgh has a similar tradition, and ribbons attached to the ball there represent the hair of the enemy's head. At Alnwick (pronounced 'Annick'), a small English town between Newcastle-upon-Tyne and Berwick-on-Tweed, the head is said to be that of a Scotsman. The contest at Atherstone, however, close to the boundary between Warwickshire and Leicestershire, claims to have originated in a struggle between the men of the two counties for a bag of gold, back in the time of King John. Haxey's claim – the village is a few miles east of Doncaster – is more fanciful: some time between the twelfth and sixteenth centuries Lady Mowbray was riding there when the wind blew off her hood. Thirteen men working in the fields struggled for the honour of returning it, and she suggested that there should be an annual contest.

Hallaton is a small upland village east of Leicester. The game there involves small wooden kegs known as bottles, and is preceded by a scramble for pieces of hare pie. Again, an elaborate explanation is offered whereby two ladies from the village were apparently returning home across the fields when they were confronted by an angry bull. They were far from the shelter of a hedge and feared for their lives, but in the nick of time a hare dashed across the bull's path and distracted him long enough for the ladies to make their escape. In thanksgiving for their deliverance they instituted the custom of giving a hare pie once a year (which, some might think, does not show much gratitude to the animal), and bequeathed land to pay for its perpetuation after their deaths. The bottle-kicking seems to have been added to the proceedings at some later date.

All these games are preceded by proclamations and processions, music and speeches, and all have unwritten rules. Teams can be very large. At Kirkwall, one side consists of people born to the south of the cathedral ('Up-the-Gates' or 'Uppies'), the other of those from the north side ('Doon-the-Gates' or 'Doonies'). Both Jedburgh and Workington also have their Uppies and Doonies, whilst Ashbourne in Derbyshire divides into Up'ards and Down'ards, with reference to the local stream. St Columb in Cornwall has Townsmen and Countrymen; at Alnwick the two parishes of St Michael's and St Paul's form opposing sides; whereas the people of Hallaton take on all comers from the neighbouring village of Medbourne. Only at Atherstone is it every man for himself.

The Uppies at Kirkwall defend a crossroads at one end of the town, the Doonies the waters of the harbour at the other end; the Workington Doonies also hold the harbour, and their opponents defend the castle, about a mile and a half away. Since 1837 the game at Alnwick has been played on part of the Duke of Northumberland's estate, North Demesne – the goals, called 'hales', are a mere two hundred yards apart, which contrasts with two and a half miles at St Columb. Play at Ashbourne and Jedburgh ranges over a considerable area of the town, but at Atherstone it is confined to the main street; at Hallaton and Haxey participants take to the fields.

The ball varies widely. A leather case filled with cork is used at Kirkwall, and the game can last for several hours of struggling scrums interspersed with brief spells of hectic open play. It ends with the first goal scored, when the winners take the ball and present it to 'the man of the match'. At Alnwick the first side to score two hales wins, after which there is a free-for-all to see who can secure the ball. And at Haxey the 'Haxey Hood' is not a ball at all but a thick piece of rope covered with leather. The object of the game is to carry the hood into a local pub, and this is usually accomplished after a huge scrum lasting for several hours. As soon as the landlord can reach out to touch the hood the game ends, and free drinks are served all round.

At Hallaton the goals are two streams a mile apart, and to win, a team must carry two out of three bottles over their opponents' line. At Jedburgh, Sedgefield and St Columb the ball used is small and hard, rather like a cricket ball; most places play only one game a day, but at Jedburgh there can be anything up to fifteen, each with a new ball. Scoring is through 'hails', and to qualify the ball must be thrown over Castle Wall (Uppies) or rolled over the Skiprunning Burn (Doonies). In addition a team scores if it succeeds in submerging the ball in specific parts of the River Jed and making a cut in its stitching – a cut is worth less than a hail, but two cuts are worth more than a hail.

All traditional football is extremely rough and hard fought, but not in the least vicious even though cuts and bruises are commonplace and broken limbs not unusual. In 1983 a man was accidentally drowned in Workington harbour during the course of a game, but intentionally malicious behaviour and deliberate violence among both players and spectators are unknown. Perhaps the conventional game with all its glitter and gold could learn something from the free-for-alls from which it is descended.

BLOOD SPORTS

Reminders of the cruel sports of the past can be readily found in the shape of town squares called 'The Bull Ring' and country pastures with such names as 'Cockpit Field', together with inn signs proclaiming The Fighting Cock or The Cockfighters' Arms. Cockpits are marked on some old maps, and the buildings themselves still exist in some places; they can be seen *in situ* at Eton in Berkshire and at Welshpool in Powys, and have been re-erected in open air museums at St Fagan's near Cardiff, and at Avoncroft near Bromsgrove in Worcestershire.

The matches or 'mains' as they were called consisted of pitting a series of pairs of birds against each other, or of having a kind of knock-out competition at the end of which only a single cock would be left alive. Great sums of money were wagered on the outcome, and any bird which turned tail would be ruthlessly and immediately killed.

Songs are still sung which celebrate epic contests and doughty champions of up to two hundred years ago, and even earlier. 'The Lee Bridge Cocking', for example, recalls a match between the birds of Shropshire and Cheshire 'cockers' held in 1779, while 'The Hathersage Cocking' is even earlier; it dates from 1715, since which

89

time it circulated widely, with changed details of people and places, including Holbeck (near Leeds), Liverpool, Oldham and Walney Island (near Barrow-in-Furness), the last version beginning:

> It's a ye cockers far and near
> I'll tell of a cock match when an' whear
> At Tumblers Hill they all did say
> The charcoal black and the bonnie gray.

Bull-baiting (also celebrated in song) took two forms: chaining a bull to a ring or post and setting dogs on to it, or releasing the animals to run through the streets to chase the young men, much as still happens in parts of France and Spain. Many thought that beef was best to eat when it came from a baited bull, and some would eat no other.

Bull-baiting was made illegal in 1835 and soon died out, yet a whole series of acts of parliament since then has failed to bring about a complete end to cock-fighting and there were several convictions in the 1980s, as well as one for quail-fighting. The RSPCA is currently deeply concerned about dog-fighting and badger-baiting – dogs fighting each other often suffer grievous injuries and have to be destroyed afterwards, but the cruelty involved in badger-baiting is even more despicable. Because the dogs are not a match for it, the badger is either chained or has a limb or two deliberately broken before the so-called contest begins. Country areas still report violent incidents when badger-diggers are challenged. Snares are another hazard, and as recently as 1989 one trapped badger was found which had worn a circular track round the snare which had caught it. At least two days must have elapsed before the wire finally succeeded in squeezing it to death.

Hunting

Hunting the fox and coursing the hare remain legal, although they face strong opposition. Fox-hunting was once justified for providing a good schooling for cavalry officers as long as they were not, in the Duke of Wellington's words, 'killed in the training'. Nowadays, people who hunt claim that they perform a useful service in keeping down not only the fox but also the mink, which is a serious threat to our native wildlife (it is, ironically, set free by Animal Rights supporters).

The cost of killing foxes in this way has not been calculated. However, in 1987 a journalist, Richard North, estimated that every serious mounted fox-hunter – and there are 200,000 of them – spends £5,000 per season on the maintenance of his horses; compared to the estimated 15,000 foxes killed, which made the cost of each fox over £66,000. However, hunt supporters argue that as well as providing glamour, excitement and also employment, their efforts to maintain a habitat beneficial to the fox help to preserve it (if only to be able to catch it later) and also the environment in general.

Hunting in many parts of the country has its traditions of 'pink' coats (in fact red in colour, but taking their name from a tailor called Pink who first made them) and black hats, its stirrup cups and its hunt balls, rowdy or stately. The expression 'painting the town red' entered the language in 1837 as a result of the actions of the Marquis of Waterford – 'The Mad Marquis' – and his friends whose hunt celebrations in that year at Melton Mowbray in Leicestershire included literally coating with red paint the White Swan Inn and other buildings in the town. Hunt followers are now usually more restrained, but many outsiders find their 'blooding' ceremony unattractive – after a kill newcomers to hunting are smeared with the fox's blood on the dead animal's brush (tail).

Fox-hunting songs have an even longer pedigree than those of cocking, with some that are still sung dating back to the seventeenth century. Others celebrate more recent heroes, like Joe Bowman and John Peel of the Lake District, where the hunt goes not on horseback but on foot. The song which John Woodcock Graves wrote in 1828 is still nationally known:

> D'ye ken John Peel with his coat so grey?
> D'ye ken John Peel at the break of day?
> D'ye ken John Peel when he's far, far away
> With his hounds and his horn in the morning?

Hound Trailing

From early spring to late autumn a dozen or more hound trailing meetings are held each week, mainly in Cumbria, but in other parts of the north of England and Scotland too. Sometimes they are held in conjunction with events such as Grasmere Sports, or Langholm Common Riding, but more often they are a powerful enough attraction in their own right. The Cumbrian branch of the Hound Trailing Association boasts well over a thousand members and some six hundred hounds. The animals are fed on chicken and beef, and also cock-loaf which as the name implies was originally prepared for fighting cocks – recipes are secret, but the ingredients usually include eggs, raisins, and sherry or port. The hounds have to complete a ten-mile course in a time of between 25 and 45 minutes, and usually average twenty miles per hour over scree and crag, fell and bog, wall and beck, following a trail laid by a man dragging a bundle of rags soaked in a mixture of aniseed, turpentine and paraffin. The hounds are cosseted and idolised, and this is not surprising, for they can earn their owners and backers large sums of money – £25,000 and more can pass through the bookmakers' hands at a single meeting.

MORE TRADITIONAL PASTIMES

Wrestling

Devon and Cornwall, Cumberland and Westmorland, Bedfordshire and Norfolk were once all famed for their traditional wrestling, although now it is only the new county of Cumbria which is the main centre. The introduction of wrestling to Cornwall has a connection with the fall of Troy, as the following story reveals:

> Britain was colonised by Brut, son of Priam and grandson of Aeneas. When Brut arrived here with his companion, Corineus, they found the island inhabited by a race of giants. They divided it, Corineus taking what is now Cornwall, but he was obliged to wrestle for its possession with the fiercest giant of all, Goemagot, and only after a terrible struggle did he manage to throw his opponent into the sea over Taw Cliff. Thus was Cornish wrestling originated.

Corineus and Goemagot were the two giant figures carried through the streets of London in the Lord Mayor's procession, though in time the name of Corineus was forgotten and the two became known as Gog and Magog. Some people, however, believe that the sport was introduced to Cumberland and Westmorland in the tenth century by Norse–Irish colonists; others that it began in the sixteenth century with a contest between a huge man from Troutbeck, Hugh Hird, and the champion of King Edward VI, a contest which Hird won. His normal diet was said to be thick porridge and milk for breakfast and the 'sunny side' of a sheep for dinner.

In both Cornwall and Cumbria the basic aim is to grapple with one's opponent and throw him to the ground, but there are variations in the rules and holds have exotic names like hype, cross buttock, and inside click. Wrestlers wear an old-fashioned costume which includes longjohns and embroidered velvet trunks. Contests are scrupulously clean and fair, but nonetheless hard fought. No wrestler makes a living from the sport, but monetary prizes (sometimes of several hundred pounds) are awarded.

Sports Days

All over the country small towns and villages hold their sports days in the summer, where the fun of three-legged running or sack races often alternates with rather more serious athletic endeavour. Some are very much local occasions, but others draw on a wide area – Grasmere in the Lake District for instance, with a population of eight or nine hundred people, regularly attracts 20,000 spectators to its sports which are traditionally held on the third Thursday after the first Monday in August. As well as wrestling and hound trailing, the events might include pole vaulting, sprinting, high and long leaping, and cycle races, and there are several fell races, the last being to the top of Butter Crag (almost a thousand feet high) and back again – the winner covers the distance in about twelve minutes. There are cash prizes for most of these events, and bookmakers take bets on them.

A similar system operates in Scotland where Highland Games meetings are held, although there is no betting. As well as conventional athletics the central features are traditional sports and pastimes such as tossing the caber, putting the shot, throwing a weight on a chain, bagpiping and fiddling, and all sorts of dancing. The general atmosphere is relaxed and pleasant, even though matters are taken very seriously by those involved. The most famous gatherings are perhaps those at Glenfinnan, with its associations with Bonny Prince Charlie, and at Braemar, which is often attended by members of the royal family.

Music and Drama

Traditional drama in the form of medieval play cycles can be seen regularly in Chester, Coventry, Wakefield and York. Here spectators pay for admission, and the formal performances are often professionally produced. This contrasts with another kind of traditional drama known variously as pace egg, souling, guising and performed informally – though not without seriousness – by local people in the streets and pubs, with no charge other than a requested contribution to a collection. A feature of the folk music scene in the last ten years has been the proliferation in all parts of the country and at all times of the year of festivals lasting from one day to a week. A huge range of traditional music and dancing can be heard and seen there, not merely from the home counties but from many others too.

In Wales there is an international eisteddfod at Lllangollen in July, and a national one in August which moves to a different town each year. The first recorded eisteddfod was in 1176, and originally the bards who gathered to perform their works were professional performers. From the late seventeenth century, however, amateurs took over, and have remained in place to this day. In 1819 the tradition of crowning the best bard of the year was introduced, the idea of Edward Williams (1747–1826) who went by the pseudonym of Iolo Morganwg (Glamorgan Ned). Williams was a remarkably versatile character, a stonemason and also a man of letters, an antiquary, romantic mythologist and laudanum addict. Many of the so-called Druidical rituals which are now shown on the television each year and which purport to go back to the mists of time, were in fact invented by Williams.

Marbles

The game of marbles has been played for several centuries but is now (where it remains at all) chiefly left to children. However, in parts of Kent, Surrey and Sussex, marbles are still played by teams of men with allegiance to their local public house. The season runs from Ash Wednesday to Good Friday. Since 1932 the British Marbles Championship – and this probably counts as the world champion-ship, too – has been played on Good Friday at Tinsley Green, near Crawley in West Sussex, outside the Greyhound Inn. The story of how this tradition started relates that in the time of Queen Elizabeth I a Surrey and a Sussex man were both competing for the hand of a young woman from Tinsley Green. To try to decide who was the better they held a whole series of contests in such sports as archery, falconry and wrestling, but unfortunately no clear result emerged. The dispute was finally settled when the suitors agreed to have a game of marbles as a decider.

Archery

The village of Meriden, between Birmingham and Coventry, is one of the places which claims to be at the very centre of England. More important for our purposes it boasts an archery club called 'The Woodmen of Arden'. We are told that in Shakespeare's time, forest once covered much of Warwickshire so well that a squirrel could travel from one end to the other without setting foot on the ground. The Woodmen can trace their history right back to medieval times

94

with only one lapse, followed by a revival in 1785. Four years after that, John Byng, the traveller and diarist, saw the archers at the Bull's Head Inn, 'all equipp'd in a green uniform, round hats and black feathers'. Two hundred years on, he would still easily recognise them if he came back to one of their monthly wardmotes (meetings) which are held throughout the summer; a grand wardmote takes place during the week which includes 1 August, and there are four days of contests. The club is exclusive, with membership being more or less hereditary, and the Woodmen insist on the traditional yew longbow and wooden arrows; spectators are few, since the archers meet for their own pleasure and recreation as did their ancestors for centuries before them.

Handball

The same might be said for the equally ancient but less exclusive sport of handball, which was played against the north wall of the local church until the revivalist fervour and the building of vestries combined to banish it in the early nineteenth century. Public courts were then built in many Welsh towns to perpetuate the sport, but of these only two survive: one is buried beneath undergrowth on the Jersey Marine at Swansea; the other – at Nelson, five miles from Caerphilly in mid-Glamorgan – is still in use. It was presented to the town by Lord Mackintosh of that Ilk, though the gift was not entirely disinterested for the intention was reputedly to attract trade from the Nelson Inn to the Royal Oak Hotel, which is nearer the court.

Handball is played with the bare hand and a rubber ball in a space enclosed by three walls, rather like a squash court; it is also played in Ireland, but with a glove and a harder ball. An English variant, fives, is popular in some grammar schools, public schools and universities. Until 1914 hundreds of people would crowd round to watch at Nelson, but now the games attract only a handful of spectators. The sport nevertheless remains popular with the players, and in 1988 there was an international match against a team from Bray in Ireland.

6

High Days and Holy Days: January to May

Calendar customs both secular and sacred continue to flourish in Britain. In character they range from turbulent fire ceremonies to the more peaceful distribution of wafers marked with the Paschal Lamb; geographically they reach from the Isles of Scilly to Shetland, and from Anglesey to East Anglia. Moreover there seems to be great interest in the ritual celebration of communal happenings, and some defunct customs have in the more recent past been revived – for instance, by the 1930s, Mothering Sunday was dead, but now it is very much alive again; similarly rushbearing in Lancashire, a procession of chimney sweeps in Kent, and 'heaving' (hoisting people up on a chair) in Herefordshire have all been resurrected.

New traditions, too, are in the making (which may sound contradictory, but then all traditions must have a beginning); one example is that morris dancers have taken to celebrating the dawn of May Day on several hills in different parts of the country. And some of the immigrant communities have made quite an impact on the traditional calendar, none more so than the predominantly West Indian Notting Hill Carnival (see Chapter 8, p140); the Chinese New

Year and the Indian Festival of Light (p125) are also part of the scene now, too.

This chapter covers the first five months of the year, in which the customs discussed are associated both with the important church festivals which run from Lent through Easter to Whitsun, and with the great secular festivals which celebrate the arrival of the new year and the coming of summer.

THE NEW YEAR

The passing of the old year and the birth of the new is an occasion which never ceases to fascinate. As the clocks strike twelve, crowds up and down the country greet the new year both at private parties and at gatherings in the streets. Bells ring the old out and the new in, and the high jinks in London's Trafalgar Square and in the centre of many other large towns on New Year's Eve are a traditional part of seeing out the old year and welcoming the new. However, they are a good deal less spectacular than the fire ceremonies held at several places in the north of England and Scotland. For example, at the remote town of Allendale in Northumberland, some thirty miles west of Sunderland, forty or fifty men set off round the streets shortly before midnight with blazing tuns (called 'kits') on their heads. After touring the town they return to the square and ignite the bonfire built there by throwing on it what is left of their burning materials. They sing in the New Year with 'Auld Lang Syne', then go first-footing round the town. In fact the fire festival dates only from the mid-nineteenth century but it gives the feeling of being much older.

The customs and ceremonies which celebrate the New Year are legion: across the border at Biggar, twenty-four miles south-west of Edinburgh, there is simply a huge bonfire. At Comrie, near Perth, a pipe band accompanies a procession of 'flambeaux' – torches made of twelve-foot silver birch poles with the upper third wrapped in paraffin-soaked sacking. At the port of Stonehaven, near Aberdeen, fireballs are swung through the streets – wire-netting baskets filled with pinecones, twigs and driftwood – then thrown into the harbour. As the blazing globes arch through the darkness and splash into the sea, the old year ends and the new begins.

In many parts of the country first-footing is still a tradition, when people go round to bring luck to neighbouring households. A dark-haired man is usually preferred, but there are all sorts of regional variations. He should carry a lump of coal (symbolising warmth for the coming year), a mincepie (standing for food in general) and a coin (ensuring that money will not be lacking). Variations are coal, iron and whisky; a piece of coal and a bunch of holly; an egg and a sprig of holly. In Worcestershire a chimneysweep is favoured, in Somerset any married man. In the Fens he must always bring something in but be careful never to take anything out. In Herefordshire and Gloucestershire he must come in by the front door and leave by the back; in Shropshire he has to enter, poke the fire and go out again, all without speaking – elsewhere, he calls out the appropriate greeting. In parts of the north of England the first-footer is called a 'lucky bird'; he carries a spray of evergreen, is let in at dawn, and is given a coin and something to eat and drink. To rouse people from sleep he calls:

> Lucky bird, lucky bird, chuck, chuck, chuck
> Master and mistress, it's time to get up.
> If you don't get up you'll have no luck,
> Lucky bird, lucky bird, chuck, chuck, chuck.

In Wales, the children used to go round on New Year's Day to collect a *calennig* or gift, beginning in the early morning, and going on until noon. They would carry an apple or orange studded with oat grains and decorated with holly and raisins, with four wooden skewers stuck into the fruit, one to make a handle and the others to form a tripod. In Chepstow the gift solicited was called a 'monty' (a corruption of 'Good morn to 'ee'), and the children would chant:

> Monty, monty. Happy New year.
> A pocketful of money and a cellar full of beer.

The giving of presents on New Year's Day goes back at least to Roman times, and was once attacked by the church as pagan – Puritans objected even to the wishing of a happy New Year. However, presents were still given in England and Wales on New Year's Day until the end of the nineteenth century, and the custom continued in parts of Scotland until the 1950s. In some areas of Wales the day was the occasion for rough-and-tumble football games, a tradition which persists at Kirkwall in Orkney (see Chapter 5).

Also in Wales, a strange episode is enacted not only over the New Year but during the whole twelve days of Christmas, and sometimes even after Twelfth Night: the figure of a horse, made of a skull on a pole with a cloak-like covering, is carried from door to door – the

Mari Lwyd, and the words may mean Holy Mary, Grey Mare, or even Grey Death. The accompanying group of people takes up station outside each house or farm and sings out first a request for cakes and ale, and then a challenge in making verses. Someone inside responds, and an exchange of comments on such alleged habits as drunkenness and miserliness follows. The verses, partly improvised and partly traditional, are sung to the same tune as before. In due course the party is invited in for refreshment and given money; then the luck-bringing visitors move to the next house on the circuit.

Twelfth Night

The night of 5 January is the twelfth after Christmas, and time for decorations to be taken down. In a few places it is known as Old Christmas Eve, since this would indeed have been Christmas Eve until 1752 when the calendar was revised. The famous Glastonbury thorn always blooms on Christmas Eve, and although it has now adjusted, it originally stuck to the old date – cuttings taken to Herefordshire still do. The thorn is said to have grown from the staff of Joseph of Arimathea, and taken root in the ground as he leaned on it on Wirrall Hill at Glastonbury. Parliament soldiers hacked it down during the Civil War (one of them cutting off his own leg in the process), but fresh trees which grew from the pieces still bloom in various parts of the town at Christmastide.

Wassailing is a traditional custom still followed in several places on Twelfth Night. For example, villagers from Curry Rivel, six miles east of Taunton in Somerset, go round the parish with their song of wassail to wish good health to people, animals and crops, and then ceremonially burn a faggot of ash sticks bound with withies outside the King William IV public house. Much Marcle, some nine miles from Hereford, is another village where apple trees are again wassailed after a lapse of many years: some three hundred people march with torches to the cider orchards where thirteen small bonfires are lit, of which one, the so-called Judas fire, is put out. Cider is poured over the base of the trees and there is music, singing and morris dancing. The ceremony was only revived in 1988 at the instigation of Weston's, a cider maker, but it was followed by one of the best crops of apples in living memory so it seems likely to continue.

A similar event has taken place on Old Twelfth Night (17 January) for very many years at Carhampton, a Somerset village on the A37 near Minehead. Behind the Butchers Arms Inn a tree is addressed in song:

> Old apple tree we wassail thee,
> And hoping thou would bear,
> For the Lord doth know where we shall be
> Till apples come another year.
> For to bear well and to bloom well,
> So merry let us be.
> Let every man take off his hat,
> And shout out to the old apple tree.

Shotguns are fired to ward off evil spirits and pieces of cider-soaked toast are lodged in the tree branches for robins, which are said to be good spirits in disguise. A bonfire is lit in the orchard, and the participants stand round it drinking freely of hot cider themselves. Fears that the grubbing up of trees might jeopardise the ceremony were ended when the publican bought the orchard to preserve it.

Twelfth Day

The twelfth day after Christmas (6 January) is the ecclesiastical feast of Epiphany. Until the beginning of this century many celebrated it as Old Christmas Day, and on the isolated and tiny island of Foula this is still the case – it is extremely remote, a speck of land only five miles square, thirty miles west of Lerwick in Shetland, and people joke that no-one thought to tell its inhabitants of the change in dates. In 1988 one of the islanders, Mrs Isobel Holbourn, described the local ways:

> Christmas here is not a religious celebration. It is closely connected with the Viking Yule, although now we have Christmas trees [flown in from mainland Shetland] and give each other presents. We spend Yule Even preparing food, like reestit [salt-smoked] mutton, Yule bread with caraway seeds, and tattie soup. On January 6, whatever the weather, we all make trips round the island to be sure of visiting everybody, and in every home there is food. At about 9pm we all end up in one house. We eat, drink, dance and play music until the early hours.

A rather more spectacular celebration of Twelfth Day takes place at the village of Haxey, about ten miles east of Doncaster: the famous hood game, described in Chapter 5. The first Monday on or after 6 January was the day when ploughmen returned to their work, and became known as Plough Monday (see Chapter 10); women resumed their ordinary tasks on 7 January, known as St Distaff's Day.

100

Old New Year

The people of Foula who still celebrate Christmas on 6 January, have their New Year a week later, on 13 January. Others also celebrate their new year at this time, namely Hogmanay on 12 January – for example at Burghead, a fishing village on the north-eastern mainland of Scotland, halfway between Aberdeen and Inverness. The people of Burghead call their New Year's Eve 'Clavie Night', and conduct proceedings according to traditional rules: a clavie is the bottom end of a huge whisky barrel filled with tarred wood and mounted on a six-foot pole, and at 6pm – the time must be precise – a glowing peat is used to ignite the contents of the barrel. The peat is taken from the fire of a particular house renowned for its magical powers, and the person who takes it is the Clavie King, an office which is kept for life, the current holder being Dan Ralph. The blazing clavie is shouldered in turn by nine men, cheered on by the crowd. Each one manages to stagger a hundred yards or so before passing his burden to the next. Stops are made at specific houses – always the same ones – to present a piece of charred wood, which is greatly prized as a luck-bringer. Finally, the clavie reaches the top of Doorie Hill where it is set up on a five-foot pedestal. As it burns, blazing fragments are thrown to the crowd.

TRADITIONAL CEREMONIES UNTIL EASTER

Mallard Day

A more sedate ceremony takes place at All Souls' College, Oxford, on 14 January, but now only once a century; it is next due in 2001. Its purpose is to celebrate the occasion in 1437 when the foundations of the building were being dug, and a mallard was found in a drain. Some say that the bird had been buried there after death, others that it was found alive, and flew away after being disturbed. At one time it was celebrated every year, when at midnight on Mallard Day the Fellows of the college, led by an elected Lord Mallard and six officers with white staves, would set off in procession singing the 'Mallard Song', which begins:

> The griffine, bustard, turkey and capon,
> Lett other hungry mortalls gape on
> And on their bones and stomacks fall hard
> But lett All Souls men have the mallard.

The ritual – and of course fruitless – search lasted till daybreak, which is perhaps why it is now only conducted every hundred years.

Up-Helly-A

A thirty-foot model of a Norse longship with great oars, heraldic shields and a dragon prow might seem out of place in the United Kingdom, but not so at Lerwick in Shetland which has historic links with Norway. Each year on the last Tuesday in January and starting at 7.30pm, the vessel is hauled through the town. The scene is illuminated by the torches of up to six hundred 'guisers' who are dressed in extravagant costumes, and sing:

> From grand old Viking centuries Up-Helly-A has come,
> Then light the torch and form the march, and sound the rolling drum,
> And wake the mighty memories of heroes that are dumb,
> The waves go rolling on.

When the ship arrives at a particular spot the guisers make a fiery ring round it, then when a certain signal is blown on a bugle they will fling their torches into its hull – as the vessel blazes, they sing again. Afterwards the revellers disperse to spend the night in dancing, and every one of the thirteen halls in Lerwick will be in use. The guisers tour the town, bringing luck wherever they go.

Candlemas Day

Candlemas is the 2 February when the Virgin Mary went to be 'churched', or purified, after the birth of Christ; the candles carried in procession give the day its name. It was in fact a pagan feast taken over by the early church, for in ancient Rome at this time the citizens used to parade through the streets with torches and candles to honour Februa, the daughter of Mars. People once kept their Christmas decorations up until this day, the fortieth after Christmas.

Shrove Tuesday

Depending on the date of Easter, Lent can begin on any Wednesday between 3 February and 9 March. The last day before Lent, traditionally a time for feasting and sport, is variously known as Shrove Tuesday, Pancake Day (for the dish still widely cooked) and in Scotland, Fastern's E'en or Bannock Night. For perhaps centuries a women's pancake race has been held at Olney in Buckinghamshire (twelve miles south-east of Northampton), and since the 1950s the idea has been imitated in many other places. At Corfe Castle, near

Swanage in Dorset, quarrymen kick a ball along the old Poole road to confirm an ancient right of way, and rough football games take place at several towns in England and Scotland (these are described in Chapter 5). In Cornwall at St Columb Major, inland from Newquay, a hurling match is held in the streets and in the far west, at St Ives, hurling takes place in a public park, though here it is on the previous day which is called Quinquagesima Monday. The town's patron saint, Ia, is said to have landed there on Quinquagesima Sunday after flying over from Ireland on a leaf.

Until the 1940s children all over the country played in streets and school-yards with whips and tops. Earlier still, the evening of Shrove Monday was one of the many official 'mischief' nights when various pranks could be expected – in Cornwall, groups of men and boys would beat on doors with clubs but run away before they were opened, taking with them anything moveable; women would make their hands all sooty and rub the faces of passers-by; people might be deluged with water; rubbish was thrown into houses, and door-knockers were banged, even wrenched off.

St Valentine's Day

On 14 February, one year in the third century, two saints called Valentine (who may in fact have been a single person) were martyred by the Romans. Neither seems to have had any particular connection with courting couples, but their day could be a survival of the Roman Lupercalia, a fertility festival held in the middle of February.

On this day at least since the fifteenth century people have taken the opportunity of choosing a partner. Valentine cards were first introduced in the eighteenth century and became extremely popular in Victorian times – enormous numbers are still sent, usually anonymously, with sentiments ranging from the earthy to the romantic. A more recent development has been the vogue for declarations of love to be emblazoned on publicity hoardings or on the sides of double-decker buses. Newspaper announcements are also favoured, and in 1989 *The Guardian* carried several pages of messages such as these:

> Mould the sand around me,
> Cast your name upon my heart,
> 'Cos foundry man, I love you,
> Even though you fart.

> Maureen – The horny independent woman with
> big pink bouncy ones and life in her veins.

103

To my touch typist. Let's get personal. Love – Rampant Sex Beast.

O Columba mea,   [O my dove,
Anima mea: My soul:
Veni, veni, veni.   Come, come, come.]

In the north of England another traditional ceremony is held every year on St Valentine's Day, less celebrated but just as important to those involved: fifteen minutes before midnight the salmon net fisheries of the River Tweed are blessed by the vicar of Norham in Northumberland. Both Scots and English fishermen attend, and join in this prayer:

Good Lord, lead us. Good Lord, speed us.
From all perils protect us;
In the darkness direct us.
Give us, good Lord, finest nights to land our fish,
Sound and big to fill our wish.
Keep our nets from snag and break.
For every man a goodly take, give us, Lord.

St David's Day

St David is the patron saint of Wales as a whole and also of many of its individual churches, besides others in Cornwall and Hereford-shire. The day on which he was born, 1 March, is marked by the wearing of leeks or daffodils. Leeks owe their status to St David because in a battle against the Saxons he suggested that Britons, fighting under Cadwallader, should sport them to show which side they were on. From then on, fighting men in Wales not only carried leeks in the belief that they would bring victory in battle, but rubbed their bodies with the juice of leeks, wild onions and garlic to keep away evil spirits. The daffodil grew in the Vale of Aeron where St David was born, and was favoured by his mother, St Non. However, it was not adopted as a national emblem for the Welsh until 1907, when Lloyd George was largely responsible for the decision.

'Taffy', the generic nickname for a Welshman, which some find offensive, comes from Dafydd, the Welsh form of David; as early as 1757 an almanack had a verse on March beginning:

The first of this month some do keep
For honest Taff to wear his leek.

In Scotland on 1 March an event known as Whuppity Stourie (or Scoorie) takes place in the little town of Lanark (Strathclyde). At 6pm one of the parish church bells signals the start of a hectic race in which the local children must run three times round the church – each carries a ball of paper on the end of a string, and while doing so they beat each other with it. After the race there used to be a scramble for pennies, but now the winner simply receives a prize. Many different explanations are offered for the origin of this custom. One unlikely story is that it re-enacts the escape of an English soldier from Wallace and his men – the Englishman shouted 'sanctuary' (scoorie), and the Scots responded with 'Up at ye' (whuppity). Another tale relates how a fairy cured a woman's sick pig, but then demanded her baby in payment unless she could discover the fairy's name. However, the woman was able to avoid the penalty because she had the good fortune to overhear it singing in the woods:

> Little kens our guid dame at hame
> That Whuppity Stoorie is my name.

A more scientific theory is that the event is a relic of some sort of mock battle in which winter was driven from the land to make way for the coming of spring.

St Patrick's Day
Irish communities in Britain never fail to celebrate 17 March, the day of their patron saint: ceilidhs are held and shamrocks are worn, though oddly enough St Patrick was born in Wales and brought up in England at the Roman settlement of Bannaventa (which some have identified with a site near the village of Norton, just outside Daventry in Northamptonshire).

Mothering Sunday
Lent is the period of forty days (not counting Sundays) which runs from Ash Wednesday to Easter Saturday; the fourth Sunday in Lent is now called Mothering Sunday. Originally, in pre-Reformation times, people made a point whenever possible of visiting their mother church on this Sunday, the one in the parish of their birth – naturally they also took the opportunity of calling on their own mothers, and ultimately the festival became a purely family occasion; various delicacies such as fig pie, frumenty and simnel cakes (see p65) were traditionally eaten. But over the years even these family gatherings gradually died away, and by the 1930s had disappeared. After World

War II, however, manufacturers once again started to produce greeting cards for Mothering Sunday; they were possibly influenced by the practice in America, where Mother's Day is celebrated on the second Sunday in May. Flowers are also now given or sent, and family reunions for meals are once more part of the occasion as they were in the past.

A relatively recent custom has been established, too, at Cookham Dean near Maidenhead in Berkshire, where the congregation of St John the Baptist Church link hands and surrounds the church to 'hug' it. The ceremony was introduced by the Rev. John Copping some twenty years ago and is a reminder of the original concept in which the mother church was the one to be fêted first on Mothering Sunday. It is akin to the church 'clipping' (embracing) held elsewhere (see p123).

Lady Day

This, the 25 March, is one of the quarter days, and the traditional time for paying rent which is still observed by tenant farmers. It is often the date chosen for buying and selling farms or changing tenancies.

On Lady Day people in the parishes of Tichborne, Cheriton and Lane End, near Winchester in Hampshire, traditionally receive a gift of flour. The custom, called the Tichborne Dole, derives from the last wish of Lady Isabella (or Mabella) Tichborne who lived some eight hundred years ago; the story is that as she lay on her death-bed she begged her husband for funds to provide an annual dole on Lady Day. He plucked a burning brand from the fire, and told her she could have as much land for her dole as she could crawl round before the brand went out. Weak as she was, Lady Isabella managed to crawl round twenty-three acres. Her husband was astonished and furious at her feat. 'Will you promise to keep your bargain?' she asked. He duly promised, but with her dying breath she warned him that if ever he or his descendants broke that promise, her curse would fall upon the family.

The plot came to be called the Crawls, and it still exists. The flour no longer comes from wheat grown there, as it was, but a gallon of it is still given to every male applicant, and half a gallon to every woman. When the dole was suspended in the 1790s all sorts of misfortunes ensued, and it was soon restored. In fact so important was this custom to the local people that when food rationing was in force in the 1940s, the Ministry of Food made a special allowance so that it could continue and the curse be avoided.

EASTERTIDE

Passion Sunday or Care Sunday, two Sundays before Easter, is still known as Carling Sunday in parts of the north of England. Carlings are small dried peas, which are soaked in water overnight and then fried in an almost dry pan – when they start to burst they are ready. Greengrocers sell them, pubs serve them, and people eat them at home in a basin with a small piece of butter and plenty of pepper and salt. There seems to be no good reason, apart from the strength of the tradition, why they are eaten on this day.

Palm Sunday is the Sunday before Easter; for people near Marlborough in Wiltshire it meant following a long-established custom in which willow hazel sprays – representing palm – were carried up Martinsell Hill, and a golf-like game was played, consisting of driving a ball up the slope with a crooked stick. Crowds of people would climb to the top of nearby Silbury Hill, and picnic on figs because the day was also known as Fig Sunday, not only in Wiltshire but in several other English counties and in parts of Wales. The connection is perhaps the biblical account of the fruiting of the barren fig tree which follows the narrative of Christ's triumphal entry into Jerusalem on Palm Sunday.

Ceremonies are now more limited – some church congregations wear small buttonholes of greenery, or carry crosses made of palm leaves. In two small Herefordshire villages – King's Caple and Sellack, both close to the River Wye – 'Pax' cakes are distributed, a ceremony which has taken place at least since the sixteenth century. The cakes are handed out by the vicar after morning service and nowadays take the form of small wafers, stamped with the likeness of a Paschal Lamb and the words 'Peace and Good Neighbourhood'.

Maundy Thursday is the Thursday before Easter: the 'royal maundy' describes the gift which for the last five hundred years or so has been given out by the sovereign on Maundy Thursday to as many men and woman as there are years in his or her age. Once it was clothing which was given out, now it is a sum of money; in odd-numbered years the ceremony usually takes place at Westminster Abbey, in even-numbered ones at a church or cathedral elsewhere in the country – though 1989 seems to have been an exception, for the distribution took place at Birmingham Cathedral in honour of the centenary of the city's incorporation.

On Good Friday, the day of the crucifixion, hot cross buns are always eaten as a sign of remembrance, and in some baker's shops and supermarkets they are on sale for many weeks before. It is a nationwide tradition, though hot cross buns were unknown in some places – Bath, for example – until the twentieth century. The buns may in fact pre-date Christianity, since bread consecrated to the Roman gods was marked with lines intersecting at right angles.

A ceremony with buns which takes place at the Widow's Son Tavern in East London is described in Chapter 1. Other events include the street football game (see Chapter 5) at Workington. The day is still widely kept as a holiday in the north, but many people in the south of England now prefer to work on it, and to take both Easter Monday and Tuesday off.

In the villages of Midgley, Hebden Bridge, Mytholmroyd, and Luddenden near Halifax in West Yorkshire, a traditional play is performed on Good Friday, in which St George engages in combat with various champions – Bold Slasher, the Black Prince of Paradine and the King of Egypt. He kills each in turn, and there is much by-play with a quack doctor who brings them back to life. The players then ask, in song, for contributions:

> Come search up your money,
> Be jubilant and free,
> And give us your pace egg
> For Easter Monday.
> I hope you'll provide
> Sweet eggs and strong beer,
> And we'll come no more to you
> Until the next year.

The 'pace eggers' have been supplied since the 1950s by Calder High School, Mytholmroyd, and during that time there have been few changes, except that clogs gave way first to shoes, then to the currently ubiquitous training shoes. Moreover thirty years ago, audiences were almost entirely local: now they include people with tape and video recorders who travel great distances to attend.

Easter Customs
The predominant custom at Easter is the giving of eggs: Easter or 'pace' eggs are thought to have a Norse origin, and in the sagas the egg symbolises the earth. They were once ordinary eggs, boiled hard and dyed yellow, violet or pink with logwood, onion skins, furze blossom or scraps of coloured cloth. Children rolled the eggs down a slope until the shells cracked, then ate the contents. Now the mass-produced chocolate egg is universal, but the old egg-rolling tradition

has been kept up in a few places on Easter Monday, for example Avenham Park at Preston in Lancashire.

One unusual Easter Sunday tradition can be seen at Radley, near Oxford, where parishioners 'clip' or embrace their church – they join hands and make a human chain round it. It is Easter Monday, however, which sees a veritable wealth of traditional celebrations throughout the country: to name but a few, there is morris dancing in many towns, including a big display at Thaxted in Essex; orange rolling, perhaps a descendant of egg rolling, which takes place on Dunstable Downs in Bedfordshire; and for perhaps eight hundred years or more there has been a distribution of food at the Kent village of Biddenden, ten miles from Ashford. Documentation is lacking, but the origins of this custom may lie in a bequest of land made by Eliza and Mary Chulkhurst, Siamese twins who were born in about 1100 and died at the age of thirty-four. The revenue from this so-called 'Bread and Cheese Land' paid for food which was distributed to the poor. Eventually a workhouse (now a private building) occupied the site, but the dole went on, and even now pensioners who present themselves at a window in the Old Workhouse receive a loaf, two pounds of tea, and half a pound of cheese. A special biscuit is also available, stamped with a representation of the Biddenden Maids, but this has to be paid for. The village is evidently proud of the association, and shows the two women on its sign.

Then there is Leicestershire's famous hare-pie scramble and bottle-kicking which also takes place on Easter Monday (see p87); and another custom kept up in many parts of England and Wales and called 'lifting' or 'heaving' was taken by some to symbolise Christ's resurrection. On Easter Monday the men lifted any woman they could find, and the women reciprocated the following day; the person was taken by the four limbs and lifted three times to shoulder height. When objections were made that this was 'a rude, indecent and dangerous diversion', a chair bedecked with ribbons and flowers was used instead – it was lifted with its victim, turned three times, and put down. A trifling payment, such as a penny, was demanded for release, but a woman might give a kiss instead. Those involved felt that the operation brought good luck, but even so, the custom was 'quite extinct' by the end of the nineteenth century. However, it was revived in 1989 at Ledbury in Herefordshire during the course of a folk festival held at the market town, and could well re-establish itself in the traditional calendar since by the following year three chairs with 'heavers' appeared.

Hocktide

The Monday and Tuesday after Low Sunday (the second after Easter) are known as Hocktide, and the time was once spent in sports and games, as well as in collecting private rents and donations for the church. Sadly the only surviving ceremony is at Hungerford in Berkshire, though very happy and colourful it is. It originated in 1364 when John of Gaunt awarded the town certain fishing rights in the River Kennett and grazing rights in the meadows; every Hocktide since then a court has been held to adjudicate on any disputes. Two elected 'tutti' men make a tour of the hundred houses with common rights, in order to collect the requisite tithe: a penny from every man and a kiss from every woman. A 'tutti' describes each of the bunches of flowers with which the staves of office are decorated, and on top of the stave is a spike with oranges stuck on it: each commoner in turn takes one orange in exchange for the tithe, and the fruit is replaced by an official 'Orange Scrambler' who accompanies the tuttimen. John of Gaunt is toasted at the civic luncheon which follows. Any man attending for the first time must have a special nail driven into his shoe, and pay fifty pence for the privilege.

SAINTS' DAYS AND HOLIDAYS

All Fools' Day

Licence for the tricks and practical jokes which are played on 1 April goes back three hundred years, and probably more. Fooling ranges from homely pranks like telling someone a shoelace is undone, to elaborate impersonations and spurious announcements in the news media. Children usually accept that their licence lasts only until midday; adults, however, often choose to mark the day by arranging visits from various forms of kissogram. In Scotland the day is called Gowking Day, the word 'gowk' meaning both 'fool' and 'cuckoo'.

St George's Day

The Scots, Welsh and Irish are happy and anxious to celebrate the days of their national saints, but the English seem more reluctant. St George's Day is 23 April and would probably pass unnoticed, were it not also the birthday of Shakespeare; not surprisingly Stratford-on-Avon has a special ceremony. St George is the patron of many churches which usually do fly his flag on 23 April. At St Neot, near Liskeard in Cornwall, episodes from his exploits are depicted in stained glass, including the slaying of the dragon.

110

May Day Traditions

The coming of May is now for most people simply the arrival of another bank holiday (the first Monday in the month). For the Labour movement however it is International Workers' Day, and has been for a century; and in the traditional calendar it marked the arrival of summer – the Celts called it Beltane, and lit fires on the hills to bring fruitfulness to crops and cattle; maypoles (usually birch trees) were brought from the woods and set up as a focus for the whole village for sports and games, singing and dancing. In former times May carollers used to go round, but where their songs have survived at all they have now largely passed to children. Many villages still have maypole dancing, but again it is the children who take the active part. On the other hand, morris dancers perform enthusiastically – indeed, they seem to be creating a new tradition by dancing on the very top of certain hills in order to greet and celebrate the dawn of May Day. Old John near Leicester, Mount Caburn near Lewes in Sussex, and May Hill near Newent in Gloucestershire are among their places chosen, and although none of these gatherings dates back many years, they all have a strong feeling of authenticity. Equally successful is the revival at Rochester in Kent, of the procession of chimney sweeps with their Jack-in-the-Green.

At the little port of Padstow on the north coast of Cornwall the whole population seems to join in the festivities on 1 May. Proceedings start on the stroke of midnight with a song, but the highlight is a fantastic hobby horse which from ten in the morning parades round the streets to the mesmeric beat of drums and the rhythmic skirl of accordions. ''Oss', as it is called, is a man inside a wide black cylinder of shiny material with a grotesque mask on top and a tiny horse's head in front – he leaps and prances, gyrates, sinks to the ground, and is revived. Local people are fiercely committed to the event. They welcome interested outsiders – and huge numbers flock in – but give short shrift to any who seek to presume. One year there was a television crew which instead of merely filming, attempted to give directions so as to secure good angles; it was summarily thrown into the harbour. Since 1919 there have been two ''osses', each with its own following; the second is known as the 'Blue Ribbon 'Oss'. Minehead in Somerset also has rival horses, the Sailor's Horse and the Town Horse.

At Oxford choristers greet May morning from the top of Magdalen Tower with a Latin hymn, *'Te Patrem colimus'* ('Father, to thee we raise'), in a ceremony well recorded since the late seventeenth century. This is now accompanied by a street festival, with morris dancing, jazz, madrigals, Punch and Judy, and even mobile discos. Meanwhile, six miles away at the village of Charlton-on-Otmoor, children are marking the day in their own style by carrying May garlands to the church.

The village of Randwick, near Stroud in the Cotswolds, used to celebrate an ancient Hocktide festival in which a mock mayor was elected, then set down in his chair in the village pond; after the singing of a weavers' song, the mayor would splash his attendants, and finally the whole party would retire to the Rising Sun Inn. The festival lapsed before World War I, but was revived in 1971; known as the Randwick Wap (or 'Runnick Swop'), it was later moved to May Day to coincide with a 'cheese roll', when three Double Gloucester cheeses are blessed and then rolled round the church. Since the revival of 1971 the combined event has been held on the second Sunday in May. In 1989 the chosen mayor was the oldest ever elected — a 73-year-old Methodist minister — and for the first time the official who traditionally soaks the bystanders with mop and pail was a woman.

Helston is a Cornish town, and Helston's Furry Dance — the word probably deriving from the Cornish *fer*, a fair — was originally a May Day celebration in which up to a thousand townspeople might have taken part; latterly the custom has become confused with the feast of the town's patron saint, St Michael, and St Michael's Day is 29 September. Some local feasts are still held on 8 May, and in this case the hypnotic music of the Furry Dance can be heard all day long; at one time if any man was found at work in the town on 8 May he was seized, set astride a pole, and carried to the river. Once there, he was obliged either to jump a wide stretch where he would be bound to fall in, or pay a sum of money. Helston's name may derive from Hell Stone, a large block of granite with which the devil was playing when St Michael came along. The devil ran away, and dropped the stone in the yard of the Angel Inn, where it remained until the end of the nineteenth century.

Finally on Old May Day (13 May) it used to be traditional for garlands of flowers to be blessed in the church at Abbotsbury in Dorset; they were then taken out and cast into the sea from the local fishing boats — this custom, it was felt, would ensure a good catch of mackerel. The mackerel are now gone and so are the local fishermen, but the children still make two large garlands each year which they take from door to door, and a collection is made (for the children themselves); one garland is then placed on the war memorial

112

and the other on the grave of a villager who used to take part in the ceremony.

Oak Apple Day

After the Battle of Worcester in 1651 the future Charles II eluded the pursuing parliamentary soldiers by hiding in an oak tree at Boscobel House, not far from the Watling Street (A5) in Shropshire; remarkably, birds perching in the tree remained undisturbed, and only flew off at the approach of the troopers who naturally concluded that no-one could possibly be hiding in the foliage. Charles' miraculous escape is commemorated on 29 May as Oak Apple Day, and until the late 1940s country boys used to sport a buttonhole of oak leaves; failure to do so would bring retribution from others in the form of stinging nettles applied to the bare legs. However, a change in fashion meant that small boys stopped wearing short trousers, and so the custom lapsed.

Other customs persist: for example at Worcester, called 'the faithful city' because of its unswerving allegiance to the royalist cause during the Civil War, the Guildhall is still bedecked with wreaths of oak leaves on Oak Apple Day; Castleton in Derbyshire's Peak District holds a procession with a garlanded man on horseback who is said to represent Charles II; and at Aston-on-Clun, some ten miles from Ludlow in Shropshire, a large black poplar tree is garlanded with flags. These are left hanging until the next year sees their renewal, though originally this was perhaps a May Day custom which gravitated to Oak Apple Day.

There are also traditional celebrations at Great Wishford, near Wilton in Hampshire, but not because of Charles II: in 1603 the villagers went to court over a threat to their rights of grazing and wood-gathering in the great Grovely Wood – they won their case, and have celebrated every year since. On 29 May they dance in Salisbury Cathedral shouting 'Grovely! Grovely! Grovely! and all Grovely!', and then there are festivities in the village with maypole dancing and the crowning of a May Queen; the local people decorate their houses with ribbons and flowers.

Spring Bank Holiday

Some traditional customs have transferred from their original days to the modern Spring Bank Holiday (the last Monday in May). For example, the Cheese Roll at Cooper's Hill, just outside Gloucester, was formerly held on Whit Monday: since the fifteenth century seven- to nine-pound Double Gloucester cheeses have been rolled down the one-in-two slope, pursued in turn by men, women, boys and girls – the winner in each category receives a cheese. The ritual is said to have been connected with the maintenance of grazing rights on the common, but is now simply an exciting happening and an excuse for a general good time. Skill and athleticism are involved, too, and also danger – in 1989 there were several injuries when runners collided with people in the crowd.

At Barwick in Elmet, near Leeds, proceedings are more sedate – and less frequent. The maypole which stands permanently in the village is lowered every third year on Easter Monday to be repaired and repainted as necessary, then raised again for dancing on Spring Bank Holiday Tuesday. The next occasion will be in 1993.

Morris dancing at Bampton, a dozen miles west of Oxford, has also moved to the Spring Bank Holiday.

Rogationtide

The date of Easter determines the timing of several events which follow: Ascension Day comes forty days later, and is preceded by Rogationside, the Sunday, Monday, Tuesday and Wednesday before Ascension Day; Whit Sunday is seven weeks after Easter. From the eighth century onwards rogationtide, together with Ascension Day itself, was traditionally the occasion when people asked for blessings on the corn harvest, and carried out the beating of parish bounds. A procession with this combined purpose in view would stop at landmarks to drink beer, eat cakes, raise a cheer, and to beat or duck small boys. The proceedings were intended to impress the scene on the memories of all those present, especially those of the small boys (who in due course would be old men, and could in turn pass on their knowledge to subsequent generations).

In certain places the clergyman would preach a short sermon, often under a tree which became known as the Gospel Oak, and the villagers would sing a hymn or psalm. Among the places where this tradition continues – without the beatings – on Ascension Day itself are Lichfield Cathedral, St Mary's and St Michael's Churches in Oxford, and the Tower of London (though here it is celebrated only every three years; the next is due in 1993). Most villages have now given up the beating of their bounds, but some are trying to revive the custom – in 1987 for example, Nailsworth (near Stroud in Gloucestershire) had its bounds beaten for the first time in a decade.

On Ascension Eve at Whitby on the north Yorkshire coast a ceremony known as 'Planting the Penny Hedge' takes place. It is in fact a fence made of strips of wood ('yedders') supported by stakes ('stowers') which is erected on the beach below high water mark – it has to be capable of standing for at least three tides. The custom originated in 1159 as a penance imposed by the Abbot of Whitby on three hunters who had beaten a hermit to death; their descendants keep up the obligation to this day.

Well Dressing

On Ascension Day itself the well at Tissington near Ashbourne in Derbyshire is 'dressed' with flowers and greenery. The practice is now very much part of the church calendar, but it probably goes back to the pagan worship of water spirits; the Romans had their own celebration of wells and springs, called *fontinalia*. The floral pictures of today usually have religious themes. Well dressings take place in various villages and are sometimes linked with other events such as carnivals; they run from May to September, mainly in the Peak District, though there is one in Gloucestershire at Bisley, near Stroud.

Whitsuntide

On Whit Sunday after evening service in the church at St Briavels (pronounced 'brevvles' – a small village on the edge of the Forest of Dean, not far from the River Wye) small pieces of bread and cheese are thrown to the crowd which gathers outside. The background is that Milo Fitzwalter, Earl of Hereford (who died in 1144), decided to remove people's rights to take timber from the forest and to graze animals in it. His wife appealed to him to restore the commoners' rights, and he agreed – but only within such a circuit as she would ride on her horse, naked. She accepted, and rode round Hudnalls Wood. In turn, she made the suggestion that as a thank offering the church wardens should collect a penny from each householder each year to provide bread and cheese for the poor. The distribution was originally made within the church, but since 1857 it has been held outside; money is now collected from all who will give. Local miners and quarrymen once carried pieces of the bread and cheese as lucky charms.

Also on Whit Sunday, rushes are strewn on the floor of St Mary Redcliffe's Church in Bristol. This has been done ever since 1486 to commemorate the first mass said there by William Conynges, a merchant who turned his back on riches to become a priest. Now that Whit Monday is no longer a bank holiday, many of its events – ram-roasting, maypole dancing, fairs – have transferred to the Spring Bank Holiday.

7

High Days and Holy Days: June to December

Calendar customs are as profuse and varied in the second half of the year as in the first; well dressings continue, rushbearings and boundary ridings are held, and the summer solstice is not only celebrated, but gives rise to great controversy. Even if midsummer itself is now fêted less enthusiastically than before, festivals like Bonfire Night still have an assiduous following. Christmas seems more frantic every year, and New Year's Eve is kept with great gusto now that the following day is a holiday in England and Wales, as it has long been in Scotland. Furthermore there are a great many fairs held in the latter part of the year; some of these are described more fully in Chapter 8.

SUMMER FESTIVALS

The Summer Solstice

In the early years of this century, only a few shepherds and labourers might have gathered to see the sun rise over Stonehenge on 21 June, the summer solstice. In the late nineteenth century, the Druids initiated an annual gathering to perform their own ceremonies – most of which are of recent invention – and in the 1960s groups of hippies began to attend; as the numbers grew the ancient monument was threatened and English Heritage called on the police to exclude them. The lines of battered vehicles, known as peace convoys, became involved in struggles with the police and in 1987 and '88 there were violent clashes and many arrests; finally in 1989, the Druids were excluded as well, much to their disgust – the police set up a 'no-go' area of four miles' radius around the stones. Mr Rollo Haughfling, archdruid of the Glastonbury order, criticised angrily: 'It is like closing Westminster Abbey at Christmas, a gross violation of religious freedom'. The action was also criticised not only by the National Council for Civil Liberties, but by local people who had gone out for a drink and found themselves unable to return home. A few hippies managed to slip through and reach the stones – so powerful is their attraction – but they were immediately arrested by police and security guards.

Midsummer

On Midsummer Eve (23 June) fires were once lit throughout the country to welcome the summer, especially in the Celtic areas. Then the custom lapsed altogether, except for Cornwall where a revival dating from the 1920s is still in full swing, and a chain of bonfires crosses the duchy as of old. The people of Whalton, too, near Morpeth in Northumberland, still have their bonfire, but they have stuck obstinately to Old Midsummer Eve (4 July).

The Mayor of Ock Street

Since at least the sixteenth century morris men have been dancing at Abingdon in Berkshire: on the Saturday nearest 19 June the dancers combine with the inhabitants of a particular thoroughfare in the town, Ock Street, to elect a mock mayor – many other morris sides attend and join in the revelry. It is interesting to notice on such an occasion that the Derbyshire morris, for example, has its own traditional style – though now represented by a single side only, that of Winster in the Peak District. It holds its annual festival on Wakes Saturday (the first after 24 June).

Bawming the Thorn

On the third Saturday in June a festival takes place at Appleton, near Warrington in Cheshire, which may be a relic of tree worship – formerly the events took place on Old Midsummer Day. A thorn tree in the village is said to be an offshoot from the famous Glastonbury Thorn, and perhaps a replacement for it. There is a procession to the tree, which is then 'bawmed' – decorated with flowers, ribbons and flags.

Rushbearing

The unpaved floors of churches, as indeed of houses, were once strewn with hay or rushes to provide some warmth for the feet. During the summer when fresh materials were available, the covering was renewed in a ceremony known as rushbearing. In certain churches the custom has been kept up, especially in Cumbria where it is a great attraction for tourists who visit the Lake District, and it can be seen in the following places: at Warcop on St Peter's Day, 29 June; at Great Musgrave on the first Saturday in July; at Ambleside; and at Grasmere where it is celebrated on the Sunday nearest 5 August. Whereas in the past those who took part were adults, nowadays it is very often mainly children. One account of Grasmere's procession, written in 1827, mentions Thomas de Quincey's presence, together with that of 'the chief supporter of these rustic ceremonies, William Wordsworth'. Recent revivals of rushbearing at Saddleworth and Rochdale in Lancashire have restored the adult emphasis, and morris dancers escort the decorated rushcart which now, as before, is central to the proceedings.

Ridings

The border country between England and Scotland is now as peaceful as it is picturesque. However, it has a long and troubled history of invasion and outlawry, which is echoed to this day in the tradition called the 'Common Ridings': between June and August hectic cavalcades set out from many of the small towns and ceremonially ride round their boundaries. A standard bearer leads the way – he is chosen for the year, and variously called a cornet, braw lad, callant, reiver or whipman – and is followed by anything up to six hundred riders. There are pauses at set points for proclamations, songs, and the symbolic cutting of peat and bracken.

The event is often combined with a fair or festival, such as at Melrose which has a summer festival and at Peebles with its Beltane festival. Langholm has both a fair and the first hound trailing of the season, and at Duns there is Reivers Week; the people of Coldstream ride to Flodden Field to commemorate the battle of 1514 in which many of their ancestors lost their lives. Most of the Ridings are annual events, both in the Borders and in some other Scots towns, but Musselburgh's takes place only once in every twenty-one years – it will next be held in 1995.

Common Ridings in Scotland

June
First week: West Linton, near Edinburgh (Border)
Friday after second Monday; Hawick (Border)
Thursday between 6 and 12 June: Lankar (Strathclyde)
Third full week: Selkirk (Border)
Third week: Peebles; Melrose (Border)
Week including 24: Dumfries (Dumfries and Galloway)
Last week: Galashiels (Border)

July
First full week: Duns (Border)
Second Saturday: Jedburgh (Border)
Middle of month: Kelso (Border)
Last Friday: Langholm (Border)

August
First Saturday: Lauder (Border)
First full week: Coldstream (Border)

The English Ridings are comparatively disappointing: Berwick-on-Tweed and Morpeth lack the spectacle of those in Scotland; at Lichfield in the Midlands there is just a Sheriff's Ride, though it is held under the provisions of a charter of Queen Mary, confirmed by Charles II; and the so-called Riding at Richmond in North Yorkshire, also laid down by ancient charter, is in fact no more than a walk over the sixteen mile boundary which takes place once every seven years (it is next due in the year 1993). Finally, the town of Laugharne in west Wales is perhaps more famous for its association with Dylan Thomas than for its walk; this covers twenty miles of boundary, and is next due on the Spring Bank Holiday in 1996.

Legal Proceedings

On the Isle of Man every law passed by its parliament, the House of Keys, must be read out in Manx and English on Tynwald Hill, St John's, on Old Midsummer Day (5 July) in order to acquire full validity. The solemn assembly normally includes the lieutenant-governor, the bishop, members of parliament and various officials, and the ceremony has varied little for five hundred years.

There is another significant hill, Worvas Hill, which stands just outside the seaside town of St Ives in Cornwall. A granite pyramid on top was erected at the expense of John Knill, a local customs and excise collector; the philanthropic Knill set up a trust to provide for a celebration to be held there every five years on 25 July – the first occasion was in 1801, and it is next due in 1991. Sums of money are given to the little girls who dance to the music of a fiddle; the mayor and officials attend, and hundreds of people sing 'The Old Hundredth' and 'Shall Trelawney Die?' The occasion is known as the Knillian Games.

Another activity with a legal background is the 'Swan Upping' on the River Thames, held every year towards the end of July. Between London and Henley all the young swans are carefully caught and marked with nicks in the beak – two nicks stand for a the Vintners' Company, one for the Dyers'. The inn-sign 'Swan with two Necks' is probably a corruption of 'Swan with two Nicks'. Any unmarked swans belong to the sovereign.

More August Traditions

Lammas, or 'Loaf Mass', is on 1 August when bread made from the first ripe corn of the harvest is blessed. It was celebrated by the early church as a kind of harvest festival – a number of places had fairs on Lammas day, and several towns still have Lammas Streets.

There is another tradition specific to the River Thames: on or near 1 August and depending on the state of the tide, Thames watermen hold a five mile sculling race from London Bridge to Chelsea. The prize is unusual: it is Doggett's Coat and Badge, and it comes from a legacy made by an Irish actor of the early eighteenth century, Thomas Doggett. It consists, in fact, of scarlet coat, cap and breeches, white stockings, black buckles shoes and a large silver arm-badge.

In Yorkshire, the small town of Ripon cherishes its customs – every night of the year at 9 o'clock the Hornblower sounds off at the market cross, as his predecessors have done probably since the year 886 when King Alfred granted a charter. St Wilfred was Abbot of Ripon even earlier, in the seventh century, and, later canonised, is remembered each year on the first Saturday in August: a man on horseback wearing episcopal vestments represents the saint; is preceded by a band and followed by floats depicting scenes from the town's history.

The Burry Man

Until the road bridge was built in 1964 there was a ferry which for some eight hundred years plied the River Forth near Edinburgh at Queensferry – a fair used to be held there which started on St James' Day (25 July); now it is held in the second week in August. On the second Friday in the month, the day before the fair opens, the Burry Man sets off to perambulate the town – his name comes from the thistle burrs which cover him from head to foot. With the help of two attendants he carries staves adorned with sprays of hydrangea, but the general impression he gives is strange and sinister. One theory is that the Burry Man was a kind of scapegoat, taking away troubles; another that he marks the landing of King Malcolm Canmore's wife, Queen Margaret, who gave the town part of its name; another that he is 'a relic of some pre-Christian figure connected with the harvest, or perhaps one transferred from the vegetation rites of May to a later date in the year'. Whatever is true, the Burry Man is an impressive figure and is welcomed wherever he goes; he is also liberally plied with whisky, which he is obliged to take through a straw.

The Festival of the Horse

The boys' ploughing match in Orkney is now known as the Festival of the Horse, and has undoubtedly been moved from Easter to the third Saturday in August for the benefit of the tourists who are much more numerous at that time. The little girls of the island of South Ronaldsay dress up as horses in amazingly intricate and colourful costumes; the larger boys parade with miniature ploughs, beautifully made of wood or metal. Costumes and ploughs are judged in the village hall at St Margaret's Hope, then for a third competition the boys go to the nearby Sand o' Right and plough a small patch of the beach. The work is carefully inspected, and one competitor is declared champion for the year.

Burning the Bartle

A rather more boisterous custom is the burning of 'Owd Bartle' at the village of West Witton in Wensleydale (close to what is now known as Herriot Country, because the adventures of a local vet were popularised by the author James Herriot). On the Saturday night nearest to St Bartholomew's Day (24 August) a large effigy is carried round, and finally burnt in a huge fire. The men involved stop at various points to recite:

> At Pen Hill crags he tore his rags,
> At Hunter's Thorn he blew his horn,
> At Capplebank Stee he brak his knee,
> At Grasshill Beck he brak his neck,
> At Waddam's End he couldn't fend,
> At Grassgill End he made his end.

From its name the effigy must have been St Bartholomew, but local people alternatively suggest a robber, a cattle-stealing giant, or simply a spirit of the forest. In any event, they resolutely continue the celebration.

Plague Sunday

There is no dispute about Plague Sunday at the little Derbyshire village of Eyam, a few miles north of Bakewell. The plague arrived there in 1665, unwittingly from infected clothes sent from London, and the people took the heroic decision to remain in a kind of quarantine until it had run its course. Out of only 76 families, 259 men, women and children died. Church services were held in the open, at a spot which became known as 'Cucklett Church', and since 1905 a commemorative service has been held there every year on Plague Sunday, which is also Wakes Sunday (the last in August).

AUTUMN

Michaelmas

As well as describing the school and university terms and a kind of daisy, Michaelmas – 29 September – has always designated a quarter day and is still the end of the farming year. Until early in this century it was customary to eat roast goose and currant-dough loaf, though the roaring old Harvest Homes (see Chapter 10) are now long gone, replaced by rather staid harvest festivals. These date from 1843 when the Rev. R. S. Hawker of Morwenstow in Cornwall revived the old Lammas thanksgiving service. Since then the practice has spread, with each church choosing its own date.

The Oldest Dance

The sleepy village of Abbots Bromley, near Lichfield in Staffordshire, is noted for its Horn Dance, said to be the oldest dance still in existence in the whole of Europe. It takes place – and one has to be precise in order to avoid a wasted visit – on the Monday following the first Sunday after 4 September, and there are six dancers together with a Maid Marian, a hobby horse, a fool, a boy with a bow and arrow, another with a triangle, and a musician. Members of a single family, the Folwells, are said to have been involved for four hundred years. The dancers carry reindeer horns which have been carbon dated to 1065, plus or minus eighty years; they may well be older than the dance, which was first mentioned in writing in 1532, and have apparently taken the place of the hobby horse as the main feature. The horns are stored in the church for the rest of the year. Performances were once held at Christmas, but changed to the Monday of the local 'Wakes' week some time before the end of the nineteenth century. From eight in the morning until after dark on the appointed day the dancers tour the farms and houses of the parish to bring good luck for the year ahead.

Children's Customs

On the Sunday on or after 19 September between two and three hundred children join hands to 'clip' or embrace the church at Painswick in the Cotswolds; they receive a bun and a new fivepenny piece for their trouble. A few days later, on or near St Matthew's Day (21 September), the boys of Christ's Hospital School at Horsham in Sussex are given rather more – a bounty of up to £5 from the Lord Mayor of London. They first travel from Sussex to a service at St Sepulchre's Church in London's Holborn, then march to the Guildhall for the presentation. The tradition dates back to the school's foundation in 1552. In fact the Lord Mayor himself has always been elected on Michaelmas Day, every year since 1192, by representatives of the city's eighty-four livery companies.

Saints and Souls

Hallowe'en (31 October) is the day before All Saints' Day on 1 November, 'hallow' being an old word for saint – but Hallowe'en parties traditionally have a spooky emphasis, with turnip lanterns and grotesque masks. Some participants dabble with horoscopes, tarot cards and ouija boards; Scouts and Guides assemble by their campfires and sing songs such as the one beginning 'Three old women, sitting in a churchyard, Oo-oo-oo-oo, aa-aa-aa-aa' – all seeming harmless enough, but apparently not to everyone. For example, in 1987 a group called the Evangelical Alliance attacked such practices as opening 'doorways to evil'; in fact for centuries Hallowe'en was associated with ghosts, spirits and witches and people felt genuinely afraid. In Wales they believed that the devil went abroad in the shape of a pig, a horse or a dog, or in the guise of an old woman spinning or carding wool; he would frequent lonely spots, prevent people from crossing stiles, and generally make a nuisance of himself. It is significant that Robert Burns' poem 'Hallowe'en' begins: 'Upon that night, when Fairies light'. Bonfires were lit up and down the country to ward off the powers of evil, though when Guy Fawkes' Night was instituted, these were trans-ferred to 5 November. One Hallowe'en festival continues to be celebrated with candles, not fire, at Hinton St George near Crewkerne in Somerset; here, on the last Thursday in October, the children go round the village with turnip lanterns and sing:

> It's Punky Night tonight,
> Punky Night tonight.
> Adam and Eve wouldn't believe
> It's Punky Night tonight.

(The tune is 'The Farmer Wants a Wife', which is perhaps now better known as 'Eee aye addio, we've won the cup'). Oddly enough, the local explanation for Punky Night cuts out Hallowe'en altogether; it relates that the men of Hinton St George used to attend the annual fair which was always held on this night at nearby Chiselborough. They usually drank a good deal and were always loath to come home, so the women would set off to look for them. They would carry home-made turnip lanterns to light the way, called 'punkies': hence, Punky Night.

Children in many towns now go round 'trick or treating' at Hallowe'en. In other words, they ask for a treat (a contribution of money), in default of which they will play a trick – this is unspecified, but probably something fairly mild such as hiding a dustbin lid or fastening a front gate with string. Some adults object and call it blackmail, and into the bargain an alien custom imported from America. In fact 'trick or treat' was probably exported to America from Britain in the first place, though the British revival of the last few years may well have been inspired from the other side of the Atlantic. Writing in November 1988 of his Belfast childhood of the 1950s and '60s, Norman Craig made these points in a letter to *The Independent* newspaper:

> We celebrated Hallowe'en by dressing as witches and ghosts and going from door to door with turnip lanterns to frighten the adults. The terrified adults would then give us sweets, money, and applecake with sixpences baked in it, to make us go away. Sounds a bit like 'trick or treat' to me. So, much as I like to blame the US for destroying much of the fabric of our society, in this case we should be thanking them for resurrecting a traditional seasonal British pastime.

At Hallowe'en and on All Saints' (1 November) and All Souls' (2 November) Days, particularly in Cheshire, Shropshire and Staffordshire, men and boys used to go round performing 'souling' plays and singing 'souling' songs. Their purpose was to gather contributions of cakes, beer, apples, money, and even left-over food. Some cakes were specially baked, and called 'soul' cakes.

> A soul, a soul, a soul cake,
> Please, good missus, a soul cake.
> One for Peter, one for Paul,
> One for him who made us all.

All this is now gone, except for one group of soulers based in the Wheatsheaf public house in the minute Cheshire village of Antrobus, just off the A559. They go out with their play at Hallowe'en, and usually the following Thursday, Friday and Saturday, too. Each evening they perform in several pubs (or, where the rooms are too small, outside). There are nine characters: Letter-in, Black Prince, King George, Quack Doctor, Old Mary, Beelzebub, Dairy Doubts, Dicky Tatton (a mock horse) and Driver. Amidst much banter and plenty of beer the old ritual of death and resurrection continues. Performing the play had been abandoned at Antrobus with World War I, but it was revived in 1926 and now attracts tremendous interest; it seems likely to go on indefinitely.

Diwali

Outside India itself, the most important celebration of Diwali takes place at Leicester, though other Indian communities in Britain organise their own festivities on the occasion. Diwali means literally 'a row of lights', and Leicester's Belgrave Road is illuminated with thousands of lights. (These serve twice, since they remain in place to be switched on a second time a few weeks later for Christmas.) Inside their houses people also have small twinkling oil-lamps, called 'divas'; doorsteps are decorated with designs made of rice and flour, new clothes are worn, and people exchange greetings and gifts. The festival is held by both Hindus and Sikhs and is mainly in honour of the goddess Lakshmi, often depicted with four arms, and always with a lotus flower; her white elephant's trunk symbolises rain, fertility and civic welfare, and she is also said to bring health, wealth and offspring. In India the festival runs for five days, the fourth day being the beginning of a religious new year, and occurs between mid-September and October. However in Leicester it is held during the first half of November.

Guy Fawkes' Night

Early on 5 November 1605 Guy Fawkes was arrested and the charge of gunpowder which he had placed beneath the Houses of Parliament was made safe; he was then tortured until he revealed his motive (the introduction of a Catholic régime) and the names of his accomplices. In January 1606 he was executed opposite the Palace of Westminster, and Parliament ordered that 5 November should be kept as a holiday, with the pealing of bells, the firing of cannon and the holding of special services. All these acts of remembrance have long been discontinued, but the story of Guy Fawkes is still universally known and the Gunpowder Plot is celebrated with bonfires, fireworks and parties. For weeks before, small boys and girls take round effigies of Guy Fawkes and ask, in time-honoured fashion, for 'a penny for the guy'; the money collected is often spent on fireworks and materials for the bonfire. In Oldham, however, boys still go round asking for coal, with a song beginning:

> We come a cob a-coalin', cob a-coalin', cob a-coalin',
> We come a cob a-coalin' for Bonfire Neet.

Enormous pyres are assembled. Inevitably every year there are numerous calls for the fire brigade when blazes get out of hand, and children and adults are injured by mishaps with fireworks. Nevertheless, the occasion still draws the crowds. At Lewes in Sussex the festival has wider implications and large numbers turn out to watch a procession which carries an elaborate guy and 'No Popery' banners: during the reign of Queen Mary, seventeen Protestant townspeople were martyred and their fate has never been forgotten. In other places Guy Fawkes is ignored altogether and the emphasis is on fire alone, a custom which may indicate a pre-seventeenth century connection with Hallowe'en. In Devon there are two instances of barrel rolling: the one on 5 November in the small town of Ottery St Mary, not far from Exeter, sounds innocuous though in fact the barrels are not rolled, but carried on people's backs – what is more, they are blazing fiercely at the time. Hatherleigh, six miles from Okehampton, has a similar event on the Wednesday nearest to 5 November in which the burning barrels are pulled through the streets on wooden sledges; a huge carnival is held on the same day.

Not far from Hatherleigh is the tiny village of Shebbear where a strange ceremony takes place on Bonfire Night, though not connected with Guy Fawkes: a discordant peal is rung in the evening by the bellringers of St Michael's, then a group of men with crowbars turn over a large boulder which lies by an oak tree, just outside the churchyard. The story is that the stone, which weighs over a ton, was dropped by the devil when he was expelled from heaven and the local belief is that bad luck will befall the village unless the stone is turned once a year. Hence the name of the local hotel – the Devil's Stone Hotel.

CHRISTMAS

Especially in Christmas tyme there is nothing els used but cardes, dice, tables, maskyng, mumming, bowling, and suche like fooleries; and the reason is, that they think they have a commission and prerogative that tyme to doe what they list, and to followe what vanitie they will.

The quotation is from the Puritan, Philip Stubbes, writing in 1583, and it shows just the sort of attack on the secularisation of Christmas which is still heard today. Even so, with its curious mixture of the sacred and profane, Christmas undoubtedly remains out most important festival. It seems timeless, yet in fact it was only in the fourth century that Christ's birthday was allocated by the church to 25 December – the date is conveniently close to that of the winter solstice (21 December), and many pre-Christian customs were incorporated into Christmas celebrations. Not all Christians were happy about this; for example mistletoe had strong pagan associations and was excluded from many churches until recent years – at the end of the nineteenth century kissing under the mistletoe was reported to be 'a dead or dying custom'. In 1644 the Puritans even abolished Christmas altogether by act of parliament; and in Scotland, although Catholics and Episcopalians celebrated Christmas, the Presbyterians refused to do so for centuries – they recognised only one feast, the sabbath, and it was not until 1952 that the first Presbyterian Christmas services were held.

Some well-loved features of the Christmas scene are of relatively recent date: pantomimes were introduced in 1702 by a Shrewsbury dancing master called Weaver; Christmas cards date from 1843, and Christmas trees (in Britain, that is) from just two years earlier. Although there are some ancient carols, most of the current favourites are of Victorian or Edwardian origin; parts of Cornwall, the Midlands and south Yorkshire have their own variations of words and tunes.

Bell ringing and sometimes burning are activities traditionally associated with Christmas. For example on Christmas Eve at Dewsbury in west Yorkshire the Devil's Knell is tolled, when relays of ringers sound the tenor bell at All Saints' Church for as many times as there have been years since the birth of Christ. The peal is carefully timed so that the last strike coincides with the chimes of midnight. The custom is said to date from the thirteenth century, when a member of the rich Saville family, enraged at the conduct of a servant who had disobeyed his orders and gone to midnight mass, struck and killed him. As a penance, Saville had to pay for the bell-ringing and the custom has continued ever since.

Another ancient ceremony, this time at the delightful north Somerset village of Dunster, was revived in 1935 and is enjoying a new lease of life: Christmas Day is welcomed in at the Luttrell Arms Hotel with a ritual known as the Burning of the Ashen Faggot – a bundle of twelve ash branches bound with the same number of green ash bands. As each band bursts a fresh round of hot punch is served, then as the wood burns the old Dunster Carol is sung by the assembled company. Finally, a small piece of the charred ash is carefully saved to help light the following year's fire.

Carols are seen as synonymous with Christmas, and one of undoubted antiquity first printed in 1521 is the 'Boar's Head':

> The boar's head in hand bear I,
> Bedecked with bays and rosemary.
> I pray you, my masters, be merry,
> *Quot estis in convivio.*
> *Caput apri defero,*
> *Reddens laudes domino.*

The song accompanies the ceremonial eating of a boar's head at Christmas, a ceremony which has been kept up at Queen's College, Oxford since 1340. It has its own story, illustrated in stained glass at the church of Horspath, just outside the city, in which a student from the college, called Copcot, was walking on Shotover Hill near Oxford when he was attacked by a wild boar. His only means of defence was a book he happened to be carrying, a copy of Aristotle. He thrust this down the boar's throat and suffocated it, then dragged the beast home in triumph to provide a feast. The theory is that the annual banquet was instituted in honour of the student's brave deed. It is more likely, though, that the banquet came first and the story second.

Boxing Day also had its share of traditions and stories. Christmas presents were once given in the form of china money boxes which were handed over on 26 December – one reason for the day's coming to be called Boxing Day. It was also the day on which St Stephen was stoned to death, the first Christian martyr; it is said that the saint was just about to escape from confinement when a sleeping guard was awakened by a bird, possibly a wren. As a result it became a custom to catch wrens on 26 December, fasten them to a pole and carry them along as part of a procession. In Pembrokeshire the poor bird was paraded round in a specially constructed wren house, of which an example can be seen in the folk museum at St Fagan's, just outside Cardiff. Wren killing lingered in the Isle of Man until the late nineteenth century, and in parts of rural Ireland until the mid-twentieth. The intention behind this practice was not to be cruel but to make a kind of worshipped sacrifice, as the wren boys' song shows:

> The wren, the wren, the king of the birds,
> St Stephen's Day was killed in the furze;
> Although he be little his honour is great,
> And so, good people, pray give us a treat.

So runs one version of what is usually called 'The Cutty Wren' or 'Hunting the Wren'. Another explanation for wren killing comes from Norse legend; the story is as follows:

There was a beautiful siren who bewitched men and lured them to their deaths in the sea. Then a charm was obtained to counter her powers, and so it was possible to capture her. She escaped, however, by assuming the form of a wren – though once a year, on St Stephen's Day, she was compelled to appear in the guise of the bird, and to be killed by human hand. The wren's body was then placed on a minute bier and buried in the churchyard. Its feathers were treasured, since they had the power of preserving from shipwreck.

8
The Fun of the Fair

Every year fairs are held at some seven thousand places in England, and there are hundreds more in Scotland and Wales, with village greens, town streets and city parks or showgrounds providing the venue. Most fairs have their origins in traditional observances of the past – sometimes the remote past – usually occasions associated with religion, employment or trade. Today they are largely held for the purpose of pleasure and entertainment, although there is still some trading, especially in horses. As well as the old fairs, there are permanent funfairs at seaside and other holiday resorts, at pleasure grounds and also in the new 'theme' parks. In addition there are events such as the Notting Hill Carnival and festivals at provincial centres which have much in common with fairs. All of these events attract interest, and some provoke controversy.

FEASTS, WAKES AND REVELS

The annual parish feast, otherwise known as the wake or revel, was one of the most important events in the year for ordinary people, and one of the few holidays. Originally the feast was in honour of the saint to whom the local church was dedicated, and the wake a vigil of prayers held on the anniversary of the dedication, or the

Sunday immediately afterwards. They were usually held between late spring and early summer (after haymaking and before harvest) or between late summer and early autumn (after harvest). Since the eighteenth century, however, the religious element has been largely absent, except perhaps for a special Sunday service, and celebration and sport have come to the fore; during wakes week the emphasis moved to eating and drinking, dancing and singing, and taking part in or watching all kinds of sport – from sack racing to catching a greased pig, from wrestling to running.

Friends and relatives would attend as well as local people, and would be welcomed with generous hospitality; itinerants might provide some of the music, and also such delicacies as gingerbread, nuts and fruit. Even large towns hung on to their old-style wakes until well into the nineteenth century – there were eight, for example, in or near Birmingham. Competitions were held for grinning, or 'gurning' (pulling funny faces) through horse collars, and for eating scalding hot hasty-pudding – though less homely was the one which involved tying a live goose to a rope so that horsemen could gallop underneath and try to pull off its head; and there was horse-racing through the streets, forerunner of the car racing currently held in Birmingham streets on the late summer Bank Holiday Monday. Foot races also featured, but these often raised considerable objection since the women, running for prizes of dresses or pounds of tea, wore only flimsy smocks, and the men and boys ran in a state of complete nudity; one report describes the men as 'bedaubed with treacle, and sometimes feathered, . . . seen competing for prizes in the principal streets of the town'.

Such spectacles were not peculiar to Birmingham, and one indignant letter writer described a race he had witnessed in 1824 at the village of Whitworth, near Rochdale:

> The runners were six in number, stark naked, the distance being seven miles, or seven times round the moor. There were hundreds, perhaps thousands, of spectators, men and women, and it did not appear to shock them, as being anything out of the ordinary course of things.

Even fifty years later, at the height of the Victorian era, races in Lancashire by naked men were 'not yet extinct . . . notwithstanding the vigilance of the county police'. The same mixture of horror and fascination was expressed by some of those who commented on the 'Flower Power' pop festivals of the 1960s, notorious for their easy-going displays of nudity and casual sexual attitudes. Wakes-goers, too, were accused of immorality and they did indeed relax their normal code of behaviour, much as many young people do today when travelling abroad for holidays; statistics usually showed a bulge in the records of births out of wedlock, nine months after the wakes.

Many wakes have died out. In some villages the population shrank so much that it could no longer support such events, and in many larger centres new, commercialised mass sport and entertainment eventually took over. The annual holiday was another factor. Wakes Week in Lancashire and Yorkshire came to mean a seaside holiday, as it still does – but nowadays this is taken at Palma or Torremolinos instead of at Bridlington or Blackpool. However, some wakes took a long time to die, and at Charlton, for example (formerly in Kent, now in Greater London), an extraordinary occasion called Horn Fair grew out of the local wakes held on St Luke's Day (18 October). St Luke is the patron saint of Charlton church and the ox is his emblem, so the horns of the ox were therefore adopted as the badge of the fair; though quite a different story gew up to explain the association:

> King John, passing through Charlton, was greatly taken by the beauty of the miller's wife. His advances to her were successful, and to compensate the husband, John awarded him the right to hold an annual fair. Neighbours, who were in the know, nicknamed it Horn Fair – a pair of horns being the time-honoured badge of the cuckold.

Whatever the truth of its origin, the fair was undoubtedly a lively occasion. It gave rise to the proverbial expression 'All's fair at Horn Fair', and was renowned for its rowdiness, horseplay and sexual permissiveness. Men dressed as women were a common feature, and they would run about carrying sprigs of furze with which they struck the real women. The event was suppressed only in 1872.

A rather more sedate Horn Fair is still held – as it has been 'since time immemorial' – on the day of St James the Great (25 July) at the village of Ebernoe, near Petworth in Sussex. Events include a cricket match, and a horned sheep roasting where visitors take it in turns with the basting, something which is considered lucky. After the mutton is eaten the head and horns are given to the cricketer who scores the most runs for the winning team.

Scuttlebrook Wake still takes place at Chipping Camden in the Cotswolds, and was said to be one of the rowdiest wakes in England.

Formerly held on the Saturday after Whitsuntide, it now takes place on the Saturday after the Spring Bank Holiday – a Scuttlebrook Queen is elected and parades, and there are many stalls and sideshows. Scuttlebrook itself, however, can no longer be seen, since it has been culverted beneath the High Street. Not far from Gloucester there is the annual festival of Cranham Feast, which continues to be held on the second Monday in August. It perpetuates many traditional events, including a tug-of-war, a deer-roasting, a mime, boundary races and maypole dancing, and there is always a fancy dress parade featuring stock village characters typical of past eras: serfs, a doctor and his wife, the vicar and his wife, the school teacher and the village idiot. The local belief is that the feast originated when villagers asserted their right to common land by roasting a deer on it in the presence of the lord of the manor.

STATUTES, MOPS AND FEEINGS

All farm workers, both men and women, and whether they worked inside or out of doors, were once hired on a yearly or half-yearly basis at fairs called statutes, mops or feeings. According to local custom these were held on May Day, at Whitsun, at Michaelmas, Martinmas or even at Christmas, and those wishing to be hired would wear emblems appropriate to their calling: a waggoner or carter would sport a piece of whipcord in his lapel or hat; a cowman would have a wisp of hay or a cow's tail; a groom, a piece of sponge; and a shepherd, a tuft of wool. Shepherds were even buried with their tuft of wool, to show at the Day of Judgement that their poor record of church attendance was because of professional commitment, not because they were lax. Indoor maids would carry a few strands from a mop, which is probably how the name 'mop fair' arose.

Then the farmer would come along, select a likely-looking lad or lass, and start bargaining over wages and conditions. If agreement were reached he would give a small advance of wages, and this was variously known as an 'earnest', an 'arles', a 'feeing' or 'fastening penny', or 'hence money'. Anyone who failed to be hired could try again at another 'statties' or 'mop', and those who regretted their bargain within a week or two – at least in some areas – could return their advance and seek a different place at a Runaway Mop.

After the hiring came the socialising, and to cater for the merrymaking there were stalls and side-shows, theatre booths and menageries, pubs which did a roaring trade, and dances which were held in the evening – or evenings, for some fairs went on for several days. In the Lake District and some parts of Ireland these hiring fairs continued to be held until World War II, and even up to the 1950s. However, like the wakes, hirings were fiercely attacked for the drunkenness, disorder and vandalism which they allegedly generated. They died out as hirings because modern employment practices superseded them, but they continued in many areas purely as pleasure fairs.

One of the most famous is the mop at Stratford-on-Avon, which has been held every 12 October since the time of Edward III or 'when the mind of man runneth not to the contrary'; the Runwaway Mop used to be exactly a week later. The attractions included morris dancing, climbing a greasy pole, ducking for sixpences, grinning through a horse's collar, and catching a pig by its specially greased tail; these have all gone, replaced long since by a mammoth funfair, but the tradition of roasting pigs and sheep continues. The mop attracts not labourers for hire, but vast numbers of people bent on pleasure who come from thirty or forty miles around.

FAIRS PROPER

Fairs were originally annual markets, and their purpose was the sale of goods, produce and animals. Many existed long before their status was formalised by royal charter, and the more ancient were held in churchyards (though only until 1285, when this was made illegal), by funeral barrows, on hilltops, and at the junction of tracks and roads. The fair on Newcastle Town Moor is said to have been started by the Romans, and Winchester Fair – sited on St Giles' Hill near the Long Barrow – was one of the most important in the country until 1337, trading in wool, tin, spices and wine; at one time it ran for twenty-four days.

The market town of St Ives, just east of Huntingdon, owes its very importance to a fair. The story goes that in the year 1001, four bodies were found buried at the tiny village of Slepe, near Huntingdon, one of which bore episcopal insignia; a peasant later dreamed that these were the remains of Ives, a Persian bishop who had come to England, had lived and died a hermit, and was later canonised. The bodies were taken to Ramsey Abbey, north of Huntingdon, and miracles subsequently occurred there, including the outflow of a spring of healing water. About a century later a mysterious beam of light began to shine at night from Ramsey Abbey back to the village of Slepe, and this was eventually interpreted to mean that the bodies of Ives' companions (though for some reason not the saint himself) should be returned to their place of burial, and a shrine built. This was done, and in 1100 King Henry I granted a charter for a fair to be held there, which led in due course to the considerable development of the village of Slepe and its transformation into the town of St Ives.

Later, other fairs were added to the annual calendar, including an Easter cloth fair where the cheaper materials were sold in St Audrey's Lane, known as 'Taudry' Lane; this is how the word 'tawdry' came into the English language. Henry's fair still survives, but only as a shadow of its former self; St Ives also has an October fair, held under a charter granted by King John in 1202.

Stourbridge Fair was once the biggest fair in the whole country, but it has now gone completely. It used to be held in a field near Chesterton, two miles from Cambridge, and had probably existed for many years before receiving a charter – again from King John – in 1211. Every year on St Bartholomew's Day (24 August) a civic procession would ride out of Cambridge to proclaim the fair which would last until 14 September, jointly controlled by the town and the university. Every year, too, an instant town sprang up on the half square mile of fair ground, its streets packed with booths, taverns and stalls, and thronged with people. Merchants came from all over Europe to buy and sell the annual harvest of hops, wool and cloth; there was considerable trade in tin, iron and lead; salt was always in demand, and the fair provided a good market for glassware and for the huge quantities of clothing which were sold. The moralising poet, Thomas Tusser, advised both merchants and the individual fair-goer who went to stock up from the goods on offer:

> At Bartlemew tide, or at Sturbridge Fair,
> buy that as is needful, thy house to repair.
> Then sell to thy profit, both butter and cheese,
> who buyeth it sooner, the more he shall leese.

Cambridge undergraduates went to buy books but also to patronise the prostitutes who flocked to the fair, an activity which the university tried to prevent, employing red-coated watchmen for the purpose – if the prostitutes were caught by the watchmen they risked being severely punished. Or to be more precise, the town crier would '. . . discipline the Ladies of Pleasure with his whip'.

Daniel Defoe visited Stourbridge Fair, a few years after writing *Robinson Crusoe*, and came to the conclusion that it was the greatest, not only 'in the whole nation, but in the world'. He concluded a lengthy account in this way:

> Towards the latter end of the fair, and when the great hurry of wholesale business begins to be over, the gentry come in, from all parts of the country round; and though they come for their diversion, yet 'tis not a little money they lay out; which generally falls to the share of the retailers, and some loose coins they reserve for the puppet-shows, drolls, rope-dancers, and such like; of which there is no want, though not considerable like the rest. The last day of the fair is the horse-fair where the whole is closed with both horse and foot-races, to divert the meaner sort of people only, for nothing considerable is offered of that kind. Thus ends the whole fair and in less than a week there is scarce any sign left that there has been any such thing there: except by the heaps of dung and straw; and other rubbish which is left behind, trod into the earth, and which is as good as a summer's fallow for dunging the land.

All that is left now is the field, called Stourbridge Common. The fair gradually declined until only the horse sale was left, and this was held for the last time in 1855. Nevertheless, even after trading had ceased a pleasure fair continued, as did the civic proclamations, although by 1933 attendance was limited to four: the lady mayor of Cambridge, one ice-cream seller, and two women with prams. That was the last Stourbridge Fair. Its descendant is the Midsummer Fair now held in Cambridge – but the epic dimension is gone for ever.

Horse Fairs

The huge increase in the popularity of horse riding in recent years has meant new patrons for some of the old horse fairs. At Weyhill, a village near Andover in Hampshire, the fair there has records going back to the eleventh century, and it is probably even older than that – there is a Bronze Age long barrow nearby, which may be significant. It is held on Old Michaelmas Day (10 October) and both sheep and horses are sold. An interesting detail is a nineteenth-century song warning horse buyers of some of the faults to look for, and some of the tricks of the sellers, and it is particularly remarkable as the advice still holds good. The same song, with a simple change of name, was made to fit another horse fair at Howden (now just off the M62, 24 miles west of Hull).

Another horse fair is held at Widecombe on Dartmoor on the second Tuesday in September; though oddly enough the celebrated

Tom Cobley of the song could not have attended since he died in 1794 (at the age of ninety-six) and the fair only began in 1850. Even so the song remains famous, and so do the Dartmoor ponies sold at the fair.

At the other end of the country the small town of Appleby-in-Westmorland thirteen miles from Penrith which despite its name is now in Cumbria is the scene of the biggest horse fair in the world. It has been held since 1685 and nowadays begins in June the day after Derby day; it lasts for a week, and each year the town looks forward to the event with some trepidation. Even the tourist information centre issues a fact sheet for visitors with the following warning: 'Do not expect to see swings and roundabouts. Bring your wellies and take care of your purses and wallets.' Some of the town's three thousand inhabitants choose to lock up and go on holiday for the week; shops shut and are boarded up; even public houses close, and those that do stay open remove everything portable from their bar rooms. This is because literally thousands of people, mainly travellers with their cars and caravans, descend upon the town from all over the country and set up a huge encampment a mile and a half away. According to a certain Geoff Smith, talking in 1989:

I am fifty-nine and I've been coming for fifty years. It is still the best place to be – we all gather here and talk into the early hours. There is nowhere like it! There might be the odd bit of bother but nothing to worry about too much. We are just friends who love this way of life.

Establishments which do remain open carry on a roaring trade. Local people talk of a tea-shop which served 110 scones in one morning, and of a fishmonger who sold 5,000 fish in a day. Horses of all colours, shapes and sizes are washed in the River Eden, cantered up and down, endlessly bargained over; and in 1989 there was the biggest gathering of animals seen for many years. Large sums of money – always in cash – change hands, then the fair-goers settle down to celebrate, and finally leave Appleby to its own concerns for another year. Other horse fairs can be found in these places:

Barnet (Hertfordshire)
Brough (Cumbria)
Belton, near Shepshed (Leicestershire)
Brigg, near Scunthorpe (S Humberside)
Lee Fair, Woodkirk, near Leeds (W Yorkshire)

Petersfield (Hampshire)
Stow-on-the-Wold (Gloucestershire)
Wibsey, near Bradford (W Yorkshire)
Worcester

Goose Fairs

Geese were once driven long distances to be sold at a market or fair; before setting off they would be made to walk through warm tar, then sand, so that they were 'shod' for the journey. Some twenty thousand birds would arrive at Nottingham for the great fair held in the market place, starting on the first Thursday in October and continuing for the next two days. Now not a goose is to be seen, but a pleasure fair is still held on the Forest Recreation Ground – it even features in Alan Sillitoe's novel, *Saturday Night and Sunday Morning*. In Devon the so-called Goosey Fair at Tavistock also carries on without geese, though its history goes right back to 1105.

More About Fairs

For students of oddity and eccentricity fairs have plenty to offer. For example, the Crab Fair at Egremont in the far west of Cumbria (held on the Saturday nearest to 18 September) takes its name from the custom of pelting those attending with crab apples. Its highlight is provided by the world championships in 'gurning through a braffin' (grimacing through a horse collar), a pastime which has been popular for centuries. At Exeter, the Lammas Fair is solemnly proclaimed each year – though this is as far as proceedings go: not only does the ceremony take place in July (on the Tuesday before the third Wednesday) – whereas the true Lammas Day is on 1 August – but there is in fact no fair at all, since it died out well over a century ago. Several other places, however, do hold true Lammas Fairs, for example Kirkwall in Orkney, and St Andrews and Inverkeithing in Fife.

One tradition does remain at the Exeter proclamation: a large white stuffed glove, bedecked with garlands and ribbons is carried through the town on a pole; this symbolised the safety guaranteed to travellers on the way to and from the fair by a law of Edward I – some existing fairs still display it. For example at Barnstaple in Devon St Giles' Fair has been held each year on the Wednesday before 20 September for seven centuries without a break, and here the glove is on show outside the Guildhall for three days. In south Devon, at Kingsbridge, the three-day July fair is also marked by the display of a glove, and local people believe that no-one can be arrested for being drunk and disorderly while the glove is on show. In fact those attending fairs are nowadays subject to the normal laws of the land; in the past, however, itinerant fair-goers received instant justice from what were called Courts of Pie Powder (from *pieds poudreux*, dusty feet). Cheats, thieves and prostitutes were summarily dealt with, at least to the end of the nineteenth century.

The first fair of the year is Kings Lynn Mart in Norfolk (on 14 February), but the main season begins with the great Easter Fair at Norwich; the last fairs of the year are in November, often coinciding with Guy Fawkes' Night, though there are always several more at Christmas (again at Norwich, and also at Northampton, Wolverhampton and Wrexham). Fairs give pleasure to many thousands of people, but for those who run them they provide a living and a very specialised way of life. The showmen and women belong to a tightly knit community with a strong sense of tradition, their unique identity reinforced by the long hours they keep – working in the evenings and at weekends – and the constant travel involved. Each change of venue means that, from great machines to small stalls, everything must be regularly dismantled, moved sometimes great distances, and re-erected elsewhere; the work involved is long, hard and also skilful.

Whilst anxious to preserve the time-honoured features of the traditional entertainments on offer, fairground people are nonetheless thoroughly alert to the innovations made possible by modern technology; for example, nothing could be simpler than the coconut shy or the hoopla, but these stand cheek by jowl with such complex machines as the Octopus or Cyclone. The traditional sense of decoration also remains, the gilt and red paint, the roses and castles associated with the art of gypsy caravans and canal boats.

Bartholomew Fair

For seven centuries from 1133 and interrupted only by outbreaks of plague, Bartholomew (or Bartlemy) Fair was held annually at Smithfield in London, starting on 24 August. In Elizabethan times it was the chief cloth fair in England, though by the middle of the seventeenth century its main object had become entertainment, eating and drinking. It provoked enormous interest in all sorts of circles; for example Ben Jonson wrote a play about it, the diarists John Evelyn and Samuel Pepys recorded their comments, and ballad writers were inspired to produce pieces such as 'Room for Company in Bartholomew Fair' and 'The Countryman's Visit to Bartholomew Fair'. Visitors included members of the royal family and aristocracy, besides many foreign notables, and ordinary people flocked to it in their thousands. The attractions the fair offered included drama in the form of puppet plays, and also lavish and spectacular productions in booths; one of the most popular attractions was the display of monsters, freaks and curiosities such as a bull with five legs, a mare with seven feet and a woman with three breasts. An alleged mermaid was probably a combination of the dried head and body of a monkey and the tail of a large fish. Even so, it attracted four hundred people a day at a shilling each, the £20 produced being a very large sum for the time.

The fair also drew beggars, pickpockets and prostitutes by the hundred, with gang warfare and hooliganism frequently breaking out. The question of suppression was raised as early as 1678, and the continuing allegations of disorder and drunkenness, crime and vice, combined with disruption to trade, eventually led to the decline of Bartholomew Fair and ultimately to its abolition, in 1855. However, in the 1970s and '80s the name has been used again by St Bartholomew's Hospital, though the events are fund-raising garden fêtes, far removed from the turbulent merrymaking of the past.

Carnivals

The carnival is another great attraction which has recently arrived on the scene, though it is surrounded by controversies similar to those thrown up by Bartholomew and other great fairs in their heyday. In many countries the carnival is linked to Shrove Tuesday – a last fling before the arrival of Lent – but it probably originated in pre-Christian times with the Roman Saturnalia which celebrated the end of winter. In the West Indies, carnivals were originally festivals for both the owners of sugar plantations and their slaves; after emancipation the festivals continued, and immigrants brought them to this country after World War II. They are currently held in Birmingham, Leeds and Manchester, and the biggest, London's Notting Hill Carnival, is the largest street festival in the whole of Europe.

Notting Hill Carnival started in 1965 as an impromptu event, and attracted seven thousand people; twenty years later the attendance was up to one and a half million, or ten times the size of a Wembley Cup Final crowd. The colour and extravagance of costume, the volume and variety of music, the brilliance and ingenuity of floats, all these rival the panache of New Orleans or Rio de Janeiro, achieved thanks to the immense skill, dedication and enthusiasm of both organisers and participants – and also support of some £300,000 in public money. The trade generated is estimated at a value of £10 million, or even more.

Unfortunately the very existence of this huge festival has been repeatedly called into question because so often it results in disorder. In 1987, for example, there were an estimated thousand serious crimes, including a murder, street robberies, and violence between youths and the police; one reveller who fell ill died because the ambulance failed to reach him through the crowds. There were suggestions in 1988 that the event should be taken off the streets and put into a stadium. Fears were expressed of 'steaming', organised theft by gangs of muggers working their way through the crowds. As it happened there was no serious trouble that year, poor weather having limited the attendance to 'only' three-quarters of a million – but what stadium could have accommodated such a number?

It is to be hoped that the carnival will not go the way of many of the old fairs. The urge to celebrate is deeply ingrained and a safety valve is vital, especially for young people. If the carnival does stop, something else will take its place, because the fun of the fair meets a need.

9
Healthy, Wealthy, Wise

The huge growth of interest in environmental issues and alternative life-styles has led to a careful re-examination of all kinds of traditional lore and practice. In the field of medicine, healers have returned to the prominent position they once occupied, yet their work in complementing or even replacing the work of official practitioners is at times fiercely resisted. For example in 1989 Michael Baum, Professor of Surgery at King's College Hospital, London, claimed that some women suffering from breast cancer had reduced their chances of a cure to zero because they had taken alternative therapy for months before turning to orthodox medicine. Herbal and folk remedies – or at least the more sensible ones – are sought again, and re-used, though some are still dismissed as mere nostrums or old wives' tales, and others are attacked as being positively harmful. Comfrey, it is claimed, is carcinogenic – yet it has a pedigree going back to Roman times for curing broken bones, sores, wounds, bronchitis, ulcers, arthritis and indigestion.

As regards the environment, the weather is anxiously studied to see if the threatened Greenhouse Effect is starting to take effect; and in general, a corpus of traditional wisdom, often encapsulated in rhyme, certainly describes things as they have been, if not as they may become. Traditional lore is revived in an attempt to make sense of the world, and to keep people same and healthy in a progressively more complex, stressful and insecure society.

HEALERS

Most places once boasted some sort of healer, such as a bonesetter, herbalist, rubber (masseur), charmer or wise woman – and no doubt there were those who combined several of these skills. The seventh of seven sons, or even better, the seventh son of a seventh son, was most likely to have such abilities; the same applies to seventh daughters, and also to all those born feet first. In most cases, though, knowledge and technique were handed on from one generation to the next. Some practitioners became very well known. Mrs Mapp was an Epsom bone-setter who became famous in the early eighteenth century for her wonder cures. 'Dame Nature hath given her a doctor's degree', was said of her by a character in a play performed at Lincoln's Inn Fields Theatre in London – though in fact she almost certainly learnt her skills from her mother, who was also a bone-setter. Mrs Mapp was ugly and strong, and as a contemporary put it: 'a more ill-favoured or a stronger-framed woman it would have been difficult to find'. She achieved remarkable feats, such as straightening a man's back which had stuck out two inches for nine years, and curing longstanding lameness. When she died (in 1737) she nevertheless had to be given a pauper's funeral in London.

John Lloyd, a bone-setter from Radnorshire (now Powys), came to an even more unfortunate end. He lived in the late nineteenth century on a sheep farm by Great Graigau in the Harley Valley, part of the Radnor Forest. He would take no money for healing, but accepted silver buttons, which gave rise to his nickname, Silver John. The buttons were sewn on to his coat, and as time went by there were a great many of them. John wore the coat when visiting patients or going to market at Builth Wells. One day, though, his horse and trap came home without him, and although anxious and extensive searches were made, Silver John was not to be found. The mystery remained unsolved until the next Radnor Candlemas Fair, held by a lake (Llyn Hilyn) near the isolated Forest Inn. Fires were lit by the side of the lake, which was frozen solid, and hot cider and cakes were on sale. Livestock changed hands, farm servants were hired, and people slid or skated on the ice. Mary, the daughter of the inn landlord, was among the skaters, and at the far end of the lake she lost her footing and fell, face down: staring up at her through the thick ice was Silver John.

The old man had been murdered for his silver, and his body thrown into the lake. Breaking the corpse out of the ice would have smashed the bones, and the people felt an overwhelming reluctance to treat their bone-setter in such a way. So they waited until the thaw, then took up the body and buried it on Great Graigau; and to this day the grass grows greener over the grave than elsewhere. The murderer was never found, and the ghost of Silver John is said to walk by Llyn Hilyn still. A plaque commemorates him in the Forest Inn, and his story continues to be told in Radnorshire; his descendants carry on the art of bone-setting to this day.

Wise Women and Witches

In the past the women who delivered babies and charmed away diseases were known as 'wise women' – the French for midwife is still *sage femme* – though the ancient arts they practised proved at times to be double-edged, and led to accusations of witchcraft. It has been suggested that 85 per cent of those persecuted in the past as witches were wise women whose work was entirely beneficial, at least in intention. As recently as 1905 Mrs Ellen Hayward, a widow living at Cinderford in the Forest of Dean, felt constrained to write to her local newspaper in these words:

> I wish to deny emphatically that I am a witch, nor am I a fortune teller or hand reader. I have no knowledge of such pagan ideas. I have no power or ability to bewitch anyone nor do I believe in any such thing.

She was in fact a wise woman, a herbalist and dresser of sores, cuts and wounds, who also claimed to be able to find lost items. However, in one case the attempt to trace £50 missing from a house apparently caused its occupants to become unbalanced, and it was from this that accusations of witchcraft arose. Mrs Hayward was prosecuted, not for witchcraft, but for deception by 'pretended witchcraft'. The magistrates, however, received many letters pointing out the good she had done, and she was acquitted. She died in 1912 at the age of seventy-four – in earlier times she might well have been burnt at the stake (see Chapter 11, p185).

Charmers

The basic requirement of a charmer from a patient is an unquestioning belief that a cure will be effected. Diseases were apparently removed by muttering a formula (usually inaudible) or by giving the sufferer special cords or thongs to tie round the affected part. The classic healer was happy to receive gifts – like Silver John's buttons – but thought that offers of money would break the spell and render the charm ineffective. However, not all adhered to this view. During a diphtheria epidemic in Sussex in 1930 a local wise woman tied a hazel twig round children's throats, and charged a shilling for doing so. If the treatment failed she gave a piece of stewed mouse and recited a charm while it was being eaten – this cost half-a-crown (12½p). The local doctor reported her to the police, who told her to desist.

Blacksmiths

At least until the 1970s blacksmiths in the Western Isles of Scotland often acted as unofficial veterinarians as well as practising their craft. In addition they treated people, their skills including setting bones, lancing boils, letting blood and diagnosing illnesses. There was one smith – a seventh son – who had a touch so powerful that an earthworm placed on his open hand would die, and he could cure any boil or cyst also by touch. Another blacksmith's remedy for boils was more complicated: people would come and ask for a quantity of the water in which he had washed his hands in the morning before eating, and would then place a sixpence in it. Three days later they came back for both the water and the coin; the water was used to bathe the boil, and the coin worn round the neck – by the time the coin fell off, the boil would be healed.

Blacksmiths were also herbalists. There was one who believed that a plant cure existed for every ailment – though he did concede that some cures might have been lost, while others awaited discovery. Some of the plants he used were nettles which he boiled in water, and the water was then drunk for rheumatism; the mariner plant, used in poultices to burst boils; and calf's plant, the ribbed side for drawing out pus, the smooth side for healing. 'Duck's Weed' and juniper were also used.

Herbalists

Herbal medicine has a very long history. A considerable knowledge is already shown in Chaucer's *Nun's Priest's Tale*, where Dame Pertelote advised her constipated mate to take centaury, fumitory, caper-spurge, hellebore, laurel, blackthorn berry and ground ivy. Simplers (dispensers of herbs) would gather large quantities of many different varieties of herb, and walk into London to cry them for sale:

Here's pennyroyal and marigolds,
Come buy my nettle tops.
Here's water-cress and scurvy-grass.
Come buy my sage of virtue, O.
Come buy my wormwood and mugwort.
Here's all fine herbs of every sort.
Here's southernwood that's very good,
Dandelion and house-leek.
Here's dragon's tongue and wood-sorrel,
With bear's foot and horehound.

Traditional herbal medicines often hold the key to the development of modern medicines. For example, near Chipping Camden in Gloucestershire an old woman was in the rectory garden gathering simples, and when she was asked what she was doing she replied 'Gathering willow bark.' 'What for?' 'To make an infusion to cure headaches.' And it was this conversation which inspired the long chain of development involving different people and processes, which led to the refinement of aspirin by the German firm, Bayer. Then there was William Withering, a brilliant Birmingham doctor of the late eighteenth century who heard of a countrywoman with a cure for heart disease. He sought her out, paid her five shillings (25p) for a handful of herbs, and then went carefully through the ingredients until he isolated the foxglove. From this, of course, comes digitalis which is still used in the treatment of heart disease – and it is interesting that, in turn, digitalis is chemically related to butafolein, the toxic principle in toad venom. Toad extract was also used in folk medicine for several purposes, including heart trouble.

Various other folk remedies have led to the development of modern medicines; for instance a pill made of spiders' webs or spiders themselves was said to cure malaria or ague – and in 1882 arachnidin was first isolated from spiders' webs, and found to be an excellent febrifuge. Mistletoe was effective against epilepsy and convulsive distempers, and the substance guipsine, derived from mistletoe, is still used in France to relieve hypertension.

Finally, bee stings were used to cure rheumatism. Only later was their nitrogenous content discovered, some other claimed effects have not stood up to scrutiny. Soon after its introduction the potato was thought – like many other foods at various times – to be valuable as an aphrodisiac. No doubt its claim was tested and found wanting in suitable human experiments.

HERBS

A complex of culinary, medicinal and magical uses surrounds herbs. Sage, rosemary and thyme, for example, are all commonly used in cooking, but if they flourish in a garden they show that the mistress is master. Rosemary is good for coughs, hoarseness or loss of voice; an infusion put in a cask of beer not only keeps it from turning sour but prevents drinkers from acquiring drunken habits; a poultice made from the leaves prevents wounds from suppurating; a spoon made of the wood makes all food eaten with it highly nutritious; and finally a sprig fastened to the doorpost stops snakes passing through, and also wards off witches.

Some Herbs and their Properties

Elecampane: is a root which helps to cure coughs and consumption; it can also be candied and eaten as a sweetmeat; and its leaves worn in the hat will frighten robbers and tricksters.

Ground-ivy: an infusion can be used for sore eyes; a sprig may be worn to prevent sorcery.

Henbane: is poisonous, but a decoction may be used in the treatment of mental illness.

Lavender: the blossom brings luck to the wearer; sprigs are said to bewilder witches and confuse evil spirits.

Leek: it is lucky to grow this in the garden, and the leek is said to frighten evil spirits; in Wales, the fighting men of old would rub the juice (and also that of wild onions and garlic) on their bodies, and they might wear the whole plant in their caps since they believed it brought victory, without injury to the wearer.

Mugwort: the juice was used against consumption; a sprig worn in the coat prevented weariness; and kept in the house it warded off witches.

Nettles: were eaten as a vegetable in the spring; they were boiled and eaten to quicken the senses, clear the brain and help the memory; and nettle broth (like marigolds) was believed to induce sleep and promote appetite:

> Drink nettle tea in March
> And mugwort tea in May;
> And cowslip wine in June
> To send decline away.

Parsley: the leaves are good for the brain; it is unlucky to give away a root of parsley or to transplant it; if parsley withers in the garden

147

it portends a death in the house, but if it flourishes there will be peace and plenty.

Saxifrage: as the name implies, it has the power of breaking rocks; and when worn near the heart is said to give the wearer victory over his enemies.

Scarlet pimpernel: as an infusion it will apparently cure low spirits; if the flower is worn in the hat, coat or bodice it will keep sad thoughts from the wearer; and if it is placed under the pillow at night it brings pleasant dreams. The plant is also used for the bite of a mad dog (see below); and it is known as the 'poor man's clock', since it opens at 7am and closes at 2pm, except when rain is impending when it closes immediately.

Sow thistle: its juice can be effectively applied to warts, and to any cut made by the hoof or teeth of a pig; if it is worn in the hat or belt the wearer will be able to run without getting tired – for the same purpose it is tied to the tails of the horses before a ploughing match; if it is thrown near the pig trough the pigs will fatten more quickly; and finally it protects from witches.

St John's Wort: is said to blossom on St John the Baptist's Day (24 June); it is a powerful protector against the devil.

Valerian: is sometimes called All-Heal; the root is used to allay pain, promote sleep, and soothe nervous strain; women used to put sprigs in their bodices to secure the admiration of the opposite sex.

Vervain: is one of the sacred plants of the Druids, who used it (in association with trefoil and hyssop) in casting lots and telling fortunes; it can be made into a love philtre as long as it is gathered as the dogstar rises, without having been 'looked on by the sun or moon'.

CHARMS AND CURES

Some of the measures taken were fruitless attempts to deal with what we now know to be incurable. Rabies, once known simply as the 'bite of a mad dog', was treated by binding the sufferer hand and foot and dipping him or her nine times in the sea. Given the fear of water which the disease inspires, this must have been an indescribable ordeal. Less traumatic treatments included taking powder from certain stones; making a decoction from the roots and leaves of buck's plantain, and mixing it with honey; and making an infusion from dried scarlet pimpernel, which could also be applied externally – it was also effective against snake bites. A particular kind of moss could be used, as could elecampane.

Magic numbers like three and nine were widely used; for example someone suffering from a feverish chill had to walk over the boundaries of nine fields in one day. One of the cures for a stye on the eye involved taking a hair from the tail of a cat on a night of full moon and pulling it nine times over the pustule; alternatively the hand of an executed criminal could be rubbed three times across it – this was called a 'dead stroke', and was possible until the end of public hangings in 1868. (A halter made of the hanging rope could also be used to cure headache.) Another cure was to rub the stye nine times with either a wedding ring (some specified a new bride's or a grandmother's wedding ring), or a sacrament shilling – one given in the collection at church and after being blessed, exchanged for other coins to the same value. A penny would also serve, provided the following formula were repeated all in one breath: 'Why one if not two, why two if not three . . .', and so on up to ten, then back again. Some of the cures for styes were similar to those for warts.

Charms of this kind, a mixture of orthodox religion and primitive belief, were very widely used. The healer himself might pronounce them, or the person involved, and sometimes even the possession of a piece of paper with the appropriate charm written on it was thought to suffice. Some charms were very simple; for example after a nettle sting, the affected part could be rubbed with a dock leaf, and these words said: 'In, dock; out, nettle'. Others, more extensive, were often set into rhyme; the following collection of verses will show the type and variety of charms traditionally employed to try and cure disease and injury:

For bone-setting:

> Lord, set it right again, right.
> Joint to joint and joint to joint,
> Marrow to marrow, bone to bone,
> So that this man [woman] can stand alone.
> Blood shall arise from skin to skin.
> Lord, set him [her] right without and within.

For the bite of an adder: Lay pieces of hazel on the wound in the shape of a cross, and say:

> Underneath this hazeldin mote
> There's a maggoty worm with a speckled throat.
> Nine double is he;
> Now from nine double to eight double,
> And from eight double to seven double . . .

149

And so on, to:

And from one double to no double,
No double hath he.

To heal a wound caused by a thorn:

> Our Saviour Christ was of a pure virgin born
> And he was crowned with a thorn.
> I hope it may not rage or swell;
> I trust in God it may do well.

For burns and scalds:

> There came two angels from the north.
> One was fire and one was frost.
> Out, fire. In, frost.
> In the name of the Father, Son and Holy Ghost.

There was also an alternative version, as follows:

> Christ he walketh over the land,
> Carried the wild fire in his hand.
> He rebuketh the fire and bid it stand.
> Stand, wildfire, stand.
> In the name . . . [and so on]

To staunch bleeding:

> Christ was born in Bethlehem,
> Baptised in the River Jordan.
> The river stood,
> So shall thy blood,
> [Name of sufferer],
> In the name . . . [and so on]

For ague: There were many charms and cures for ague; here are just three:

1. To be spoken up the chimney by the oldest female in the family on St Agnes' Eve (14 January):

> Tremble and go.
> First day, shiver and burn,
> Tremble and quake.
> Second day, shiver and learn,
> Tremble and die.
> Third day, never return.

2. To be written on a three-cornered piece of paper and worn round the neck:

> Ague, ague, I thee defy.
> Three days, shiver,
> Three days, shake,
> Make me well for Jesus' sake.

3. To be said while unwinding a rope from the body, and coiling it round an aspen tree:

> Ague, ague, I thee defy.
> Ague, ague, to this tree I tie.

The notion of transferring one's disease to some other thing or person (as in the third ague charm) was widespread. Until within living memory, a ringworm sufferer in Shetland would take a pinch of ashes from the fire on three successive mornings before eating, hold it to the affected part and say:

> Ringworm, ringworm red,
> Never mayst thou speed or spread,
> But aye grow less and less,
> And die away among the ase [ash].

In Hertfordshire ague was cured – or so it was thought – by the sufferer's pegging a lock of his hair to an oak tree, then with a sudden wrench pulling it out, leaving it attached to the tree. A less painful expedient was to catch a spider and put it in a box – as it died, the disease waned. A child suffering from thrush would have a young frog held with its head in his mouth for a few seconds, so that the disease could transfer to it; in Cumberland a fish was used in similar fashion. The traditional cure for convulsions was more involved: parings from the nails, together with hair clipped from the eyebrows and the crown of the head, were bound up in a cloth with a halfpenny; the bag was then set down at a crossroads, and whoever picked it up would take on the disease. For this reason, people were at one time very reluctant to pick up any mysterious parcel at a crossroads.

These conceptions occur again and again in the common ailments and diseases of the past, such as cramp and nosebleed; chilblains, boils and swellings; fits and snakebite. Most common of all must have been toothache, rheumatism, warts and whooping cough, and the remedies recorded and presumably attempted were positively legion. Just a few are given here; it would be possible to compile an extensive catalogue.

151

From amongst the many remedies thought to bring a cure for toothache the sufferer could either cut his gum with an iron nail, then drive the nail with his blood on it into a beam or a tree; or he could bathe his tooth in holy water; or scrape a horseradish root, then bind it to his wrist. He might try inserting a piece of onion in his tooth; putting a plaster on his wrist on the side opposite the painful tooth; or wear a corpse's tooth in a bag round his neck; or he could take a sharp willow twig, prick his gum till it bled, then throw the twig into a running stream . . . and so on.

There were almost as many cures for rheumatism: the sufferer could choose whether he carried the right forefoot of a hare in his pocket, or a small potato, nutmeg or conker; he could wear a loop of catgut, or he might prefer to whip his body with nettles – he could even strip naked, arrange to be buried up to the neck in a churchyard, and stay there for several hours . . . and so on.

For whooping cough the cures, remedies and advice seem to be almost endless, though they are mainly for an adult to administer to a suffering child: the adult could, for example, take hairs from the child's neck, roll them into a piece of meat or bread and butter, and give this to a dog; if the dog coughed on eating it, the disease would have transferred. Alternatively, the assistance of a piebald horse would be required, since it was believed a cure might be effected if the child were passed under its belly – or if the horse were caused to breathe on the child – or if the child were given any remedy suggested by the rider of a piebald horse. If these failed, the patient could be given plain currant cake made by a woman whose maiden surname was the same as that of the man she married; or fried mouse (also good for quinsy), preferably eaten in a spoon made from horn taken from a living animal; or roast mouse, with the patient kept in ignorance of what he is eating, and seated on a donkey facing the tail . . . and so on.

WELLS

Water from certain wells and springs was used extensively for its healing properties. In the heart of London, Sadler's Wells Theatre is on a spot once called Holy Well, which was renowned for its curative powers. It has long since disappeared but elsewhere healing wells continue to be patronised, especially – but by no means exclusively – in the Celtic areas.

In the Highlands and islands of Scotland epilepsy was once a great curse, possibly because of in-breeding. One of the many remedies tried was the combination of water from a healing well, drunk from a skull – that of a suicide did nicely, and otherwise the skull of an ancestor would be specially dug up from the graveyard. A well which does combine the two influences can be found in the remote township of Wester Ross in the north of Scotland (the precise location has been withheld because the local people do not want publicity; in addition, they believe that the curative powers are finite, and should not be used any more than necessary). The well is called *Tobar a' Chinn* – the Well of the Head – and the story goes that some two hundred years ago a local woman committed suicide; because of this she could not be buried on consecrated ground, so she was interred on the moor. Shortly afterwards the woman's skull appeared, lying on the ground. The wise men or healers of Wester Ross took this as a sign that the skull would help in curing epilepsy, so it was taken to the well and kept there in a stone container. The skull is still there, and a local charmer acts as its guardian.

A person seeking a cure must go through a careful ritual: first he goes to the guardian's house and gives an assurance that he has complete faith in the water's power. Then he must climb the hill to the well with the guardian, between sundown and sunrise. He walks three times round the well, and three times is given water by the guardian which he must drink from the skull in the name of the Trinity. The whole procedure must be carried out in complete silence.

Another cure for epilepsy – though without a skull – is (or was) effected at St Tegla's Well in the tiny village of Llandegla (just off the A525 between Wrexham and Ruthin). The patient had to go to the well after sunset, wash in it, throw in fourpence, walk round it three times, and say the Lord's Prayer three times; it was important that a man carried a cockerel in a basket, and a woman, a hen. Then the patient would go into the church, creep under the altar and stay till dawn, using the bible as a pillow; in the morning a further offering was made, this time of sixpence. The hen or cockerel had to be left in the church – if it died, a cure followed.

St Bridget (or Bride) is the patron of poets, blacksmiths and healers, and there are many ancient churches dedicated to her in England and Wales. In addition there are St Bridget's or St Bride's wells up and down the country, though it is possible that some of these were originally dedicated to Brigantia, the Celtic goddess of fertility, and were taken over by the church. One early statue of Brigantia, dating from the third century BC, comes from Dumfriesshire. Certainly, women prayed to St Bridget to ease the pains of childbirth, and also visited her wells to seek help in becoming pregnant. The Well of Fertility (*Tobat an Torraidh*) on the Isle of Skye is thought to cure barrenness in cattle and is used quite openly for this, but its water is also used secretly by women with the same problem.

St Walstan's Well at the village of Bawburgh (pronounced 'Baber') in Norfolk was renowned for curing sick animals, and its bottled water was sold in nearby Norwich. St Walstan is the patron of farm workers and sick animals, and was born at Bawburgh in 965, the son of a king of East Anglia; legend relates that at the age of twelve he renounced riches, and started working as a labourer on the land. One day when he was mowing a meadow an angel came to warn him that death was at hand; he therefore asked his master and fellow workers to place his corpse on a cart, yoke two oxen to it, and allow them to go where they wished. This all happened as predicted; but when the wagon came to water its wheels passed across the water surface leaving a track as if they had been on dry land; twice the oxen rested, and twice a spring burst from the ground. The end of their journey was at Bawburgh, where Walstan was buried; a church was raised over his grave. St Walstan's Well lies a short distance from the church, and amongst its many curative powers it was thought to be able to restore lost genitals to both men and beasts.

Sprains and bruises, sores, rheumatism and even toothache – every problem could potentially find its cure at some well or other. If a pin was stuck in a wart, then thrown into the appropriate well, it would take the pustule with it. Even insanity could be cured. One town, though – Cambuslang, on the outskirts of Glasgow – was reputed to make its people mad with the water of Borgie Well:

> A drink of the Borgie, a bite of the weed [fungus],
> Sets a' the Cam'slang folk wrang in the heed.

St Govan's Well is situated close to St Govan's Chapel, a few miles south of Pembroke on the Welsh coast, and its water was used both for eye troubles and rheumatism. The area is linked with Gawain of the Arthurian tales, who apparently hid here from pirates, using enchantment to protect himself – the rock opened to admit him, then closed behind him. When his enemies had gone, the cliff re-opened, leaving behind the impression of Gawain's body. Wishes made in the cleft of the rock will be granted, and any hopes in a person's mind when going up to or down from it will be fulfilled – and the steps, incidentally, cannot be counted. Below are magic stones which ring like bells when touched; and in the arch above the chapel there used to be a bell which had hung there for centuries and which often rang of its own accord, signifying a death or disaster at sea. Earth from fissures round the chapel was sprinkled round farmsteads and homes to avert the evil eye.

Other wells, too, were renowned for their beneficial effects on diseases of the eye. For example at Aconbury, a few miles south of Hereford, the first water taken from St Anne's Well after midnight on Twelfth Night was applied to styes or sore eyes. Others improved the general health. The town of Holywell on the Dee Estuary in Flintshire (now Clwyd) owes both its name and existence to St Winifred, whose home was there in the seventh century; the legendary tale says:

> A prince called Caradoc saw the saintly and virginal Winifred and tried to seduce her; he promised marriage if she would submit to him, but she still refused. He was so enraged that he struck off her head with his sword – but he was immediately cursed by St Beuno, Winifred's uncle, and melted away like a candle in a fire. Beuno then took up Winifred's head, miraculously replaced it, and brought her back to life; only a thin red line round her neck remained of the wound, and at the spot where her head had fallen a healing spring gushed forth.

Winifred spent many years as abbess at a convent at Holywell. When she died her remains were first buried there, then taken (in 1138) to Shrewsbury. The healing well acquired great fame, and was visited by a whole string of monarchs, including William the Conqueror, Henry II, Edward I and James I. There were many ordinary visitors, too, and those that were cured – as they frequently were – left behind crutches, sticks and even handcarts of which they had no further need.

Rag Wells

All over Britain there used to be wells where people left a scrap of cloth – hence the name 'rag' or (in Scotland) 'clootie' wells – because they believed their disease would be left behind with the piece of rag. In England and Wales the practice seems to have died out, but in Scotland it flourishes at three wells, all near Inverness: St Mary's Well is close to the site of the battle of Culloden, the other two are a few miles away across the Moray Firth on the Black Isle – Craigie Well on the north shore of Munlochy Bay, and St Boniface's Well close to the roadside between the villages of Munlochy and Tore.

The first Sunday in May is thought to be a particularly good time to visit them, but their powers are available all the year round. The trees and bushes by St Boniface's Well, for example, are festooned with a multi-coloured tangle of rags which at first sight is perplexing. However, those with an ailment take a small amount of water three times from the well and spill it on the ground; then they tie a piece of cloth to a tree, make the sign of the cross, and drink from the well. Tradition maintains that the person who removes a rag will take the misfortune left behind with it, and that is why the rags remain until they rot in the rain or the wind blows them away.

WEATHER LORE

The health and welfare of people, animals and crops are very much affected by the weather, and there is a great deal of traditional lore on the subject. Expert meteorologists accept some aspects of this, while questioning others; for example, Dick File of the London Weather Centre rejects out of hand the predictive value of the St Swithin story with regard to rain. Swithin, Bishop of Winchester, was famed for his charitable work and for his efforts in organising church building. When he died (on 2 July 862) he left instructions that he was to be buried in the cemetery just outside the west door of the Old Minster at Winchester. Despite his wishes, the decision was taken about a century later to move his remains inside the cathedral. When this was done (on 15 July 971) the occasion was marked by miraculous cures but also by heavy rain, and ever since then it is claimed that if rain falls on 15 July, St Swithin's Day, it will continue for forty days.

Not according to the records, says Dick File. Yet he acknowledges that 'there is some sound advice in other weather sayings, and particularly those which describe the sky itself' and these, after all, must have been based on long observation. For example 'rain before seven, dry before eleven' is usually well founded because 'not many frontal rain bands last more than a few hours, so if the rain has started early there is a good chance that the prediction will come true'. Another saying runs 'As the day lengthens, the cold strengthens', and this is an accurate reflection – obviously based on people's experience – of the cooling which normally takes place after the shortest day on 21 December, and through into January and February. If this fails to happen, as in 1989, a whole series of further predictions comes into play:

March in Janiveer,
Janiveer in March, I fear.

A January spring
Is worth nothing.

Of all the months in the year,
Curse a fair Februeer.

If Candlemas Day be fair and bright,
Winter will have another flight.

Candlemas Day (2 February), half-way through the winter, appears in many rhymes and sayings:

If Candlemas Day be clouds and rain,
Winter is gone and will not come again.

As far as the sun shines on Candlemas Day,
So far will the snow blow in afore old May.

On Candlemas Day if the sun shines clear
The shepherd had rather see his wife on the bier.

The farmer should have on Candlemas Day
Half his stover [winter forage] and half his hay.

Methods of farming and husbandry have obviously made some of these inapplicable, and climatic changes may in due course render other weather lore obsolete, but in the meantime it continues to fascinate. It is interesting, too, that as with local forecasts, so can local rhymes be more accurate than national ones – at Norwich, for example, it is suggested that the following is a reliable prediction: 'When three [jack]daws are seen on St Peter's vane together, Then we are sure to have bad weather'. In Northumberland they say:

When Cheviot ye see put on his cap,
Of rain ye'll have a wee bit drap.

Worcestershire people have something similar about a landmark of their own:

When Bredon Hill puts on his cap,
You men of the vale beware of that.

And there are parallels in many parts of the country. Besides these local sayings there are all kinds of good advice provided for the person who is working or walking out of doors. There are good signs

157

– 'A red evening and a grey morning Sets the pilgrim a-walking' – and bad – 'A rainbow at eve sends the ploughboy home with dripping sleeve' or 'In the decay of the moon A cloudy morn, fair afternoon'.

Excellent counsel is offered to those caught in the open by a thunderstorm:

> Beware of the oak it draws the stroke;
> Avoid the ash it courts the flash;
> Creep under a thorn it can save you from harm.

Popular lore recognises, though, that in the final analysis:

> To talk of the weather is folly;
> When it rains on the hill it shines in the valley.

LUCK AND MISFORTUNE

Sheer chance continues to play an inevitable part in life, and hopes of averting misfortune often used to be expressed in superstitious beliefs. Not many people nowadays have a wide range of superstitions, but very few have none at all – and even those involved with the technology of the late twentieth century do not escape because there is a so-called virus which attacks computer programmes, and removes 1,813 bites at a time from a memory's files. On Friday 13th, it is widely believed that the virus is more likely to attack than on other days.

Signs of good luck seem to be far less common than the reverse, and signs of bad luck often come to be interpreted as harbingers of death. Nevertheless, it is lucky:

to find a piece of old iron, such as a nail
to find a horseshoe
to find and pick up a piece of coal
to find and pick up a pin ('See a pin and pick it up, All the day you'll have good luck')
to pick up dropped gloves
to tread on dug-muck
to receive a deposit from an over-flying bird
to see three magpies
for a black cat to cross one's path
to see a piebald or skewbald horse
to see the head of the first lamb of spring
to meet a chimney sweep (provided one speaks to him)

158

to meet a sailor (provided one touches his collar)
to see a load of hay (provided one wishes, and watches it out of sight)
to turn the money in one's pocket on hearing the first cuckoo in
  spring
for a child to be born on the first day of spring
to have a crooked sixpence or a copper coin with a hole in it
to bring the flowers of elder into the house
to have flowering myrtle in the window
to stir the Christmas pudding when it is in the making
to fall downstairs
to have widely-spaced teeth
to have meeting eyebrows
to have an itching palm (because it means money to come)

The omens which presage misfortune are far more numerous, however, and a person would have to be fairly careful if he wanted to avoid doing something which would incur ill-luck. It is unlucky:

to meet a squinting woman (unless one speaks to her)
to meet a white horse (unless one spits)
to see a single magpie (unless one crosses oneself)
to see the tail first of the first lamb of spring
not to catch the first butterfly seen in spring
to kill a ladybird, a spider or an owl (an owl is said to have shared
  the tree in which King Charles II took refuge, and by flying out
  when searchers approached convinced them that no-one was
  there)
to harm a robin or a wren ('God Almighty's cock and hen')
to pick up dropped flowers (because this is to pick up sickness)
to cut one's nails on a Friday or Sunday
to bring eggs into the house after sunset
to burn eggshells without smashing them
to break a mirror (it brings seven years' bad luck)
to help to salt (because this helps to sorrow)
to spill salt (unless one throws a pinch over one's left shoulder)
to leave a house by a door other than that by which one entered
to turn back after setting out, then resume one's journey
to bring feathers into a house
to trip on entering a house (unless one kisses one's thumb)
to stumble when going upstairs
to pass another person on the stairs
to burn elder
to cut down a holly tree
to wear green

to change a garment put on inside out
to turn a bed on a Sunday
to leave a white cloth on a table overnight
to boast (unless one knocks on wood)
to put shoes on a table
to sit down thirteen at table (unless one person is pregnant)
to bring blackthorn, hawthorn or gorse into the house (because of their association with the crown of thorns)
to uproot periwinkle ('plant of the dead', which used to be grown on graves)
to cross knives on the table (this indicates a quarrel)
to put anything other than a prayerbook on top of a bible
to open an umbrella indoors
to drink another's health in water
to mend an article of clothing while wearing it
to throw out soapsuds on a Good Friday (or for that matter to wash at all on a Good Friday)
to sweep dust out of the house (as opposed to collecting it and carrying it out)
to burn green holly (brings a death in the family)

There are also particular omens which it is even more unfortunate to encounter, since they are signs of death:

a hen crowing like a cock
a bird flying or falling down the chimney
the prolonged nocturnal howling of dogs
a mouse running over part of one's body
a mouse squeaking behind the bed of an invalid
the sight of three butterflies
a swarm of bees alighting on a dead tree
the blossoming of fruit trees, especially the apple, twice in a year
a picture falling from the wall
a clock striking thirteen
a coffin-shaped crease in a tablecloth or sheet
a hole in a loaf
a dream of a wedding

10
What About the Workers?

Work plays an important part in most people's lives and has its share of custom and ritual which are sometimes overlooked by folklorists; for example it was – and still often is – traditional to put a new hand through an 'initiation'; or to celebrate when an apprentice came out of his time, or to mark with due ceremony a strike or a trade union rally. All such events, and more, in many cases still have their associated lore and customary practices, and give occasion for ceremonies which are not always popular.

CEREMONIES AT WORK

Initiation

Starting work is a significant stage on the road to adulthood, and established workers in many different occupations might mark the arrival of a newcomer in various ways; they could well send him (sometimes her) on a wild goose chase, and there is a great variety of these traditional to individual professions. For example, a new railwayman might be told to go for red oil for a tail lamp, or a bucket of steam for cleaning things off; a carpenter or builder might be sent to fetch a bubble for a spirit level, and a miner, a bucket of compressed air; an engineer might be given a small wheelbarrow to go and collect what turns out to be a huge, weighty machine.

The fool's errands for sailors were legion, and a new boy could well be sent off to fetch green oil for a starboard light, or to collect old bread for the mules which would pull the ship through the Panama Canal (the mules are in fact railway engines); he was very often detailed to watch out for the equator and holler when he saw it, or to report when he heard the dogfish barking. More generally, several professions would send a new apprentice for a tin of elbow grease or a left-handed saw, screwdriver or spanner; or insist that he found a glass hammer – or one of rubber, leather or cloth – and a selection of rubber screws or nails; or he might be told to go at the double and fetch a round square or a tin of striped paint: the list of possible errands is long and varied.

Newcomers were also subjected to practical jokes – though these might be played on anyone, especially a person to whom other workers had collectively taken a dislike. For example a beginner is sent to an ill-tempered foreman with instructions to call him by a nickname he is known to detest; an established but unpopular worker has his toolbox screwed to the bench or filled with heavy castings; the teapot is carefully drilled with holes in such a way that the damage is not obvious until hot water is poured in; or clothes and tools may be hidden.

Practical jokes are often part of an initiatory ritual which is partly intended to see whether a person is 'a sport'. In 1902 a certain Harry Pollitt started work at the tender age of twelve at Benson's Mill in the Lancashire town of Droylesden, where the women weavers played polite, ladylike tricks on him – but the buxom lasses in the cardroom went to the length of taking down his trousers 'and daubing my unmentionable parts with oil and packing me with cotton waste'. Half a century later, new apprentices in the Austin foundry at Longbridge, near Birmingham, had their private parts encased in clay by the women core-makers, and the ceremony would be repeated on birthdays if the dates were found out. In Northern Ireland, women spinners and weavers would subject a new lad to similar treatment, removing his trousers and anointing his vital parts with either oil or paint. New girls were not taken to such lengths, but they were victim to various pranks; for instance, one was told that for the medical examination she was due to attend at the end of the day she had to fill a bucket with her own urine.

As recently as 1989 some sixteen year olds on the Youth Training Scheme (which they dubbed the Youth Trauma Scheme) complained of degrading initiation ceremonies. In some car repair shops and factories trainees had a mixture of glue and iron filings poured over their genitals, or paint sprayed on them; others were locked in car boots or suspended over inspection pits for hours at a time. A parental complaint to one company director elicited a response which underlined the traditional nature of such rough treatment: 'Your letter brought a smile to my face, having experienced a situation similar to that of your son when I was an apprentice at Rolls-Royce.' Some trainees left their placings in protest, and one, a Mark Hepworth of Horbury near Wakefield in West Yorkshire, took three workmates to court for subjecting him to a ceremony in which they pinioned his arms, then poured silicone sealant over his testicles whilst he was helpless. Each was fined £100.

Entrants to the police and fire services face particularly fierce practical jokes and initiatory ordeals. Usually little is heard publicly of these, but as recently as 1989 a case in London made newspaper headlines after an enquiry was set up. This involved a woman firefighter who complained that as part of the introduction to her first fire station she had been forcibly compelled to watch a group of male colleagues masturbating. Other cases involved a young Manchester policewoman handcuffed overnight in freezing temperatures to some railings, and army recruits in Colchester forced to call out musical notes as a sergeant hit them on the bare buttocks with a baseball bat.

Again in 1989 a new employee at a London printing works was stripped by his workmates, tied to a chair, daubed with ink and flour, and left in the cold for three hours. And Tony Tucker, aged 17, died as a result of an initiation which went badly wrong. At a factory in Skelmersdale, near Liverpool, his trousers were doused with two litres of paint thinner by larking workmates – this should have been the end of the ceremony, but two young colleagues began to strike matches to frighten Tucker. His clothing caught fire and he died of 80 per cent burns three weeks later; the two young men were sentenced to youth custody for manslaughter.

Paying One's Footing
Of late the apprentice has become a rare breed. In the past, a boy would start his seven years' apprenticeship at the age of fourteen when he would have to pay his 'footing' of one shilling (5p). The same applied to a new journeyman starting work, and there were many other pretexts for collecting beer money: beginning or finishing a batch of piece work (which was, if paid in advance, called 'dead horse'), being promoted, having a child born, getting married, even

merely wearing a new jacket. The other workers would have to make a (smaller) contribution, too, and the money was allowed to accumulate until it was sufficient to pay for an evening out at a public house. Then healths would be drunk, songs sung, stories told, and recitations delivered, and on such occasions the lore of the trade would be passed on, tales would be told of journeymen on tramp, and accounts given of strikes and lockouts of the past.

Blacklegs

'Knobsticks' and 'black sheep', later called blacklegs, have always been particularly hated. A certain Jack Elliott from the village of Birtley, near Chester-le-Street in County Durham (now Tyne and Wear), recalled how miners used to 'tin-pan' blacklegs out of the street: that is, beat tin pans and baths, shout, and throw stones and 'all sorts' up at their windows. In 1985 a man blacklegging during a strike of footwear workers at Rossendale, Lancashire, was treated to another time-honoured display of communal disapproval: he was carried along astride a pole, known as 'riding the stang'.

Weddings

Those about to be married are often given an elaborate send-off by their workmates in factory or office. Women's coats have their sleeves and bottoms sewn up and are then filled with odd objects, and the bride-to-be may be presented with dolls and also a beribboned rolling pin which has both culinary and sexual symbolism. In addition, a chamber pot is decorated, filled with such items as a packet of salt, and inscribed:

> Wash my face and keep me clean,
> And I won't tell what I have seen.

Then the lady is put into a handcart with her gifts and wheeled into the street.

In Scotland, especially Glasgow, a wheelbarrow is used for this purpose, and the chamber pot ('chanty') contains a doll. The procession is accompanied by rough music on tin cans and saucepans, and also by the singing of 'bottling songs', so called because they are sung at the exclusively female pre-wedding parties known as hen or send-off parties to which all those attending bring bottles, usually of whisky. In July 1989 a hen party was observed in Albion Street, Glasgow, in which the L-plated, mini-skirted bride-to-be carried a 'chanty' containing a packet of salt, a jar of Vaseline and a baby's dummy, together with money collected from passers-by. A group of female companions sang 'Ha'd up, kick the can' and 'Down in Yonder Meadow'.

The male counterpart of such ceremonies is usually less elaborate. The day before his wedding a man may be festooned with streamers, tied to a lamp-post outside his workplace, and showered with confetti – a photograph taken in 1982 shows a man called Brian Deacon in just such a position outside the Portland shoe factory at the Newarke, Leicester. Tied to his chest is a placard bearing the words: 'Getting Married Tomorrow', though at least he has kept his clothes on – one variation on the ceremony requires their removal. Following a similar pattern, one John Hall was given a lively send-off in Gloucester before his wedding when workmates from Severn Joinery Ltd fastened a yoke round his neck, from which a notice hung with the words: 'I'm Getting Married in the Morning'; then a group of them led him round the streets of the city centre. The bridegroom's stag party on the eve of his wedding is still a very well established occasion, though what is new nowadays is that various forms of 'strippogram' might well enliven the proceedings.

Out of Time

The successful completion of an apprentice's time was also cele-brated; the period used to be seven years, and its end would coincide with the formal attainment of adulthood at the age of twenty-one. One of the rituals, said to be five hundred years old, is called 'trussing the cooper': the apprentice must stand in a barrel of his own making, and he is then showered with a mixture of soot, shavings, feathers, treacle and beer. Next he is rolled round the workshop in the barrel before being taken out and tossed three times in the air. Injuries sometimes occur when the participants become over-enthusiastic, but since most barrels are now cast in aluminium the days of such ceremonies may well be numbered.

The same could be said of printing, where new technology has substituted computer keyboards for hot metal. Formerly, journey-men banged heavy objects while apprentices were led out of the composing room, smeared with ink, and taken in procession through the various departments of their firm – on at least one occasion such a procedure stopped the traffic in Fleet Street as a party crossed the road to an outlying department. Now, though, newspaper printing is almost entirely gone from that historic street. However in Birmingham, and as recently as 1986, an employee called Christopher Southall was given the traditional ducking in flour and slops after completing his apprenticeship as a bookbinder at a firm in Barford Street. Many school pupils, too, mark their departure at the age of sixteen by sewing up sleeves, wearing streamers, carrying balloons, autographing each other's shirts or blouses, and dousing each other with flour and eggs. Ritually slashing school uniforms also features, though this caused an injury on one occasion, leading to a subsequent court case – and sometimes, it must be said, such rituals come to light only as a result of a mishap.

THE MINER'S WORLD

Mining does not require a formal apprenticeship, though its skills nevertheless have to be learned. Not all miners rise to the top of the hierarchy of pit work and become hewers at the coal face, and those who do have to work their way up. Like sailors, miners work in a hostile and unfamiliar element; the mine has been described as 'a strange world', with 'silence like infinity or the bottom of the ocean', in which 'you can feel the darkness pressing in', and not surprisingly, the fears and anxieties of men in such circumstances result in a large number of taboos and superstitions. By no means all miners subscribe to all such beliefs, but most accept at least some of them, and they apply at home, on the way to work, and in the pit.

Cornish tin miners tried in various ways to bring themselves good fortune. Until well into the twentieth century a little image made of clay would be placed over the timbers by the entrance to a new level; and when work began each day, these words were said: 'Synt Meryasek my a'th prys' – Saint Meryasek [the patron saint of Camborne] we pray thee'. Such ways are also remembered in the Forest of Dean, where for example at the Favourite Mine near the village of Ruardean, a figure representing St Piran, patron of the tin miners, was carved into the living rock in 1976 by Vanilla Beer. The mine is now closed, but the sculpture can still be seen by the locked entrance.

Back in Cornwall, a bottle of whisky would be broken over the engine bob when a new mine was christened; then every year a green bough was tied to the top of the sheerlegs on St John's Day (24 June), and a holly bush hung on the pit headgear at Christmas. In Wales at Christmas, miners carried a board covered with clay and stuck with candles from house to house on a wheelbarrow. The men called this board their 'Star of Bethlehem', and would stop with it in front of each house where they would kneel to sing a carol, then ask for a Christmas gift. In the Black Country of the Midlands the colliers

toured with a sword dance and a song; and on Christmas Day –
known as Yule-do-day – in County Durham, the coal hewers
brought a flatty cake (one made with left-over ends of pastry) to give
to the putters for good luck.

Pit Ghosts

Pits are dangerous places, the scene of many deaths and disasters.
The perils of mining, added to the mysteries of underground work,
have produced a number of customs and beliefs, and also many
stories.

As a mark of respect to the dead, miners always stop work after
a fatal accident, though formerly where they remained idle until the
victim was buried, now they wait only for the remainder of the shift.
Nevertheless, the custom is still strongly upheld, and one pit in
Leicestershire which continued to operate during the miners' strike
of 1984–5 did shut down on one occasion during it for a fatality;
upon which a miner was heard to remark: 'Arthur Scargill couldn't
stop this pit, but the death of a miner did'.

It was considered unlucky to take the place of a miner killed in a
pit accident. In County Durham at least until the 1950s no miner
from the same colliery would work where a 'marra' (workmate) had
died, so new men had to be brought in who were unaware of the
accident. A dead miner's ghost was thought to haunt the pit until his
funeral, and furthermore it was believed that it would remain even
after this if any item stolen from him in life were not returned to his
relatives, or if any of his tools were inadvertently left down the pit.
Some ghosts do seem to have stayed for long periods, and carried
out malign actions; for example at Ruardean Hill in the Forest of
Dean, sometime in the 1840s, there was a mason known as 'Get-it-
and-go' who employed a number of miners, but was always loath to
pay their wages. One day there was a quarrel by the pit shaft, and
Get-it-and-go fell to his death, or perhaps was pushed. The colliers
abandoned the pit, but said nothing about the incident – Get-it-and-
go simply disappeared.

A year later a family living nearby reported the sound of hammer
and drill from the pit, but although the parish constable searched
underground, he found nothing there. Eighteen months later the
noises increased, but a second search also proved fruitless. Only at
the third attempt were the remains of Get-it-and-go found – they
were shovelled into a coffin and brought to the surface, and only
then did the mysterious and frightening sounds cease.

Another instance was at Kingswood, near Bristol, where a

phantom in the first half of the nineteenth century was 'the cause of the death of several persons, by cutting the rope with an Hatchet as they were descending the Pit'. A similarly unpleasant spectre was reported from Cotgrave Colliery in Nottinghamshire as recently as 1987, when on Friday 9 October front page banner headlines in *The Star* newspaper proclaimed: 'Terror of the coalface phantom. GHOST SENDS MINER MAD. Panic as dead pitman prowls again'. The accompanying article revealed in fact that the miner in question – nineteen year old Gary Pine – was hardly mad, but only 'too shocked to speak about his experience'; workmates explained that he had seen a man wearing overalls and carrying a miner's cap and lamp, who had apparently disappeared through a concrete wall.

Nevertheless, during the twenty years of the pit's existence a dozen miners have been killed; the ghost has been seen for at least eight years, and several injuries are laid at its door. A pit deputy recalled the time when two of his friends were injured underground by a haulage truck: 'When I turned round I saw a man standing by the button that sends it – I ran towards him but he vanished, and it must have been a ghost because no-one could have got at the switch without passing us.' A letter in 1989 inviting the manager to comment received no reply – he was no doubt pre-occupied with the news that the workforce at his pit was to be reduced by five hundred men.

There have been attempts to exorcise such ghosts. An apparition in Staffordshire was confronted by a party of men who went down the pit at midnight because their leader had been told by a wise man that they could get rid of it if they followed a certain formula: he was to carry a bible in his right hand and a key in his left and was to say:

> Matthew, Mark, Luke and John,
> God bless this errand we've come on.

Then he was to repeat the Lord's Prayer. The leader carried out the instructions, but the ghost did not give way as expected. Then one of the miners noticed that the leader was 'caggy-handed', and was carrying the bible and key in the wrong hands – as soon as they were changed over and the ritual repeated, the spirit vanished. Other spirits are more benevolent, and give warnings to miners. At one Cornish pit there was a woman called Dorcas who in the late nineteenth century committed suicide by throwing herself down the shaft. However, her spirit was later thought to have saved one miner's life: he heard a voice repeatedly calling his name – it persisted until he left his work and walked towards it; as soon as he had done so a massive fall of rock came down where he had been working.

Other signs were perhaps less helpful, merely pointing to the inevitability of disaster. The miners of Yorkshire and the East Midlands believed that when the broad beans were in flower was a time when accidents were particularly liable to happen. Rats and mice leaving their old haunts in the pit constituted a bad sign – so was the appearance there of a white rabbit, hare or rat. A pigeon perching for a long time at the pithead, a dove hovering, a robin lingering – all these gave warning. For example, a robin was seen in a pumphouse underground before the explosions at Llanbradach pit (where it survived, and was brought up and liberated) and also at Senghenydd in 1901. Unfortunately, the signs were either ignored or came too late, and twelve miners died in the first disaster, eighty-one in the second.

The Seven Whistlers

In the Midlands as well as in several other places, the Seven Whistlers are thought to predict danger – the difficulty is that no-one seems very sure as to what they are. Some say whimbrels (which pass twice a year on migration), others curlews, and swifts are another possibility as they have a piercing cry; they are otherwise known as devlins. The story goes that seven colliers were drunk on a Sunday, and whistled for a wager to pay for more drink. However, they were carried up into the clouds, and their spirits doomed to roam the heavens and whistle a warning when fatal accidents threatened. As early as 1686 Robert Plot described a similar belief in the mining town of Wednesbury in Staffordshire:

> The *Colyers* will tell you that early in the morning as they go to their work, and from the *Cole-pits* themselves, they sometimes hear the noise of a *pack* of *hounds* in the *Air*, which has happened so frequently that they have got a name for them, calling them *Gabriels hounds*, though the more sober and judicious take them only to be *Wild-geese*, making this noise in their *flight*.

Both the Seven Whistlers and Gabriel's Hounds are vestiges of an ancient belief in the Wild Hunt, a company which rides across the sky to announce impending disaster. The Hounds were among the items listed on a board once displayed at the Cockfighter's Arms Inn, Old Moxley, near Wednesbury.

Y^e Colliers Guide of Signes and Warnings

1st – To dreame of a broken shoe, a sure signe of danger.

2nd – If you mete a woman at the rising of ye sun, turne again from ye pit, a sure signe of deathe.

3rd – To dreame of a fire is a sure signe of danger.

4th – To see a bright light in ye mine is a warning to flee away.

5th – If Gabriel's Hounds ben aboute, doe no worke that day.

6th – When foule smells be aboute ye pit, a sure signe that ye imps ben annear.

7th – To charme away ghosts and ye like: Take a Bible and Key, hold both in ye right hand, and saye ye Lord's Prayer, and they will right speedily get farre away.

Death Tokens

Until well into the twentieth century Welsh miners believed in a whole series of death signs: the 'corpse candle' was a light seen following a particular route which would shortly be taken by a funeral cortège; in the pit the sound of feet trampling as though people were carrying a heavy burden indicated that a dead man would soon be borne that way, and that miners should stop work immediately.

There is also another spectre called the *lledrith* which invariably predicts a death: Walter Haydn Davies tells how it appeared to a miner from Bedlinog near Merthyr Tydfil, whose name was Shoni Pengwyn; as a result his hair went white overnight. The apparition indicated a part of the rock face, then pointed silently at a body lying dead and maimed in a phantom tram (wagon) pulled by a phantom horse: next day, the body of Pengwyn's butty (workmate), Shinkyn Jenkins, was taken out of the pit on just such a tram, after being dug out of a fall of rock at the very spot shown by the *lledrith*. Davies' own father had died of a stroke in 1910 at a place in the pit where a strange and unexplained light had been seen the day before by one of his workmates.

The Big Hewer and Tiny Newman

North-eastern miners had a semi-mythical hero, an industrial superman called either Towers or Temple, although he was known as the Big Hewer. He weighed eighteen stones, without fat, and was as good as two men, or even ten. He had exceptional pit sense, and could perform great feats of strength – for instance, for plug tobacco, he could pull a rivet out of a tub and chew that; and the blows of his pick followed a rhythm as relentless as that of a clock's ticking.

Some say this was a management ruse to bring down the price of piecework: a highly skilled man would be sent in to work for a short time to the absolute limits of his strength, and would then be rested; but the prices for the work of the ordinary miners would be set on this basis. One is reminded of Stalin's superworker, Stakhanov, whose achievements turned out to be faked. For a long time, though, they served their purpose of encouraging ordinary workers to greater efforts. Perhaps the cynical assessment of the Big Hewer is confirmed by the Midlands miners, for they refer to him simply as 'a pacemaker', 'a slogger' or 'a big hitter'.

Car workers at Cowley, near Oxford, had a genuinely powerful hero in the 1930s. His real name was Newman, but he was always known as 'Tiny' – and he is still remembered. He was strong enough to fit motor tyres with his hands alone. He was a quiet man, but once became enraged with a workmate during an argument; they were on the upper deck of an open-topped 'bus, and Tiny took him by the scruff of the neck and held him over the side, which very soon settled the disagreement.

Pit Humour

The danger and hardship of mining were often relieved by jokes and stories, and miners tell many tales of the resilience of ordinary men in adverse circumstances. At Chasetown, not far from Lichfield in Staffordshire, some men were cut off by a roof fall in the Fly Pit. They managed to survive for fourteen days before being rescued, and during that time 'Gammy' Whitehouse, one of their number, took charge. For food he killed a pit pony called Nobby, and distributed his stomach (the tenderest part) to be eaten raw. For water they gathered seepage.

Nearby, in the Black Country at Nine Locks Pit, ponies and their harness were eaten in a similar way after a disaster in 1869. When rescuers still failed to arrive, the men decided that their only hope lay in cannibalism, so lots were drawn to select the first victim. This turned out to be a boy – either by chance or good management – but the colliers had not the heart to carry the plan through. They nevertheless survived, and afterwards the boy was pointed out in the streets as 'the one that should have been eaten'.

Another Black Country miner, trapped with others, is said to have prayed: 'Lord, if thou'll only get we out of this lot, we woh (won't) bother yo agen for a bloody long while.' And Jack Elliott, from the pit village of Birtley in County Durham, used to tell the story of two miners who worked together, one an atheist and the other a lay preacher:

To avoid constant argument the two men made a pact not to discuss religion. However, it so happened that there was a heavy fall of rock, which left them uninjured but trapped behind a thirty-yard blockage.

'Could we set aside our agreement?' asked the preacher. 'I'd like to pray.' 'By all means', replied the atheist.

'O Lord Jesus . . .', began the preacher, but stopped when the atheist tapped him on the shoulder. 'Listen', he said. 'This is a big job. Shouldn't you be getting hold of the Old Man?'

A Working Vocabulary

Close-knit communities of workers produce their own jargon which can be impenetrable to the outsider. Railwaymen, for instance, spoke in the days of steam of a 'banjo player' (fireman), a 'bugler' (driver who used the whistle a lot), 'green fire' (unburned coal), 'navvies' wedding cake' (bread and butter) and a 'whispering baritone' (noisy person). The Eastern Region was 'Indian Territory' and Clapham Junction, 'the Maze'. Railway companies were known as 'Elluva Mess' (LMS), 'Late, Never Early' (London and North-Eastern), and 'God's Wonderful Railway', 'Greatest Way Round' or 'Go When Ready' (GWR).

Miners' talk – pitmatic – varies from region to region. 'Marra' (workmate) in the north-east is replaced by 'butty' in the Midlands and Wales. In turn, the Midland 'ripper' or 'lipper' (worker who makes the underground passage behind the coalface) in Scotland is a 'brusher'. Even within the Midlands a miner in charge of a section of such a roadway is variously known as a 'corporal', a 'doggy' or a 'coddie'. A simple activity such as lowering the floor level to provide greater overall height is 'baiting' or 'dinting' in the Midlands, 'pavement brushing' in Scotland, and 'pocking' in Wales.

The Welsh are renowned for picturesque and inventive nicknames. One miner was called Dai Damn-and-Bugger-it, from a phrase he habitually used when a tram went off the rails. However, after experiencing a religious conversion he changed the formula to 'Jam-and-Butter-it', so the nickname was revised accordingly. Other baptisms came from appearance (Tom Duck's Legs, or Charlie Fat), eating habits (Billy Welsh Cake, Dick Iron Stomach), pace of work (Dynamo Dan, Tom Dead Slow), or character (Ned Fair Play, Tom the Careful Tom Cat). Such names were often used so habitually that a man's official name was more or less forgotten, even by members of his own family. There is a story told of one man who arrived in a Welsh pit village looking for a particular person.

'Do you know Thomas Davies?' he asked a villager. The man thought carefully. 'I can't bring him to mind, boy bach', he said. 'Is he known by any other name?' 'I think some call him Twm Bara Brith' [Tom Bread and Butter], said the stranger.

'Good Lord', came the reply. 'That's me. What can I do for you?'

The name 'Tom Dead Slow' provides a reminder, if such is needed, that miners are not invariably keen or hardworking; and that there is the occasional downright lazy man of whom it is sometimes said: 'Throw some bread about and set the hens scratching. They'll shift more stones than him.' Beyond any question of slacking, though, there was always an ingrained reluctance in many miners to do more work than they had to, a feeling which perhaps dates back to pre-industrial times. Welsh pitmen wishing to decide whether to go to work or not, would throw a stone in the air: if it stayed up, they went to work, otherwise they went home. Boilermakers in Lancashire had a similar custom, using a brick. An alternative with a somewhat less predictable outcome was to throw a cap into a tree – if it lodged in the branches the miners would go to the pit, and if it fell to the ground they would go home.

In Shropshire, miners took a holiday called a Gaudy Day or a Cuckoo Morning signalled by the sound of the first cuckoo in spring. Another day off was traditionally taken when the first crop of peas in their gardens was ripe for picking in the early summer. Until World War II a ballot for workplaces was held four times a year in some Northumberland and Durham collieries. This was known as 'cavilling', and on those days it was considered lucky to place a cat in the oven – cold, of course – at home. The first Monday of each quarter was therefore set aside for miners to move their tools and gear to the new workplaces, and eventually came to be taken as a holiday, called 'Cavilling Monday'.

Monday in general was an unpopular day for working, not only with miners but with other trades, and absence from work on this day was a long tradition, known as 'keeping Saint Monday'. Charles Shaw, a potter from Tunstall in Staffordshire (died 1902) wrote in his autobiography: 'This saint was the most beneficent patron the poor pottery children ever knew', and other upholders of Saint Monday included toolmakers, pearl buttonmakers and gunsmiths in Birmingham, English and Scottish handloom weavers, Whitby jet workers, Sheffield cutlers, iron workers in the Black Country and Wales, woodworkers and tailors everywhere, and all Cockneys;

shoemakers remembered St Crispin. However, work left undone might well have to be made up by longer hours later in the week, and the Kidderminster carpet weavers wryly reflected:

> Dingle dangle,
> Play by day,
> Work by candle.

As the five and a half day week gradually came in, starting in the mid-nineteenth century, Saint Monday declined, and after World War II the five day week was instituted. However, miners' absences were still regarded as 'the gaffer's plague'. Five shifts were expected; but when one exasperated manager asked a meeting of miners: 'Why do you only work four shifts a week?' the answer came back in a flash: 'Because we can't live on three'. British Coal's drive to reinstate six-day working is being strongly resisted, even though time off in compensation is proposed, because weekends are sacred to miners for their leisure pursuits. Favourites still include the classic whippet racing and pigeon flying, and on the musical side, brass bands and male voice choirs remain popular. In the north of England miners are not only fervent followers of Rugby League, they also provide many players – indeed, it is said in Yorkshire that if a team is short someone goes to the top of the nearest pitshaft and shouts down 'Send up a forward' or 'Send up a three-quarter', as the case might be.

The mining industry and many of the communities based on it are now in decline, but the famous annual galas in Yorkshire and Durham continue, with their bands and banners, speeches and celebrations. The traditional mixture will surely continue as long as mining itself.

THE BLACKSMITH

Other trades have their traditions, too. The blacksmiths' patron was St Clement, or Old Clem, and on his day (23 November) smiths would fill a hole in their anvils with gunpowder and ceremonially fire it, then take the rest of the day off. In the evening there was a supper, called a 'wayzgoose', and until the beginning of this century some employers – in Brighton, Bristol, Liverpool and London, for example – provided a roast leg of pork for the occasion. The oldest smith would take the chair and propose toasts to Vulcan, to Tubal Cain, and to:

> True hearts and sound bottoms,
> Checked shirts and leather aprons.

The association between St Clement and the smiths goes back to the time of King Alfred: legend tells that Alfred wished to decide which of the trades was best and therefore called for a representative of each to present himself with a specimen of his work. The blacksmith brought his hammer and a horseshoe; the tailor showed his shears and a new coat; a saw and a deal trunk represented the carpenter, while some chisels and a cornerstone stood for the mason. Finally, the butcher flourished a cleaver and a joint of meat. Alfred was so impressed by the coat that he declared the tailor as winner, and installed him as king of the trades. The blacksmith was very angry at the decision, and went on strike.

Some time later – on St Clement's Day, as it happened – Alfred found that his horse needed shoeing so called at the smithy; he found it closed, and while he was wondering what to do the four other tradesmen turned up, each with tools needing repair. Eventually they decided to force their way in and do the work themselves, but the forge soon became a shambles. Then the blacksmith arrived, accompanied by St Clement – Alfred confessed his error in choosing the tailor as king of the trades, and the smith was named in his stead; so the blacksmith gave up his strike, shod the horse and mended the tools.

ON THE LAND

If they had been present with King Alfred, agricultural workers might have argued their own supremacy, maintaining they provide the food necessary for life itself. Their festivals run throughout the year, starting in January with Plough Monday, the first Monday after Twelfth Night: until well into the twentieth century groups of farm labourers would customarily disguise themselves – either with simple reddening or blacking of the face, or with elaborate costume – and drag a plough round their home village. Contributions were requested from householders – in default of which lawns, doorsteps, footscrapers or footpaths might be ploughed up – and a short play, or dances or songs (or all of these) would be performed:

> Tramp, tramp, tramp, the boys are marching,
> Cheer up, the boys are at your door.
> If you do not let us in we will kick the door in,
> And you won't see your mother any more.

175

Accusations were made that this was at best hooliganism and at worst criminal damage, and the custom almost completed died out – its last vestige seems to be the practice of taking a plough to church to be blessed on Plough Sunday (the Sunday after 6 January) at Exeter and Chichester Cathedrals. The Plough Stots still perform at Goathland near Whitby in North Yorkshire on the Saturday after Plough Monday, but nowadays they have no plough, and confine themselves to a sword dance. The old Plough Monday play has been revived at various places, including Harpenden in Hertfordshire, though the people involved are no longer ploughmen but teachers, office workers and computer programmers. Nevertheless, some of the old ceremonies can be seen once again.

At the other end of the farming year, in September, were the Harvest Homes. Their former glory has been described by a host of writers, including Flora Thompson and A. G. Street, when they were celebrated with abundant food, copious drink, and lengthy sessions of song. However, their importance dwindled until they became no more than a plain supper held on the last day of harvest or soon afterwards, the farmer merely providing a good meal for his workers, both permanent and casual, with little ceremony. And finally the huge reduction in the numbers working on the land helped to ensure that these, too, died out, leaving only the staid Harvest Festivals held in church.

Nevertheless, the true Harvest Home, with all its jollity, food and drink, dancing and singing, has been successfully revived in at least one place; it is celebrated, for instance, in the small Herefordshire village of Putley, near Ledbury – both folk enthusiasts and ordinary people join in, and even though most of them cannot feel the deep satisfaction of having brought home the harvest themselves, the event has a strong appeal.

Hopping

The same village is still part of the hop-growing area of Herefordshire, though the acreage is now much reduced and most of the picking is done by machine. George Orwell picked hops in Kent in 1931, and described both the drudgery and the joys of the work in his novel *A Clergyman's Daughter*. At the end of the hop harvest the head pole-puller, gaily decorated with ribbons and sprays of hops, walked in front of the last load to the hopyard; behind him came the chosen king and queen of the pickers, also festooned, and the farmer provided a meal and a dance:

176

When hop-picking was over and done
The farmer he gave them a treat.
They danced like rams in a halter
When each jolly couple did meet.
Young Roger the black chimney sweeper,
The grinder and his bonny lass,
And Betsy they made her so drunk
She was forced to lie on the grass.

After all this merrymaking, the hops used for decoration were dried and hung in the farm kitchen to bring luck until the next year; in Herefordshire, pillows stuffed with dried hops were considered good for insomnia; and a few whole bines were always cured in the kilns and used at harvest festivals, as indeed they still are. Some are kept in pubs to adorn the bar for a year.

Picking went on by hand until the 1960s or '70s; the picked hops were put into a crib, a large sacking container on a wooden frame – when a crib was full it was emptied and the contents measured and logged to the pickers. Throughout this time a custom called 'cribbing' was celebrated at the end of each season: as the last bines were pulled down for picking, the pole-pullers took hold of any unmarried woman, picked her up, and dropped her into a crib – photographs show a fairly decorous version of what was in fact vigorous horseplay with clear sexual implications. The women would sometimes band together and retaliate by up-ending the binman into a crib. George Dunn of Quarry Bank in Staffordshire (died 1975) was one who remembered the Herefordshire and Worcestershire hopyards as being 'full of singing'; he described the time he spent there as 'the best of my days'.

11

Other Worlds

Outside the pages of children's books one would now be hard put to find anyone who believed in fairies, though they feature in plenty of stories from the past. Similarly, there are a great number of stories told about the devil but not many people who now believe in his existence. However, ghosts seem to be a different matter: sightings seem to be abundant and stories are plentiful, and many of these are set firmly in a twentieth-century context, as well as in the traditionally haunted mansions of the past. Witchcraft, too, seems to be enjoying a vogue – its confessed practitioners are probably in part merely sensation-seeking, perhaps even play-acting, yet some claim they can influence, possibly even threaten, British Rail over its choice of route for the Channel Tunnel. Finally there is the Flying Saucer fraternity, which, with its tales of little green men, kidnappings into outer space and multiple sightings of Unidentified Flying Objects, might seem laughable to many; yet it attracts a large following, and some of its stories do seem to defy scientific explanation.

GODS AND SPIRITS

Especially in Wales and northern England, many stone sculptures of heads survive from the remote past – the highest concentration of all is in what was the Celtic kingdom of Elmet, now part of west Yorkshire near Leeds. To the Celts the head was of supreme importance, since it was believed to contain a person's spirit. The heads of enemies slain in battle were therefore greatly prized and would be put on display; a favoured subject for sculpture was the head of the horned god, Cernunnos; other carvings, sometimes with two, three or four faces were used as altars and oracles, or simply to keep evil forces at bay and to bring good fortune. Furthermore, in adorning its buildings with gargoyles and grotesques (see Chapter 3), the Christian church also took over the cult; and in parts of Cheshire, Derbyshire and Yorkshire stone heads have, until quite recently, been used in the old way – to cure illness, to promote fertility and to combat ghosts. Some people still identify them with the 'Old Ones', the ancient Celtic gods and spirits.

In 1971 Dr Anne Ross, a Celtic scholar and archaeologist, took into her house for study two stone heads which had been unearthed near Hadrian's Wall. Soon after their arrival she got up in the early hours of one morning and was terrified to see a dark figure on the stairs, part man, part animal; but although her husband searched the house, he found no-one. Then one afternoon a few days later Dr Ross's daughter also saw, again on the stairs, a menacing shape – huge, dark and inhuman. The heads were quickly returned to the museum, but even so, certain phenomena continued for a time – a cold presence was felt, a dark figure seen, the padding of feet heard.

Fairies

The expression 'a fairy tale' has come to mean an untruth, which only goes to show how far belief in fairies has declined. At one time mothers in Scotland felt it necessary to leave an open bible next to a baby when they went out of the room, so as to protect the child from the fairies. The Isle of Man, too, had several traditions to prevent fairy intervention; for instance, a woman taking a child to be christened would make sure she had with her a piece of bread and cheese, and would give it to the first person she met, believing this obtained protection for her child from fairies and witches. Other customs included placing salt under a milk churn; throwing stale water over the plough; tying a cross of twigs to the tail of a cow; picking hedgerow flowers, especially those coloured green and yellow, and bringing them into the house; and finally the last cake from a batch of baking would be left 'behind the turf-flag for the little people'.

Many people believed implicitly in fairy luck, too. At Edenhall, near Penrith in Cumbria, the Musgrave family carefully preserved a glass beaker for many years. It was probably brought to England in the thirteenth century by a returning Crusader, but the story is that a group of fairies were making merry round a well – St Cuthbert's Well – near the hall which gives the village its name. When some people approached, they ran away and left the cup behind, but as they fled one of them called out:

> If this cup should break or fall,
> Farewell the luck of Edenhall.

Whatever the truth as to its origin, the cup was very carefully treated by the Musgraves. For some reason, though, they lent it (in 1926) to the Victoria and Albert Museum in London, where it can still be seen – but eight years after it left Edenhall the hall was demolished: apparently the luck had indeed run out.

Other Cumbrian families also had their 'lucks', including the Penningtons of Muncaster Castle, which stands near to the coastal town of Ravenglass. Theirs is an enamelled glass bowl supposed to have been given to a Pennington by Henry VI for sheltering him after the battle of Towton in 1461. King Henry blessed the bowl and said that the family would flourish as long as it remained intact. The bowl is still in one piece and is on display at Muncaster Castle, though it was probably made at least three hundred years later than the story suggests.

There is no documentary evidence to prove the existence of fairies, though at one time it was thought that there was. In 1917 two girls who lived at Bingley in west Yorkshire were scolded for being late, but their excuse was that they had been playing with fairies in a place called Cottingley Dell. When they were challenged they offered to bring back photographic evidence, which they did, and when the film was developed it showed a number of tiny winged creatures dancing round one of the girls. National, and even international, publicity followed: some cried fake, and Sir Arthur Conan Doyle, the creator of Sherlock Holmes, was called in. He pronounced the photographs to be genuine, however, and suggested into the bargain that one of the fairies had a navel, thus proving that they reproduced themselves in the same way as humans. Not until 1983 did one of the girls involved – Frances Griffiths, then aged 76 – confess that the pictures were faked. The fairy figures had been cut from books and held in place with hairpins, and Conan Doyle had missed a prime clue by mistaking the end of a pin for the fairy navel.

Demon Dogs

People in certain parts of the country once lived in fear of various spectral presences which were thought to roam the land and be full of menace. For example, if the Wild Hunt (see p169) rode through the sky it was a presage of death or disaster. In Wales there were the *Cwn Annwn* (Dogs of Annwn, king of the underworld) which went howling through the air, especially on the eves of St David's Day and St Agnes' Day, All Saints' Day, New Year's Day and Good Friday – anyone walking a lonely lane or byway would desperately hope not to meet the pack, especially at a crossroads. The hounds were in fact inhabited by the souls of those doomed to wander in purgatory, especially those of 'drunkards, scoffers, tricksters, attorneys, parsons' wives and witches'. A person unfortunate enough to encounter *Cwn Annwn* would be sure to die within the year.

In many English counties a spectral black dog with fiery eyes performed a similar function: the Devonian variety inspired Conan Doyle to write *The Hound of the Baskervilles*; in Lancashire it is called 'Trash' or 'Skriker'; on the Isle of Man the 'Mauthe' Dog; in Norfolk 'Shuck' and in Suffolk 'Shock' (from the Old English word, *scucca*, a demon). His claw marks are pointed out on the north door of Blythburgh Church in Suffolk, a few miles inland from Southwold (though it is more likely to have been lightning which caused the indentations). In Cornwall there was a spectral huntsman with a whole pack of hounds, known by all as the Devil and his Dandy Dogs; one of the stories related about this pack goes as follows:

A poor herdsman was making his way home across the moor, one dark and windy night. Suddenly he heard in the distance the baying of hounds, and realised to his horror that the Dandy Dogs were out. There were still several miles to be covered before he reached home so he stumbled on, as fast as he could. The yelping came nearer and nearer. Finally the man ventured a look back, and saw both huntsman (with horns, tail and saucer eyes) and dogs (snorting fire, and howling balefully) – but just as they were about to catch up, he fell to his knees and prayed aloud: the hell hounds stopped immediately. The huntsman waited impatiently for a moment, then called off his dogs and went in pursuit of other victims.

SATANIC FORCES

Although the devil inspired extreme fear there were some bold enough to outwit him. One of these was John of Kentchurch,

otherwise known as Sion Cent or Jack of Kent – Kentchurch is a
small Herefordshire village close to the River Monnow, which marks
the border with Wales. As a boy Jack had apparently sold his soul
to the devil in return for special powers, and until well within the
twentieth century a whole string of stories were told about Jack and
his deeds. In one of these, he was sent by a farmer to keep the crows
from the corn. The farmer then went off to Hereford Fair, but was
furious to meet Jack there: 'I thought I told you to scare the crows.'
'Aye, maister. The crows be all right. They be in the barn', he said.
Sure enough, when the farmer returned he found the crows all sitting
in an empty barn with no roof, with one particularly big old bird
perched on a crossbeam keeping them in order until Jack came back.

Then it is said that with the help of the devil Jack built a bridge
over the Monnow at Kentchurch (some say at Monmouth) in a single
night. The agreement was that the soul of the first living being to
cross would be claimed by the devil – but John threw a bone across
and a dog ran after it (obviously, the devil was thinking to have a
human soul). Yet another story relates that the devil once challenged
Jack to thresh a whole bay of corn in a day – so Jack took off his
boot and put it on top of the stack: it kicked down the sheaves one
by one. Then he took the flail and set it on the floor, and it threshed
the corn by itself while Jack sat and played his fiddle, murmuring
from time to time:

> Nobble, stick, nobble.
> Play, fiddle, play.

Jack also had a stable full of horses with which he hunted on
Sundays, and he would force the local people to join in. Apparently
he once left his horse in a wayside barn for three weeks, and no-one
could remove it; yet as soon as Jack passed, the horse sprang from
the barn and joined his cavalcade. On his deathbed he gave
instructions that his 'liver and lights' should be placed on three iron
spikes projecting from the church tower. Some say this was at
Kentchurch, others at Grosmont, just over the river in Wales, where
such spikes could at one time be seen. He predicted that a dove and
a raven would come and fight over the remains; if the dove won, his
soul would be saved – but if the raven was victorious, then it would
go to the devil. In fact the original bargain was that the devil should
have both Jack's body and his soul, whether he were buried inside a
church, or outside. Jack cheated the devil by making sure that he
was buried beneath the church wall, that is, neither in nor out. So

the dove must have won the battle with the raven.

At Grosmont Church a stone in the south wall of the nave is said to mark Jack's grave, and a half-finished effigy is supposed to be of him. There are several suggestions as to his real identity: Sir John Oldcastle (also a possible model for Shakespeare's Falstaff), Owain Glyndŵr, Sion Cent (a Welsh bard) and John Kent (vicar of Kentchurch in the reign of Henry V).

No doubt it was his wilder exploits which mothers had in mind when, right up to the 1930s, they told misbehaving children to mind their manners – or 'Jackie Kent'll have you'.

Witchery

The wrinkled and bearded crone with tall hat and sinister cat, riding on a broomstick or muttering spells over a bubbling cauldron, is an image which owes much to Walt Disney and arouses fear only in the very young cinema-goer or television-viewer. By way of contrast, a survey taken in 1989 showed 250,000 British people to be interested in occultism, and this was defined to include astrology, herbalism, mind power, ritual, paganism, kabbala, spells and satanism (though satanism only appealed to a quarter of the number). Modern witches, it seems, are mainly middle-class, intellectual, well educated and white. Witchcraft or Wicca, as they call it, from the Old English word for wizard, claims to be a mystery cult based on the ancient nature religion of Europe. However, its current rituals were cobbled together from the writings of such twentieth-century figures as Aleister Crowley and W. B. Yeats, and some adherents frankly admit that they 'write their own rituals round old stories' and mythology.

Others take themselves much more seriously. Just north of Maidstone lies the Kent village of Aylesford, and nearby are two groups of ancient stones: one is Kit's Coty (Cottage), consisting of three large slabs capped by a fourth and thought to have been the burial place of Prince Catigern, who was killed at the battle of Aylesford in 455. The second is a collection of tumbled stones called Little or Lower Kit's Coty, or alternatively the Countless Stones. Once a local baker did attempt to count them by placing a numbered loaf on each, but long before he reached the end he found that his loaves were disappearing behind him, so he gave up the attempt in a hurry. Another belief is that if the stones are indeed counted, and counted twice, and if the same result is obtained, the devil will appear.

It may be significant that the stones are on a ley line; they are also close to the route proposed by British Rail for the link to the new

Channel tunnel: they might be missed by yards, or they could disappear beneath the proposed new Parkway station, and in May 1989 several witches met to try to charm BR away from a place they held to be sacred. They somewhat ludicrously drew the outline of a railway track in flour, put on it a small plastic carriage with a runic inscription, and chanted: 'BR, begone. BR, begone'. This group chose the full of the moon, but there is another which prefers it to be waning for a threat. These witches are anxious to help campaigners prevent Avon County Council from allowing motor access to its green lanes, one of which (passing through North Stoke, near Bath) was the Roman Via Julia. The procedure was described by one of the witches:

> When we're doing a protection for the land we need all the help we can get. So we start off calling up the oldest spirit we know, who is Puck, and we do this in the time-honoured way by clutching oak, ash and thorn in our hand, and explain what we are going to do. We call up all the heroes who've ever fought for the land. We always call up Merlin. We always call Arthur, and Old Herm, the keeper of the crossways.

It will be very interesting to see whether BR and Avon County Council will be duly influenced.

The malevolent powers of witches, deriving from the devil, were once widely accepted, and witches were tortured and burnt at the stake because of them. They confessed to such activities as sexual intercourse with the devil, flying through the air, preventing women from giving birth, depriving men of their virility, afflicting people with infirmities, injuring cattle and raising storms. In 1590 several Scotswomen, known as the North Berwick witches, admitted raising a storm to sink the ship in which King James VI (later James I of England) was returning from Norway with his bride, Anne. The storm duly came, but sank the wrong ship.

James himself was deeply interested in witchcraft and even wrote a treatise on it. On this occasion he interrogated some of the witches personally. One of them, Agnes Sampson, described a great assembly of two hundred witches addressed by the devil in North Berwick Church. When the king flew into a rage and called her a liar she took him to one side (this was at Holyrood Palace in Edinburgh) and whispered in his ear the words Anne had said to him on their wedding night. James was so astonished at the accuracy of her report that he concluded that Agnes must be in possession of supernatural powers, and so she was burnt at the stake. One wonders why she should wish to convince the king, knowing the horrific fate which awaited her – perhaps she had lost the will to live because of torture, or she might have convinced herself that she was in fact a witch. Before being arrested she had been a midwife and herbalist in the town of Keith; perhaps she had experimented with hallucinogenic plants.

Concoctions made from such things as mandrake, henbane and belladonna (deadly nightshade) would certainly have induced the fantasy of flying. Potions made from some of these poisons would have been lethal, but small amounts rubbed under the armpits could have entered the bloodstream and induced hallucinations and other traditional witchlike symptoms such as dilated pupils, bloodshot eyes and a lack of saliva. Like hundreds of other innocent women, Agnes Sampson probably went almost willingly to her death.

A woman suspected of witchcraft was subjected to various tests which in themselves were degrading and even dangerous. If every part of her skin were pricked with a pin, and no insensitive spot found (which was unlikely), a suspect could be declared innocent. If she were weighed against a church bible and found to be heavier, she might be set free. Another test involved casting her into water: if she floated she was a witch, if she sank, she was not. Neither outcome was particularly happy because if she floated she would be burnt, and if she sank she might drown – the ordeal was carried out winter and summer.

In 1717, Jane Clarke of Wigston, a village just outside Leicester, was suspected of witchcraft, together with her son and daughter. They were publicly stripped and 'swum'; evidently they floated 'like a cork, a piece of paper, or an empty barrel' despite trying very hard to sink. They then had blood drawn 'above the breath', an operation believed to take away their powers as witches, and were indicted for trial at the assizes. Despite the willingness of twenty-five people to testify against the Clarkes, the grand jury threw out the indictment, and they were set free. This was the last recorded indictment for witchcraft at a secular court in England, though it was not until 1951 that the offence was completely removed from the statute book.

Legal or no, witchcraft remained a force for many people. The story of the witch who assumes the shape of a hare is told with variations all over Britain: a large hare is frequently seen by hunters, but always eludes them – though many shots are fired at it, they all seem to miss. One of the sportsmen has his suspicions, and makes a bullet from a silver coin (witches are vulnerable to silver); with this he manages to wound the hare, but it dashes into a cottage garden and escapes. The old lady who lives there does not appear for a day or two, and when she does she walks with a limp.

Until recently, people in some isolated communities thought witches had the power of 'overlooking' or 'ill-wishing', which enabled them to stop horses in their tracks, prevent cows from giving milk, bring illness to animals and humans – in other words, to achieve all sorts of malevolent purposes. Even in less remote parts of the country various curses have come to light in recent years. In 1960 a house in East Street, Hereford, was found to have a doll of the late nineteenth century in a wall cavity. With it was a piece of paper bearing these words:

Mary Ann Ward

I act this spell upon you from my holl heart wishing you to never rest nor eat nor sleep the rest part of your life. I hope your flesh will waste away and I hope you will never spend another penny I ought to have. Wishing this from my whole heart.

Both doll and paper are now on show in Hereford Museum.

There is another curse in the museum, this one taking the form of a little wooden coffin with a human effigy, the body firmly pinned by a nail to the bottom of the coffin. The curse dates from the middle of the nineteenth century, but was found only in 1987, at a house in the village of Woolhope, a few miles from Hereford. Soon after it had come to light, the lady of the house was visiting friends when an entire window fell out, from three storeys up – mercifully she was dealt only a glancing blow, but she could easily have been killed. Then her daughter fell mysteriously ill, and at this point the lady thought it advisable to take the curse to Hereford Museum. The curator kept it in her office for a short time, and almost immediately her husband was involved in a serious car accident. The object was hurriedly moved to the impersonal surroundings of a glass case in the museum, where it can currently be seen.

Of course these events could have been coincidental, but the result was that even people in the late twentieth century were given pause to think. And if these objects, obviously imbued with real hatred, still succeed in shocking people of today, how much more powerful must their effect have been a hundred or two hundred years ago? Since some of them have only just come to light they cannot have been discovered by those for whom they were intended, so those who made and planted them must have believed that they had an awesome power.

HAUNTED SITES AND BUILDINGS

'Ghosts are innumerable, and their number is added to every day.' Without a doubt, Christina Hole's remark could be illustrated by whole libraries of books all full of stories, and every ancient house, pub, lane and wood seems to have its tale of some kind of apparition or presence. The British Tourist Authority even issues lists for those who wish to stay in haunted hotels and inns; a recent edition includes some fifty establishments – though surprisingly there is only one each given for Wales and Scotland. All sorts of unexplained manifestations are included, described variously as feelings of sudden cold or apprehension, the sound of footsteps, or noises of objects or furniture being dragged or moved about. There are places which report fiddle playing, others which boast of ghostly carousing; places where doors open and close, where duelling occurs and where knockings are heard. There have been sightings of ladies in green, grey or white; of a headless coachman and his team, of an old lady working at a spinning wheel.

Some of these reports and rumours are no doubt carefully cultivated for their publicity value, but others seem genuine and are even played down. At the Five Bells, for instance, in the village of Wickham, six miles from Newbury in Berkshire, the landlady tried to avoid talking about the supernatural in order to avoid upsetting the staff. When her two daughters were small they refused to sleep in a bedroom previously used a hayloft, and in the same room her baby son would wake up every night at midnight. The children are now grown up but they still refuse to sleep there, and cats and dogs avoid it altogether. Several visitors who stayed in it and had been told nothing in advance reported seeing a smiling young woman dressed in white – one man was disturbed enough to insist on moving into a different room in the middle of the night.

Some influences are even more sinister. Tony Nacey was the landlord of the Old Gantondale Inn between the villages of Foxholes and Staxton on the B1249 road between Scarborough and Great Driffield in north Yorkshire, and in 1989 he explained how a series of unpleasant happenings there had caused his family to break up. The inn had a local reputation for being haunted by a grey lady, and also the sound of a coach and horses had been heard. Then in 1985 it was gutted by fire, and the firemen reported seeing an apparition among the flames which caused them feelings of profound unease. Shortly after this Mr Nacey took over and began restoring the building, and immediately sensed a malevolent presence; he described it in these words:

187

It was as though the building was crying, if that doesn't sound stupid. I'd put things down and then never be able to find them. I was frightened when I worked here at nights, and I can tell you, I've worked in some unbelievable places; isolated churches and derelict buildings. I used to dread coming in to work – the sight of it turned my stomach at one time. My wife absolutely detested the place and it culminated in our breaking up. The building has lost me a wife and three daughters.

There were stories of an eighteenth-century murder over a bag of gold, and workmen drilling through a wall did in fact find bones concealed there. Perhaps they were the remains of the victim, but whatever their origin, after their discovery the atmosphere changed for the better. 'I'm not frightened when I sleep here now', said Mr Nacey. 'The spirit isn't malevolent any more. After my wife went, too, things seemed to change, as if the house had decided to accept me for what I was doing.' Bad luck seemed once more to get the upper hand though, and by the end of 1989 the Old Gantondale Inn stood boarded up and empty once again.

Certainly it seems that the sufferings and wrongs of the past can linger on in some form. The lonely shell of Hermitage Castle is all that remains of a place with a bloodthirsty history – it stands in Liddesdale, some fifteen miles south of Hawick in the Scottish Borders. Mary Queen of Scots visited the wounded Bothwell there, and almost died of fever herself; and the Queen's Mire nearby is still pointed out as the spot where Mary's horse became bogged down. A local song still refers to her escort:

> A ghostly band may cross the hill,
> And none will see them come.

However, the macabre associations are with another tenant of Hermitage, Lord Soulis; he lived there in the eighteenth century, and was thought to be a warlock. He desired a beautiful woman called May, and so abducted her, together with her sweetheart, Lord Branxholm. Then Soulis turned for advice to his familiar spirit, Redcap Sly, who told him to 'Beware the coming tree'; however, Soulis failed to realise that this was a reference to Branxholm's men who had camouflaged themselves with branches and were advancing rapidly. The castle fell, and Soulis was taken out to a stone circle called Nine Stane Rig where he was wrapped in lead, and then boiled to death in a large cauldron. This may have been to avoid shedding noble blood, or because as a suspected warlock Soulis was thought to have the means to protect himself from other forms of destruction. Redcap Sly haunted the castle in the guise of an old man with fang-like teeth, and until quite recently the local boys would shout defiantly (from a safe distance) into the ruins: 'Redcappie-dossie, come out if ye dare'.

Certain battles seem to give rise to curious phenomena, sometimes centuries after taking place. Ghostly armies are seen from time to time marching across the moor at Culloden where such great slaughter of Highlanders took place in 1745. In England the Civil War seems to have left a particularly strong atmosphere. For example, on 14 June 1949 a man and a woman out cycling paused for a rest near Naseby in Northamptonshire; they saw some carts passing down an old drovers' road with weary, dusty men in leather jerkins helping to push. Both cyclists suddenly felt apprehensive, and without saying anything to each other they quickly moved on; only later did they discuss what had happened, and realised that they had seen the same things, and experienced the same reaction. Later they discovered that that day was the precise anniversary of the battle of Naseby. There are now plans to drive a big new road through the battlefield, so it remains to be seen whether problems other than those of engineering will be encountered by the workforce.

The first great battle of the Civil War was fought in 1642 near Edgehill in Warwickshire, between Stratford-on-Avon and Banbury. Two months after the fighting, shepherds witnessed a ghostly re-enactment in the sky, a phenomenon which went on for several nights; it was fully described in a contemporary pamphlet. Furthermore ever since then phantom horses have been seen from time to time, and during World War II unexplained terrors gripped hardened soldiers on sentry-go at the nearby army ordnance depot which covers part of the battlefield site.

Peter Young describes another episode in his book *Edgehill, 1642*: as recently as 1960 a concert pianist travelled specially from London to see the battlefield, but was seized by deep apprehension when he was visiting the grave mounds in the army camp. He immediately returned home, but he felt then an unseen, hostile presence went with him, and lived in a state of terror for a month, until it began to fade. Later, he decided that this was the spirit of a Roundhead soldier pursuing him because his family had fought on the other side in the war.

'This mile of countryside contains An air the centuries will not expunge'. So wrote the poet, Jan Weddup, on Edgehill.

Many ghosts derive from personal tragedies, rather than from public events. The village of Pluckney is set among pleasant orchards and hopfields near Ashford in Kent, yet it has been called the most haunted village in Britain. First of all there is a white lady who walks St Nicholas' churchyard; she is said to be the ghost of a lady who died over four hundred years ago. Her husband, a member of the Dering family, was utterly distraught at her death and, seeking to preserve her beauty, he had the body embalmed and carefully sealed in a lead casket. However, according to ancient belief, excessive mourning on the part of the living can cause the dead to be restless.

There are three public houses in Pluckney and they all have stories to tell. At the Dering Arms the figure of an old lady in old-fashioned clothes can sometimes be seen in a corner of the bar; on other occasions the dog's hackles rise when no-one is apparently there. Then the Blacksmiths Arms has the ghost of a Cavalier's wife who died at the hands of the Roundheads, possibly under torture. Then the Black Horse, near the church, has a room which is not used because people continually complained that it was eerily cold.

There are plenty of phenomena besides these in the same village – for example a spectral coach and horses, which once forced a woman motorist off the road and caused her to storm into the Black Horse to ask for the name and address of the driver; a cloaked and headless figure; and two girls who seem substantial, but then disappear. There is also a screaming man, the ghost of an employee at a local brickworks, who fell to his death down a deep clayhole; and a gypsy woman who made a living by gathering and selling watercress – she can be seen on the bridge where she fell asleep in a drunken stupor, ignited herself with her pipe, and burned to death. Finally there is the village schoolmaster, whose body can sometimes be seen swinging from the tree on which he hanged himself in the 1920s (his body was found by his pupils). Pluckney's reputation is such that ghost coach tours are run there by a tourist operator from Maidstone.

If Pluckney is the most haunted village in Britain, then the rectory at Borley, a tiny Essex village near Sudbury, must have been the most haunted house. The rectory itself no longer exists, burned down fifty years ago, and the last of its rubble was used in 1942 as hard core for a wartime airstrip. Five successive rectors who lived there testified that they saw, heard and felt strange things. The chief apparition was the figure of a nun, who had walked in the area before the rectory was built. Some say that she had been walled up alive as a punishment for having a sexual relationship with a monk; others that

190

she was strangled for some reason – possibly to conceal her pregnancy – by a member of a local family, the Waldegraves. The rectory was built in the nineteenth century and disturbed the nun's walks, so she took to gazing sadly in through the windows. A more spectacular apparition was that of a phantom coach which would thunder across the dining-room and disappear through the wall.

The nun walked even by day, and was seen by the postman and the gardener, and in the 1930s the rector's wife started to find messages pencilled on the wallpaper: 'light – mass – candles' or 'please get help'. Vases shattered; keys fell from locks; candlesticks flew through the air, and a marked chill would suddenly descend. Seances were held at which the nun identified herself as Marie Lairre – she stated that she had been strangled in 1667, and buried in the garden. Another spirit predicted that the house would burn down: and in 1939 it did, a lighted paraffin lamp having apparently toppled over of its own volition. As the rectory blazed, figures were seen silhouetted against the flames – and one was that of a nun. Four years later the bones of a young woman were found below what had been the cellar floor. They were given decent burial, but the nun still walks. At least, according to some; but local people now dismiss such stories as media hype.

TWENTIETH-CENTURY APPARITIONS

Modern Ghosts

Not all ghosts by any means are of ancient origin, though sometimes the old and new combine. For example, this story is told on both sides of the Atlantic:

A young woman on her way to town breaks her journey with friends who live in an old manor house. She does not sleep well, and as the clock strikes midnight she hears the sound of wheels and horses' hooves outside. She looks out, and sees an old-fashioned hearse; it is crowded with people, but there is no coffin – then the coachman looks up from his box in the direction of the woman and says: 'Room for one more'. She is terrified, and jumps back into bed.

Next morning she is not sure whether she has dreamed the incident or not, but is glad to leave the house. In the city she goes shopping in a department store, and on the top floor makes her way to the lift to go down. It arrives crowded with people, but the attendant says: 'There's room for one more'. When she looks at him she sees that he has the face of the coachman. 'No, thank you', she says. 'I'll walk down.' The lift doors click shut. Then there are screams, a distant crash, and silence: the lift has fallen to the basement, and everyone in it is killed.

There are a great many stories of phantoms associated with the road, travel and driving, and they are found throughout the country. For example, a mini-skirted woman waits beside the road in pouring rain. Motorists stop to offer a lift, but she disappears – later they find that a woman pedestrian was killed in an accident at that very place. Another version of the story, found in many parts of the country, is that a woman hitchhiker accepts a lift. The driver stops for coffee but she chooses to remain in the car and when he comes back he finds she has gone. She did happen to mention her name and where she lived, so he phones her parents to check that she has reached home safely. They tell him that their only daughter was killed three years earlier, outside the café.

On certain stretches of road motorists drive into cyclists – or think they do – but when they stop to look for the victims there is no-one there. Some swerve to avoid a lorry backing out onto the road, and accidents ensue, but subsequent police investigations find no opening at that point on the road from which any vehicle could have emerged. This story lies behind a series of accidents which have occurred on the A57 near Manchester, between Hyde and Mottram.

Near Coventry there was a three mile stretch of the old A45 near Knightlow Hill and the crossing with the Fosse Way which was haunted by a phantom lorry – it would appear on the wrong side of the road, threatening a catastrophic, head-on collision, and then vanish, leaving drivers in a state of abject terror. Even policemen confessed to seeing the phantom. However, the stretch of road was made into a dual carriageway in the late 1950s and the appearances seem to have come to an end.

At Blackpool the tramway system has several ghosts. A figure with a lantern seen on the promenade on dark nights is said to be the ghost of an old pointsman who spent his whole life working on trams. There are even phantom trams – an inspector saw one rattling along at 6.30 one morning, and put out his hand for it to stop: it vanished instead. Another was invisible; it could be heard passing, and rainwater was seen to be thrown up between the rails by its wheels, but no actual tram was seen at all.

In Devon, the road between Two Bridges and Postbridge (the B3212) runs across Dartmoor and the devil is said to ride out hereabouts with his black hell hounds – he has been known (they say) to stop for a drink at the Tavistock Inn (locally known as the Old Nick) at Poundsgate. The beer boils as it reaches his lips, and his empty glass scorches the wood of the bar. However, it is not the devil who harasses travellers on this stretch of road but a pair of hairy, disembodied hands. In 1921 Dr Ernest Helby, doctor at the nearby Princetown gaol, was going along the road by motorcycle with the governor's two children in his sidecar. Suddenly he shouted 'Jump!', then the machine swerved off the road and he was killed. The children survived, and reported seeing a pair of huge hairy hands on the handlebars. In the same year a young army officer came off his motorbike; he also reported that 'A pair of hands closed over mine . . . large, muscular, hairy hands'.

Similar stories have been repeated over the years. In 1989 a Dartmoor warder described how on the same stretch of road he suddenly felt a tremendous force trying to wrench the steering wheel so as to pull his car into the ditch; he was obliged to struggle for some time before he could regain control. 'The most frightening experience of my life' was how he described it. Mundane explanations – the camber of the road, excessive drinking – have been put forward, but not very convincingly. Mike Cutler, blacksmith at the Powder Mills forge believes the phantom hands can be related to an incident: 'In the 1800s, in the days when [the forge] was a gunpowder factory, there was an Italian who worked there, and he came into a lot of money; he went down the pub to celebrate and came back with the lads, they were "three sheets to the wind" and the Italian forgot to take off his hobnail boots. He created a spark and blew himself to kingdom come, all that was left of him was his hands.'

UFOs

Interest in 'unidentified flying objects' began in 1947 with the sighting of a formation of strange objects by a civilian pilot in the United States. Five years later in this country the Air Ministry (now Ministry of Defence) began to keep records of such incidents, and since that time some three thousand have been logged.

Officially, every sighting can be explained by one of four causes: astronomical or meteorological phenomena, mistaken identification of aircraft or balloons, optical illusions, or hoaxes. Philip Mantle runs a UFO hotline from his home in Batley, West Yorkshire, and agrees that most can be explained satisfactorily. In 1987, for example, there was a big upsurge in reports occasioned by the prominent showing in the sky of Mars and Jupiter. However, he believes that 'there is no rational explanation for between 5 and 10 per cent' of incidents reported.

Two of the most mysterious were first reported by Air Force personnel. In 1952 several men at RAF Topcliffe, near Thirsk in North Yorkshire, noticed a Meteor fighter plane being shadowed by a silver disc which eventually accelerated away, faster than a shooting star. The second incident was just after Christmas in 1980, when three US Air Force patrolmen saw unusual lights outside a gate at RAF Woodbridge in Suffolk. A strange metallic object, triangular in shape and two metres high, was moving in a nearby wood, emitting an intense white light which illuminated the whole area. Then it maneouvred through the trees and disappeared.

Extravagant claims are made about little green men, and thousands of people kidnapped and taken to outer space. Then in the dry summer of 1989 mysterious circles appearing in certain fields were ascribed to extra-terrestrial visitations, and marks on a remote Welsh hillside near Hay-on-Wye were described by Colin Andrews of the Circle Phenomenon Research Unit at Sussex University as 'perhaps the most significant development in seven years'. 'Tadpole tails' – tracks a few yards from the circumference, and similar to configurations seen in Peru – were thought to be especially significant. Unfortunately, the reality was more prosaic. The landowner, Sir Andrew Duff-Gordon, had arranged for the circles to be cut so as to make for better shooting, since young grouse need to feed on freshly cut heather, with denser undergrowth nearby, for protection. The 'tadpole tails' were caused 'by the tractor moving off to cut the next circle'.

Conclusion

Like other living things, folklore can be attacked by decay and disease, and is subject to all sorts of influences. The very word is used by some as a synonym for the archaic, the unsubstantiated or the irrelevant, and some of its manifestations are still under active attack from officialdom in various forms. For instance, teachers discourage schoolchildren's rites of passage on leaving school – egging and flouring is one – for the understandable reason that they are usually messy; and the autumn game of 'conkers', with its litter of broken horse chestnuts and its damage to trees, is also a target for reproof.

In October 1989 Hallowe'en came under fire, or at least the children's practice of dressing up to go 'trick or treating' (allegedly imported from the United States, but having indigenous roots). Kent County Council went to the lengths of issuing a circular to all heads of school asking them to discourage children from dressing up as ghouls and demons, and the police joined the debate, too, suggesting that old people might be frightened, not so much by the ghouls and demons as by the threat, real or implied, of the trick which would follow the refusal of a treat. The Association of Christian Teachers joined in with the view that the 'medieval and pagan' festival of Hallowe'en had become linked with both vandalism and the occult.

It is not only national traditions which are attacked. In Sutton, near Epsom, a rare custom has recently been terminated by the rector of St Nicholas Church. Since 1794 the Gibson Mausoleum in the churchyard has been ceremonially unlocked on 12 August every year; few people bothered to attend, though numbers gradually rose in the 1980s to about a hundred. There were local stories that the ceremony originated as a precaution against grave robbers, and some said that the key was taken afterwards to the Holy Land to be thrown into the River Jordan – though this would have effectively stopped the annual gatherings. Some believed that from time to time a ghost emerged from an urn on top of the tomb.

Since 1990 this curious little ceremony has therefore disappeared, because the rector feels that it is inappropriate for Christians to pay so much attention to the body in the coffin instead of the spirit in heaven. He has also pointed out that the ceremony of opening the tomb was not specifically laid down in the Gibson will, but was something that just grew up – though that might have seemed a very good reason for keeping it.

Local officials and the police sometimes combine to oppose traditional observances. For example in some places children are occasionally prevented from collecting for Guy Fawkes on the grounds that the practice constitutes begging. Ancient fairs often come in for criticism, and many have been driven from the streets where they used to be held; some have managed to survive in their original locations, especially in small towns, but the police say they encourage litter, drunkenness and pick-pockets, shopkeepers claim that they interfere with legitimate trade, and motorists complain that they disrupt the traffic. Yet how sad if this opposition were to result in the fairs being driven out altogether, for usually they operate in a given town for a few days at the most, and are nearly always well patronised.

On the other hand, both private and public interests sometimes do recognise the value in traditional activities, and seek to promote them. Hoteliers and publicans, for example, love a good ghost story or a telling association – there is a 1980s housing estate in York which boasts a new public house called the Dick Turpin, and it is odd to think that Turpin's name and fame are remembered in the city where he was hanged well over two hundred years previously. And the story which has brought fame and prosperity to the village of Beddgelert in Snowdonia was the brainchild of an enterprising landlord. Visitors are shown a cairn marking the grave of a dog called Gelert (Beddgelert could mean 'Gelert's grave' in Welsh), and are told this story:

Prince Llywelyn the Great went out hunting and left his dog, Gelert, to guard his infant son. When he returned the room was in disorder and the cradle overturned. The child was nowhere to be seen, but the dog sat licking blood from its chops. Thinking the dog had killed his son, Llywelyn drew his sword and killed it. He then righted the cradle and discovered the baby safely asleep beneath it. In a corner of the room behind a curtain he found the body of a wolf, killed by the faithful Gelert.

Very touching, but more or less a confidence trick since the village's name is probably derived from that of a Celtic saint, Gelert, who lived there. Although the story has a pedigree going back to the ancient Orient, it was unknown in the Welsh village until 1798; it was in fact put into circulation quite deliberately by David Pritchard, landlord of the Royal Goat Inn, and the cairn was erected to lend veracity to the tale, which – as intended – was remarkably good for trade. Yet few of those who now hear or read it doubt its authenticity.

A sort of modern equivalent might be seen in the grants given by local councils and regional art bodies to those who promote folk festivals and ceremonies – a well dressing, a mumming play, a sweeps' procession, rushbearing, or perhaps a morris dance meeting. Such events may simply be a form of promotional activity, with paid actors – one scholar has called them 'folklorism' – yet if local people take part in and run such an event, if the community comes to expect it to have the inevitability almost of the seasons, if it takes place irrespective of outsiders – then we are back in the realms of folklore. The evidence is that even if happenings of this kind are consciously revived or even invented, they can take root and flourish as though they were completely traditional.

Once every village had its stock of traditional lore, but much of this is now under threat. Young people leave the villages of their birth to look for cheaper housing, work, entertainment, and behind them the landscape changes as fields are amalgamated, hedges bulldozed, ponds filled, woods and orchards grubbed out. Names fall into disuse and are then forgotten. With them, stories and associations disappear. Nevertheless, against such forces are ranged the energies of people who are determined to seek out, preserve and pass on village lore. Sometimes they are local, sometimes incomers; they may glean valuable information from the collective memory of a village, or they may look for printed records.

Sixpenny Handley – the name is a corruption of Saxpena Hanlege

– is in north-east Dorset, just off the A354, and is a good example of a village whose wealth of traditional lore has been recorded. In the years 1939–41 a certain Aubrey Parke noted the large number of stories and anecdotes there, and took the trouble to put them in writing – though oddly enough he makes no mention of Isaac Gulliver, a smuggler notorious in the eighteenth century (p40) who was married in Handley Church and spent an affluent retirement in the village. Parke's records include stories of a boot full of sovereigns buried in Harley Wood by Dick Turpin (and still to be discovered); a secret passage to the church from the Old Vicarage, and a crowd of little people in leather jerkins seen dancing on one of the barrows on Bottlebush Down; also Kit's Grave, a copse so called either because a highwayman was hanged and buried there, or after a gypsy who was buried there because local parishes refused to bear the costs of her funeral. Parke also describes a man in armour seen riding a white horse near a big oak tree – this ghost, however, thought to be a guardian of treasure, in fact ceased to appear when a hoard of Roman coins was found by the tree and removed. He mentions the ghost of the Duke of Monmouth seen at a coaching inn at East Woodyates, where the duke is thought to have spent the night after his defeat at the battle of Sedgemoor in 1685; and also a path in the woods known as Susan Gibbs' Walk, from the ghost which appears there of a maidservant from nearby Rushmore House who hanged herself from an oak tree.

There are many more tales included in Parke's collection, though one wonders how many of them are still current in Handley, fifty years on – and also whether new ones will emerge during that time.

Traditions such as these are by no means confined to rural areas. Towns large and small have their civic customs and also their stories of murders and battles, ghosts and witches. They also have a sense of humour as characteristic as their local accent. The Black County, a collection of industrial towns and villages to the north-west of Birmingham, seems to be steeped in local lore which continues to evolve. A large body of stories involves two men, Enoch and Eli (pronounced 'Aynoch' and 'Ayli'), who seem stupid on the surface, but in reality are rather logical. Sometimes they occur in a story singly, as when Aynoch ruins a pair of boots by drying them in the oven when they are wet. He then advertises them for sale as riding boots, and a toff calls to see them. He takes one look and exclaims 'These are not riding boots, my man!' 'Well, yo try walkin' in the buggers, then', says Aynoch.

More often, Aynoch and Ayli are together, one acting as a foil to

198

the other. Late one Saturday night, Aynoch rouses Ayli from his sleep by throwing small 'bibbles' (pebbles) at his bedroom window. Sleepily Ayli puts his head out of the window and asks what he wants. Aynoch asks: "Ow am the Baggies [West Bromwich Albion] got on?' 'They drew, none-none.' A quarter of an hour later Aynoch returns to waken Ayli once more. 'What d'yer want this time?' asks Ayli, wearily. 'Ah forgot, t'ask th' 'alf-time score.'

Other stories deal with such matters as car sales, motorbike accidents, marriage (with a kind of Andy Capp morality), pigeon flying, and working life; they are jocular and fictional, though not without reflections of reality. Many other tales are true, or purport to be so. Most ghost stories, for example, would lose their *frisson* if the hearer felt they were made up merely to entertain.

The same is true of many stories which are essentially folk tales in a modern setting. There is no intention to deceive, as those involved are convinced that what they are passing on is true. Yet they invariably claim – and this seems to be an infallible indicator – that it happened to 'a friend of a friend'. And if that person is sought out, it usually turns out that it was not he or she personally, but a further friend. When it transpires that other friends' friends in other places (and even in other countries) appear to have had markedly similar experiences, one begins to realise that these are not realistic narratives after all. 'The Stolen Corpse', for example, is widely told with many variations. Essentially, a family holidaying in Spain find one morning that their aged grandmother has died. They are worried about the formalities, so they place the body in a large hamper on the roof of the car and set off to find the British consul. On the way they stop for coffee or a meal – but when they return to the car, the hamper and its contents are missing.

'The Cement Car' is a story of excessive jealousy involving the driver of a ready-mix lorry who happens to see a smart sports car stop in front of his house. A well dressed young man gets out and is warmly received by the lorry driver's wife. 'So that's the game', he thinks. He takes his vehicle alongside the open sports car, fills up the interior with concrete, and drives away. When he returns in the evening the car is still there, with the concrete set inside it. His wife meets him tears. 'I saved up to buy this car for you as a surprise. While the dealer was giving me the papers some idiot came and did this to it.'

Ready-mix lorries are very much a late twentieth-century pheno-menon, so the story must be of recent origin, whereas 'The Stolen Corpse' dates perhaps from the 1940s – it was first printed in 1953, and achieved wide circulation both in Britain and America by the 1960s. There are several instances, in fact, of apparently recent tales which nevertheless have a long history. For example, during the 1970s the story was told of a young woman who gives a lift in her car to an old lady with a heavy shopping bag, but as the passenger reaches out to place her bag on the back seat the driver notices that her hands seem large, hairy and masculine. She asks the passenger to get out and check that the rear lights are working, and then drives off to a police station. The bag proves to contain a blood-stained hatchet. In the seventies the story was stimulated by fears of the Yorkshire Ripper, and by electricity blackouts caused by strikes, but essentially the same story was reported in 1834, when the driver of a gig found a brace of pistols in a supposed female's bag.

Other stories cover incidents in late twentieth-century urban life involving baby-sitters, joggers, plumbers, car and lorry drivers, hitchhikers, alligators in sewers and petfood in restaurant meals. Those who pass on such narratives would probably be surprised to learn that they are relating folk tales, but this is the case – and the same could be said to apply to the plethora of jokes about Lada, Skoda and Yugo cars. Yet these have no known author; they are exchanged by word of mouth from the West Country to Scotland, and vary considerably in the telling. For example:

What do you call a Skoda rally? A scrapyard.
Why do Lada cars have heated rear windows? To keep your hands warm when you're pushing.
Did you hear about the man who went into a motor parts shop and said: 'Can I have a fanbelt for a Yugo, please?' The person replied: 'It's a deal'.

And there are dozens more. Apparently they have no adverse effect on sales – after all, they say, there's no such thing as bad publicity. Such exchanges undoubtedly lack both the quality of the classic tales and also the story-teller's art in presentation, but they nevertheless show that folklore lives.

As long as traditional song and story, music and dance, custom and ceremony continue to appeal – and to do this they must balance change against stability – they will have a future. Enormous numbers of people are preoccupied with their heritage and roots, of which folklore with its colour, drama, pleasure and meaning, is a vital part.

Bibliography

Alexander, Marc *British Folklore, Myths and Legends* (Weidenfeld, 1982)
Baker, Margaret *Folklore and Customs of Rural England* (David & Charles, Newton Abbot, 1988)
The Folklore of the Sea (David & Charles, Newton Abbot, 1979)
Barber, Chris *Mysterious Wales* (Paladin, 1987)
Baring-Gould, S. *A Book of Folk-Lore* (Collins, n.d.)
Barrett, W. H. *Tales from the Fens*, ed by Enid Porter (Routledge, 1963)
Bignell, Alan *Kent Lore. A Heritage of Fact and Fable* (Hale, 1983)
Black, William George *Folk-Medicine; a Chapter in the History of Culture* (Elliot Stock for the Folklore Society, 1883)
Blakeborough, Richard *Wit, Character, Folklore and Customs of the North Riding of Yorkshire* (EP Publishing, East Ardsley, 1973)
Boase, Wendy *The Folklore of Hampshire and the Isle of Wight* (Batsford, 1976)
Bord, Janet and Colin *The Secret Country* (Elek, 1976)
Briggs, Katharine M. *A Dictionary of British Folk-Tales* (Routledge, 4 vols, 1970–1)
A Dictionary of Fairies (Penguin, Harmondsworth, 1977)
The Folklore of the Cotswolds (Batsford, 1974)
Brockie, William *Legends and Superstitions of the County of Durham* (EP Publishing, East Ardsley, 1974)
Brunvand, Jan Harold *The Choking Doberman and Other 'New' Urban Legends* (Penguin, Harmondsworth, 1987)
The Vanishing Hitchhiker. American Urban Legends and their Meanings (Pan, 1981)
Burne, Sophia Charlotte (ed) *Shropshire Folk-Lore: A Sheaf of Gleanings* (Trubner, 1883)
Butcher, David *The Driftermen* (Tops'l Books, Reading, 1979)
Cawte, E. C., Helm, Alex, and Peacock, N. *English Ritual Drama. A Geographical Index* (Folklore Society, 1967)
Cawte, E. C. *Ritual Animal Disguise* (D. S. Brewer, for the Folklore Society, 1978)
Chamberlain, Mary *Old Wives' Tales. Their History, Remedies and Spells* (Virago, 1981)
Chambers, Robert (ed) *Popular Rhymes of Scotland* (3rd ed, Chambers, London and Edinburgh, 1870)
Choice Notes from 'Notes and Queries' (Bell and Daldy, 1859)
Crawford, Phyllis *In England Still* (Arrowsmith, 1938)
Crossley-Holland, Kevin (ed) *The Riddle Book* (Macmillan, 1982)

Dacombe, Marianne R. (ed) *Dorset Up Along and Down Along* (Dorset Federation of Women's Institutes, Dorchester, n.d.)

Davies, Lynn 'Aspects of Mining Folklore in Wales', in *Folk Life*, 9

Ditchfield, P. H. *Old English Customs Extant at the Present Time. An Account of Local Observances, Festival Customs and Ancient Ceremonies yet Surviving in Great Britain* (George Redway, 1896)

Dunkling, Leslie *A Dictionary of Days* (Routledge, 1988)

Dunning, R. W. *Arthur, the King in the West* (Alan Sutton, Gloucester, 1988)

Farmer, David Hugh *The Oxford Dictionary of Saints* (Oxford University Press, Oxford, 1987)

Firor, Ruth A. *Folkways in Thomas Hardy* (University of Pennsylvania Press, 1931)

Folklore, Myths and Legends of Britain (Reader's Digest, 1973)

Gorman, John *Banner Bright* (Penguin, Harmondsworth, 1976)

Greenoak, Francesca *All the Birds of the Air. The Names, Lore and Literature of British Birds* (Penguin, Harmondsworth, 1981)

Grinsell, L. V. *The Rollright Stones and their Folklore* (Toucan Press, St Peter Port, 1977)

Harland, J. T., and Wilkinson, T. T. *Lancashire Legends* (Routledge, 1873)

Harrowven, Jean *The Origins of Rhymes, Songs and Sayings* (Kaye and Ward, 1977)

Harte, Jeremy *Cuckoo Pounds and Singing Barrows* (Dorset Natural History & Archaeological Society, Dorchester, 1986)

Hazlitt, W. C. *Dictionary of Faiths and Folklore* (2 vols, Reeves & Turner, 1905)

Henningsen, H. *Crossing the Equator: Sailors' Baptism and Other Initiation Rites* (Munksgaard, Copenhagen, 1961)

Hinde, Thomas *Forests of Britain* (Gollancz, 1985)

Hobsbawm, Eric, and Ranger, Terence (eds) *The Invention of Tradition* (Cambridge University Press, Cambridge, 1983)

Hole, Christina *British Folk Customs* (Hutchinson, 1976)
   Witchcraft in England (Batsford, 1977)

Holloway, John (ed) *The Oxford Book of Local Verses* (Oxford University Press, Oxford, 1987)

Holt, J. C. *Robin Hood* (Thames & Hudson, 1982)

Hopkins, Harry 'What's behind the church door?' in *Reader's Digest* (September 1989), 65–71

Hopkinson, Jean (ed) *A Pocketful of Hops* (Bromyard and District Local History Society, Bromyard, 1988)

Hughes, Thomas *The Scouring of the White Horse* (Macmillan, 1859)

Hunt, Robert (ed) *Popular Romances of the West of England* (Chatto & Windus, 1930)

Jones-Baker, Doris 'The Graffiti of Folk Motifs in Cotswold Churches', in *Folklore*, 92 (1981), 160–7

Judge, Roy 'May Morning and Magdalen College, Oxford', in *Folklore*, 97 (1986–7), 15–40
   The Jack in the Green (D. S. Brewer for the Folklore Society, 1979)

Leach, Maria (ed) *Funk and Wagnall's Standard Dictionary of Folklore, Mythology and Legend* (New English Library, 1972)

Leach, Robert *The Punch & Judy Show. History, Tradition and Meaning* (Batsford, 1985)

Leather, Ella Mary *The Folk-Lore of Herefordshire* (Jakeman & Carver and Sidgwick & Jackson, Hereford and London, 1912)

Legend Land. Being a Collection of some of the Old Tales told in those Western parts of Great Britain served by the Great Western Railway (Great Western Railway, 2 vols, 1922)

Lockhart, J. G. *Curses, Lucks and Talismans* (Bles, 1938)

Long, George *The Folklore Calendar* (Philip Allan, 1930)

The Mabinogion, trans by Jeffrey Gantz (Penguin, Harmondsworth, 1976)

Marshall, Sybil *Everyman's Book of English Folk Tales* (Dent, 1981)

Marwick, Ernest W. *The Folklore of Orkney and Shetland* (Batsford, 1975)

McEwan, Graham J. *Sea Serpents, Sailors and Sceptics* (Routledge, 1978)

McKenna, Frank *The Railway Workers, 1840–1970* (Faber, 1980)

McNeill, F. Marian *Scottish Folk-Lore and Folk-Belief* (Maclellan, Glasgow, 1957)
  A Calendar of Scottish National Festivals (Maclellan, Glasgow, 3 vols, 1959)

Menefee, Samuel Pyeatt *Wives for Sale* (Blackwell, Oxford, 1981)

Messenger, Betty *Picking up the Linen Threads. A Study in Industrial Folklore* (Blackstaff, Belfast, 1978)

Moore, A. W. *The Folk-Lore of the Isle of Man* (Brown & Son and D. Nutt, Douglas and London, 1891)

Newall, Venetia *The Encyclopedia of Witchcraft and Magic* (Hamlyn, 1974)
  (ed) *Folklore Studies in the Twentieth Century* (Brewer and Rowman & Littlefield, Woodbridge, Suffolk, and Towata, New Jersey, 1980)

Newman, L. F. 'Some Notes on the Pharmacology and Therapeutic Value of Folk Medicines', in *Folk-Lore* (1948–9), 59–60, 118–135 and 145–156

Opie, Iona and Tatem, Moira (eds) *A Dictionary of Superstitions* (Oxford University Press, Oxford, 1989)

Opie, Iona and Peter 'Certain Laws of Folklore', in Newall (q.v.)
  (eds) *The Oxford Dictionary of Nursery Rhymes* (Oxford University Press, Oxford, 1977)

Orwell, George *The English People* (Collins, 1947)

Owen, Trefor M. *Welsh Folk Customs* (National Museum of Wales, Cardiff, 1974)

Palmer, Roy *A Ballad History of England* (Batsford, 1979)
  The Folklore of Leicestershire and Rutland (Sycamore, Wymondham, 1985)
  The Folklore of Warwickshire (Batsford, 1976)
  A Gazetteer of Warwickshire Folklore (Drinkwater, Shipston-on-Stour, 1991)
  The Sound of History. Songs and Social Comment (Oxford University Press, Oxford, 1988)

Parke, Aubrey L. 'The Folklore of Sixpenny Handley, Dorset', in *Folklore*, 74 (1963), 481–7

Parry-Jones, D. *Welsh Legend and Fairy Lore* (Batsford, 1988)

Patten, R. W. *Exmoor Custom and Song* (Exmoor Press, Dulverton, 1974)

Porter, J. R., and Russell, W. M. S. (eds) *Animals in Folklore* (D. S. Brewer for the Folklore Society, 1978)

Raven, Jon *The Folklore of Staffordshire* (Batsford, 1978)

Ringwood, Margaret 'Some Customs and Beliefs of Durham Miners', in *Folklore*, 68 (1957), 423–5

Rollinson, William *Life and Tradition in the Lake District* (Dent, 1974)

Ross, Anne *The Folklore of the Scottish Highlands* (Batsford, 1976)

Samuel, Raphael (ed) *Miners, Quarrymen and Saltworkers* (Routledge, 1977)

Sanderson, Stewart F. *The Modern Urban Legend* (Folklore Society, 1982)

Sawyer, F. E. ' "Old Clem" Celebrations and Blacksmiths' Lore', in *Folk-Lore Journal*, 2 (1884), 321–9

Seal, Graham 'A "Hussiting" in Berkshire, 1930', in *Folklore*, 98 (1987), 91–4

Sharpe, Charles Kirkpatrick *A Historical Account of the Belief in Witchcraft in Scotland* (London and Glasgow, 1884)

Shaw, Charles *When I Was a Child* (1903)

Shuel, Brian *The National Trust Guide to the Traditional Customs of Britain* (Webb and Bower, Exeter, 1985)

Sikes, Wirt *British Goblins* (Sampson Low, 1880)

Simpson, Jacqueline *The Folklore of Sussex* (Batsford, 1973)

The Folklore of the Welsh Border (Batsford, 1976)

Smith, Alan *The Folklore of Industry* (Shire Publications, Tring, 1969)

Smith, Laura A. *The Music of the Waters* (Kegan Paul, Trench, 1888)

Starsmore, Ian *English Fairs* (Thames & Hudson, 1975)

Swinford, George *The Jubilee Boy. Recollections of George Swinford of Filkins*, ed Judith Fay and Richard Martin (Filkins Press, Filkins, 1987)

Swire, Otta F. *Skye. The Island and its Legends* (Blackie, London and Glasgow, 1961)

Sykes, Homer *Once a Year. Some Traditional British Customs* (Gordon Fraser, 1977)

Thomas, Keith *Religion and the Decline of Magic* (Penguin, Harmondsworth, 1973)

Thomson, David *The People of the Sea. A Journey in Search of the Seal Legend* (Paladin, 1980)

Trent, Christopher *The BP Book of Festivals and Events in Britain* (Dent, 1966)

Trevelyan, Marie *Folk-Lore and Folk-Stories of Wales* (Eliot Stock, 1909)

Tyack, George S. *Lore and Legend of the English Church* (William Andrews, 1899)

Vyvyan, C. C. *The Scilly Isles* (Hale, 1953)

Walvin, James *The People's Game. A Social History of British Football* (Allen Lane, 1975)

Waters, Ivor *Folklore and Dialect of the Lower Wye Valley* (Chepstow Society, Chepstow, 1973)

Westwood, Jennifer *Albion. A Guide to Legendary Britain* (Paladin, 1987)

Whistler, Laurence *The English Festivals* (Heinemann, 1947)

Whitlock, Ralph *Here Be Dragons* (Allen & Unwin, 1983)

Wilks, J. H. *Trees of the British Isles in History and Legend* (Muller, 1972)

Williamson, Duncan and Linda *A Thorn in the King's foot. Stories of the Scottish Travelling People* (Penguin, Harmondsworth, 1987)

Witchell, Nicholas *The Loch Ness Story* (Corgi, 1989)

Wright, Thomas *Some Habits and Customs of the Working Classes, by 'A Journeyman Engineer'* (1867)

DISCOGRAPHY

All Round England and Back Again. English Customs and Traditions (Saydisc SDL 332, 1982)

The Big Hewer (Argo DA 140, 1967)

Calennig. Songs and Tunes from Wales (Greenwich Village GVR 214, 1980), Mick Tems and Pat Smith

Here is a Health Songs, Music and Stories of an Ulster Community (Arts Council of Northern Ireland cassette, 1986)

A Jug of This. An Introduction to English Folk Music (Sussex Publications cassette, M11, 1987), Roy Palmer

The Leaves of Life. Songs, stories, tunes and a play from eight counties of England (Vaughan Williams Memorial Library cassette (VWML 003, 1989), various artists

Maypoles to Mistletoe (Trailer LER 2092, 1975), various artists

The Songs and Stories of a Durham Miner (Leader LEA 4001, 1969), Jack Elliott of Birtley

Songs from the Sailing Barges (Topic 12TS361, 1978), Bob Roberts

Songs of Ceremony (Topic 12T197, 1971), various artists

The Streets of Glasgow (Topica 12TS226, 1973), various artists

Tales in Trust (cassette TT1, 1989, Beech Cottage, Langdale Rd, Grasmere, Cumbria), Taffy Thomas

The Wide Midlands (Topic 12TS210, 1971), various artists

Index

206